To Carole

CRIMINAL JUSTICE IN MIDDLE AMERICA

Criminal
Justice

David W. Neubauer
University of New Orleans

In
Middle
America

GENERAL LEARNING PRESS
250 James Street
Morristown, New Jersey 07960

Manufactured in the United States of America.

Published simultaneously in Canada.

Library of Congress Catalog Card Number 73–89094

ISBN 0-382-18040-2

Preface

Popular concern with criminal justice has prompted scholars to reexamine their traditional neglect of the lower courts. Until recently, few ventured into studies of them, either believing one had to be a lawyer to study the law or that the lower courts did little of interest. Fortunately, both of these assumptions have been rejected and, as a result, we have a growing number of studies on how justice is administered. Where once scholars were content to study appellate court cases (largely assuming that lower courts automatically applied the correct rule of law), now concern has shifted to deciphering exactly the type of justice being meted out on the working level. Studies of the administration of justice, however, have not been evenly distributed across the spectrum of the criminal justice process. Rather, the focus has been on either end of the spectrum. We have studies of crime and police—the basic inputs into the criminal courts. At the other end of the spectrum we have studies of prisons, corrections, and rehabilitation.[1] What happens between arrest and prison, however, has been largely neglected.

Between a citizen's arrest for violating the law and the final sanctioning of that activity, a number of important decisions are made. After an arrest, charges may be filed; bail must be posted or the defendant will await trial in jail; a lawyer may be hired; if a felony is involved, a preliminary hearing may be held and/or a grand jury convened; guilt or innocence will be determined, and finally the guilty will be sentenced. Each of these decisions is important, because they involve determinations of the type of justice that will be handed out.

---

[1] Several other works provide a more detailed analysis of the gaps in the literature: Herbert Jacob, *Justice in America*, Little, Brown, 1965, pp. 206–207; John Gardner, *Traffic and the Police*, Harvard University Press, 1969, pp. 1–3; Abraham Blumberg, *Criminal Justice*, Quadrangle Books, 1967, pp. vii–viii.

This is a study of how one court system makes these decisions. The community is Prairie City, a fictitious name I have given to a medium-sized industrial town in Illinois. The decision to study one particular community was made on a basic assumption about how justice is administered. Although usually we refer to the criminal justice system as a collective, in reality this collectivity is several disparate organizations tied together by a common denominator, the defendant. A wide variety of officials (and some non-officials) make the decisions. No one actor has sole responsibility, although some have more power and influence than others. A case study of one community is uniquely suited to the task of discovering who wields the power and influence in the administration of criminal justice.

The goal of this study is to describe and analyze one particular community, but the study has a wider relevance. Prairie City is not approached as a unique place. Instead, an attempt is made to see what the experiences in Prairie City can tell us generally about how justice is administered. Where appropriate, we attempt to point out not only the practices in the study city, but also how the practices of other communities may be different. The overall goal is to develop some theoretical insights into the administration of justice, insights that can aid in future examinations of the courts.

This study focuses on the people who apply the law and their importance in the administration of criminal justice. Ours is a political-sociological perspective on the administration of justice. Until recently, most studies viewed the criminal courts from an apolitical, almost antipolitical, orientation. Their approach has been described best as legalistic and mechanistic.[2] Their focus has been on the structures and institutions of the courts, not on the people who run them. Even minimal consideration of the political, social, and economic factors affecting the administration of criminal justice has been omitted.

In contrast, the legal realists provided much of the impetus for studying the law as part of the larger social system. For the legal realists, the key to the legal system was not the black letter law, but the people who applied that law. Thus judges were portrayed as *makers* of law, not just finders of law, as mechanical jurisprudence had insisted. The legal realists have provided the intellectual fountainhead for political scientists, anthropologists,

---

[2] James Klonoski & Robert Mendelsohn, eds., *The Politics of Local Justice*, Little, Brown, 1970, p. 6.

sociologists, and others interested in how the legal system functions.[3]

But despite the probing of the courts from a political-sociological perspective, until recently the criminal justice system has been virtually neglected. Klonoski and Mendelsohn summarize the deficiencies of past studies as well as the overall goals of the present study:

> An examination of available source material on local legal systems and how they function produces almost immediate awareness that the process and roles concerned with allocating justice within the legal subsystem have not yet really been subjected to full and systematic investigation by persons prepared to ask theoretical questions.[4]

Thus, basic questions require asking before they can be answered. A case study allows for the exploration of areas that have not been studied previously. This case study seeks to avoid the major pitfalls of many case studies—too much narrative description and too little analysis—by concentrating on central questions about the administration of justice. The goal is to isolate general factors that explain the court's operation.

But the goal of exploring new areas does not obviate the need for the proper testing of ideas. Some explanatory and heuristic studies have concentrated on generating insights to the exclusion of such testing.[5] Here, however, we make an attempt to validate the findings, using a variety of statistical data gathered from the court records of the community.

Our focus on how justice is administered also distinguishes it from many current endeavors to reform the courts. This is not a study that proposes to call for court reform, although in the view of the author and many others, reform of the system does seem necessary. Before we reform the courts, however, we should have some idea of how they operate. Unfortunately, much of the current rhetoric calling for court reform seems uninterested in investigating basic questions about how the courts operate.[6] These

---

[3] For a good discussion of the legal realists see: Edwin Schur, *Law and Society*, Random House, 1968, pp. 43–50. Among the most important works have been: Karl Llewellyn & E Adamson Hoebel, *The Cheyenne Way*, University of Oklahoma Press, 1941; Jack Reltason, *Federal Courts in the Political Process*, Random House, 1955.

[4] Klonoski & Mendelsohn, *The Politics of Local Justice*, p. 4.

[5] Robert Emerson, *Judging Delinquents* (Aldine 1971), p. xi.

[6] Jacob, *Justice in America*, p. 206.

reformers have a bible of proposed changes but seem to overlook the need for examining whether their reforms would have the desired results. The most massive effort along these lines has been the President's Task Force Reports. In ten volumes, the Task Force not only describes what is happening but also proposes changes.[7] It is particularly troublesome that the Task Force and other reformers appear unconcerned with the need to examine the factual basis they use for proposing reform.

A note on the tone of this study is appropriate. Criminal justice has become a very emotional issue. People have strong opinions on justice and the role of the courts. Most researchers on the court show a marked bias in favor of the courts acting to protect individual liberties. Often these personal value judgments come to the fore in the author's description of how justice is administered, for many studies condemn the injustices they perceive. Unfortunately, such condemnations of the observed practices obscure the analysis of what is happening and just as importantly, why it is happening. As a result, it is difficult for researchers to separate value statements from factual assessments.

In this study, then, the reader will be free to make his own assessments about the quality of justice under investigation. Those who have read parts of this manuscript, and students who have observed courtrooms as part of their class assignments in my courses, share one thing in common—they reacted to different aspects of criminal justice in varying ways. What shocks one person is accepted, sometimes even praised, by another. It is up to the reader, therefore, to draw his own conclusions about the goodness of the justice produced. The author, however, does think it appropriate to offer some of his thoughts in the concluding chapter, where they stand apart from the empirical findings of the study.

This book is intended for the students (and teachers as well) in a variety of fields that are increasingly interested in how the criminal law is administered. A growing number of courses in criminal justice are being offered in a wide range of disciplines: political science, sociology, criminology, criminal justice, police science, and, not least, law. Each of these disciplines to one degree or another has ignored the criminal court process and thus this book can be a useful supplement. The book is also aimed at the more traditional courses such as judicial process (political science)

---

[7] The President's Commission on Law Enforcement and Administration of Justice, *The Challenge of Crime* (Government Printing Office, 1967).

and sociology of law, where there is a growing awareness that trial court activities require greater attention. But no matter what the student's academic home, the goal of the book is the same. Hopefully by examining one community in depth, he or she will want to investigate his own community, to take a close look at local justice. If the materials in this book suggest questions about how the student's own community administers justice and if the concepts advanced begin to suggest ways to answer those questions, then the book will have served its purpose.

A short preface cannot fully express the debt the author owes to many people. A project of this sort necessarily involves a large number of people. The field research alone involved over fifty people. The preface, also, does an injustice to those who cannot be thanked by name because they have been promised anonymity, and any but a personal thanks is inadequate.

The author owes a special thanks to Dr. Fred Coombs, Dr. Stephen Douglas, and Dr. Stuart Nagel, all of the Department of Political Science, University of Illinois, and Dr. David Bordua of the Department of Sociology. They gave freely of their time and advice but most importantly, took an interest in the project. Also, they provided the flexibility necessary in taking an idea from the germination of imprecise thoughts to completion. Others at the University of Illinois gave of their time. Mr. Wayne LaFave of the Law School and Mr. John Kleberg of the Illinois Police Training Institute suggested lines of inquiry and analysis that greatly aided the study. Mr. Paul Wice offered advice and suggestions at several junctures, as well as comments on the draft of Chapter 7.

Colleagues at the University of Florida should not go unmentioned—Mr. Hank Balyoria and Mr. Jesse Marquette provided valuable assistance in mastering a new computer complex, as well as aiding in the data analysis. Tom Henderson also deserves a word of thanks for hearing out my research problems and offering suggestions and encouragement.

Obviously, a study such as this can succeed only with the cooperation and good will of the community being studied. One cannot imagine a more hospitable research site than the place I have named Prairie City. The prosecutors, defense attorneys, judges, and police proved both cooperative and interested. They answered my questions, allowed me to look over their shoulders, and went out of their way to call my attention to important events. The prosecutors—Bill, Gary, Larry, John, Jack, Jerry, and Tom—at times put in extra hours in order to answer my questions. The defense attorneys—Fred, Norm, Aussie, Al, and Glen—were just a few who discussed their views of criminal justice in Prairie City. The judges also aided greatly, often spending hours with me. I am grateful also to the detectives and command personnel of the Prairie City Police Department who allowed me to spend two weeks observing their operations.

Whether any of these people agree with the final results is problematical. The author takes sole responsibility for the descriptions and analyses offered. But without the cooperation and encouragement of all these people, there could have been no descriptions or analyses.

Contents

Studying Criminal Justice

The courtroom was full. Most people had found seats on the old church pews, when the sheriff directed a short line of defendants, clad in blue gray, to sit in the unused jury box. It promised to be a typically busy Monday morning as the arraignment court set about the task of advising the weekend arrestees of their right to counsel, bail, and the charges against them. To speed up the process, the judge asked all defendants to rise (about three-fourths of those sitting met the specifications) and advised them of their rights *en masse*. The first defendant from the sheriff's bluish-gray line to appear before the judge individually was Terry Boldt. Boldt was a fairly typical burglary defendant—young (seventeen); a first offender; not rich but not necessarily from impoverished parents; and, at this point, somewhat apprehensive. "How plead you, Terry Boldt?", the judge asked, using the archaic phraseology of the law. Boldt's parents, who also appeared to be somewhat apprehensive, stood behind their son, ready to post bond so that he would not have to await trial in jail.

The traffic courtroom, just a few feet away from arraignment court, was also in heavy use that morning.[1] At first glance, the major contrast appeared to be the decor. The arraignment court was decorated with an imposing bench and wood paneling. The walls of the traffic court featured peeling paint. But once the traffic judge began to speak, it was obvious that the judges, as well as the decor of the courtroom, provided a study in contrasts.

---

[1] Although some people do not include traffic cases when they think of the criminal courts, the serious traffic cases should be considered in the same category as misdemeanors. The normal traffic violations, such as speeding, do not involve the courts, because the violator normally pays his fine and the case ends. Serious traffic cases—drunken driving and driving without a driver's license—do require a court appearance. In addition, serious traffic cases also involve the possibility of significant penalties: a large fine; a jail sentence; and/or a loss of driver's license for a year.

Whereas the arraignment judge wore robes, was courteous, and made an effort to see that each defendant understood his rights and what was happening, the traffic judge was more curt. Rights were less fully explained and never to individual defendants.

Mrs. Altman, like Boldt, was waiting to be called by the judge. Her speech and her dress marked her as a typical middle-class citizen. She might have been a potential juror waiting to hear a burglary case much like Boldt's. But she was not in court to serve as a juror. Rather, she waited to answer a traffic violation—driving without a driver's license. Arraignment court and traffic court that day, that week, that year, would hear many cases like Altman and Boldt.

Boldt, the accused burglar, and Altman, the forgetful renewer of her driver's license, obviously have little in common. Yet the contrasts are instructive. While one is relatively poor, the other is relatively well off. One faces a major charge, the other a fairly minor one. Altman and Boldt (fictitious names, but based on actual cases) typify the variety of people who pass through the criminal courts. Every year thousands of suspects like Boldt and Altman are adjudicated innocent or guilty, sentenced to prison, placed on probation, or fined large amounts or small. The cases range in seriousness from the average speeder to the drunk driver; vary in intensity from the family squabble that disturbs the neighborhood to the family fight that ends in a homicide; and reflect backgrounds ranging from that of the ghetto dweller to the bank official. Most of these cases are minor, perhaps even mundane. They will rarely make the papers or the local TV news. Rather, such drama is reserved either for the higher courts or for the popularized versions of justice portrayed in television dramas.

Most Americans equate justice and the courts with the higher tribunals. We have associated justice and equal protection of the laws with the higher courts. Higher courts write reams of court opinions, adapt ancient legal protections to changing times, and cases are appealed to these courts to decide which direction the law will take. But for Altman and Boldt, and thousands like them, justice will not proceed to these higher tribunals. For them the crowded pews of arraignment court and the curt judge of traffic court are the realities of justice. As a rough estimate, the criminal courts yearly decide about 5,000,000 felony and misdemeanor cases similar to Altman and Boldt.[2] These totals make the courts

---

2 The President's Commission on Law Enforcement and Administration of Justice, *Task Force Reports: The Courts* (Government Printing Office, 1967), p. 31 & p. 154.

one of the most pervasive of governmental institutions. Indeed, for a sizeable proportion of the population, especially for those at the lower end of the economic ladder, the only contact with government will be through the criminal courts. The criminal courts far surpass the more dramatic actions of the president or congressional legislation in terms of how they affect the daily lives of the American citizen.

The lack of drama of the lower criminal courts masks the large amount of contact they have with the citizenry. The lack of drama and the mundane nature of the cases involved also obscure the nature of these citizen-government interchanges. Most contemporary governmental institutions are marked by the benefits they offer the citizenry, but not the courts. The courts seldom hand out direct benefits to the citizens (except in the form of revenge for the aggrieved party). Instead, the courts apply negative sanctions and serve as a crucial agency of social control. Simply put, the criminal courts enforce community norms.[3] They apply negative sanctions (either a fine or a term in jail, and sometimes a restriction of activities such as probation) to prohibited activity. It seems that when all else fails the criminal courts are called upon to take action. Thus, a large number of social problems end up in court. Problems as diverse as alcoholism, drug abuse, deviant sexual behavior—problems that are seemingly insolvable, at least in the short term, by other societal institutions—become entries in the court docket. Economic difficulties, marriages that are breaking up, abrasive interactions between landlord and tenant, or strangers in the bar wind up as the *People* vs *Boldt* and the *State* vs *Altman*. To a large extent, the failures of other contemporary institutions are given to the courts.

Thus, the courts in American society are called upon to execute a complex task. How well they perform these tasks has mushroomed within a decade into a prominent political issue. Increased crime, the politics of law and order, urban riots, and controversial court decisions are just a few of the factors that catapulted criminal justice to the forefront of national concern. Commentators representing a wide variety of political opinions seem to agree that the courts are not functioning properly. All agree that something is wrong with the way in which the criminal courts administer justice, but such consensus really masks more *fundamental* disagreement on what has produced these ills.

---

[3] For example, see Herbert Jacob, *Justice in America*, 2d edition (Little, Brown, 1972), pp. 21–29.

For example, a common criticism of the criminal courts has been that they coddle criminals. The courts are said to hamper effective law enforcement. It is somewhat anomalous that the questioning of the role of the courts as crime fighters arose at the same time that the opposite concern surfaced. Some criticized the courts for focusing too much on crime fighting and not enough on the administration of equal justice. The .courts have been pictured as dispensing one type of justice to the rich and another type to the poor and minority groups. In the caldron of the 1960s and 1970s, the criminal courts have been buffeted by the somewhat contradictory charges that the courts do not fight crime and do not administer fair and equal justice.[4]

No matter what the ideological perspective (and the issue of law and order, as well as court reform, involves switching traditional alignments), all agree that the criminal justice system presents some basic contradictions. While the Constitution guarantees a speedy trial, in some communities the defendant (as well as the victim) may wait over a year before his case comes to trial. While the Constitution guarantees a jury trial, most cases are disposed of without a trial through the mechanism of plea bargaining. Thus, the contradictions are many, but most reduce to a basic duality—although the law is premised on an individual adjudication of cases, the overriding reality of criminal justice is its assembly-line approach. A man's day in court often involves waiting with scores of other people for a momentary encounter with the judge before being sent to jail, placed on probation, or fined. But this discussion of the importance of the courts as a social institution may be reduced to the basic question: what type of justice will Altman and Boldt receive? How will the criminal courts handle their cases and thousands like them?

This study investigates how one community—Prairie City— dispenses justice in the criminal courts. The focus is on the work of the criminal courts after the police have made an arrest and forwarded the defendant and the police report to the prosecutor's office. Because the focus is on the courts we do not examine the work of the police in depth. This should not be taken as a reflection that what the police do is unimportant, but rather as a reflection that one has only limited resources. However, throughout the book we shall discuss how the work of the police bears on

---

[4] For an interesting discussion of different perspectives on the purposes of the criminal law see Packer's discussion of the crime control and due process models. Herbert Packer, *The Limits of the Criminal Sanction* (Stanford University Press, 1968).

what the criminal courts of Prairie City do. Thus we are concerned with how the criminal courts dispense justice, how they
decide which suspects should be charged with a crime, who will
be released prior to trial, who is innocent, and what penalties the
guilty must pay. To begin answering these questions we need to
examine the relationships between law and politics.

Law and Politics

Unfortunately, the social and political importance of the criminal courts have been obscured by the American belief that law
and politics are separate. A familiar phrase of American democ-
racy is "a government of laws and not of men." As a metaphor,
it is a good guide to the values of American society, but it is
hardly a good guide to the application of these values. It points out
the central importance of formal law in America, but it omits the
people who apply that law. The administration of justice, especially the application of criminal statutes, involves much more
than the laws in statute books, appellate court cases, court procedures, and rules of evidence. Statutes and their interpretation,
and rules of evidence and procedure, form the written law. But the
written law is not self-executing. It must be transformed into
living law, law that affects people. The difference between the
written law and the "law in action" is the people who apply that
written law—and in the process transform it.[5]

To illustrate this point, let us consider in greater detail the
cases of Boldt and Altman. In Mrs. Altman's case the facts are
likely to be straightforward—either she had a driver's license or
she did not. If she has failed to renew her license, Illinois law
provides an automatic penalty of three days in jail. Court officials,
however, usually view such a penalty as too harsh, particularly in
a case like Mrs. Altman's. Not only has she never been in trouble
before, but she has two preschool-age children at home. Will justice be served by depriving the children of their mother for several
days? In such situations the court officials (usually the judge,
but often the prosecutor) *circumvent* the law. Thus, Mrs. Altman,
and those like her, will be placed on probation. Although the
charge involved is relatively minor, it illustrates how the officials
who must apply the law and interpret it may make a decision at
variance with what the legislators intended.

Terry Boldt's case similarly involves such discretion by court
officials. However, since Boldt's case is more serious, the number

---

[5] Edwin Schur, *Law and Society* (Random House, 1968), p. 141.

of people who will decide his fate are greatly increased.[6] Judges, prosecutors, defense attorneys, probation officers, and perhaps a jury will be called upon to make judgments about the evidence, assessments about the type of persons involved, and also make discretionary decisions. Consider, for example, the decisions involved if he is found guilty and is to be sentenced. Under Illinois law, a convicted burglar can be sentenced to prison for an indefinite period of from one to ten years. Alternatively, the suspect may be placed on probation. But who decides between prison or probation? If the decision is made to send him to prison, who determines whether the term should be one to ten years or nine to ten? Here the beliefs and values of the participants come into play for there are obvious grounds for disagreement. One person might argue that Boldt has never been in trouble before and sending him to prison will be a hindrance rather than a help because prisons are often schools for crime. Someone else might approach the case from a different perspective and argue that the community has experienced a rash of burglaries, in which case a long prison term for this defendant will be a warning to others that crime does not pay.

Situations such as these arise in virtually every case, and often several times in each case. The administration of justice is not simply a question of applying the law to the facts. Rather, the law creates situations where decisions must be made. Should charges be filed? How much bail shall be required? Is the evidence sufficient to hold the suspect for trial? Is the suspect guilty? And finally, what sentence should be imposed?

The consequences of these decisions are quite important. It means some suspects will have to await trial in jail, while others will be free to return to their jobs and families until their case is decided. The question of who should be sent to prison and who should be placed on probation needs no elaboration. All of these decisions, plus others, involve a fundamental distribution of benefits and sanctions. Some suspects receive a different type of justice than others. Klonoski and Mendelsohn nicely summarize this point when they speak of the criminal courts as allocators of justice.[7]

Because the court systems make decisions with important con-

---

[6] In Illinois, seventeen-year-old defendants such as Boldt are tried as adults since state law specifies that juveniles are those sixteen and under. Other states, however, vary in their definitions of juveniles.

[7] James Klonoski & Robert Mendelsohn, eds., *The Politics of Local Justice* (Little, Brown, 1970), p. 3.

sequences and in the process allocate justice, the courts should be viewed as a political institution. In this context politics is not synonymous with partisan politics but has a broader meaning. A commonly accepted definition of politics is David Easton's statement that "Politics is the authoritarian allocation of values." [8] We can easily apply this definition to Congress or the presidency— both make major decisions about the distribution of goods and services in American society. Congress may pass laws giving subsidies to farmers but deny money for day-care centers. The president may decide to normalize diplomatic relations with Cuba, and press for tax reductions. All of these decisions are identified easily with politics. Yet because the courts deal with a large supply of nondramatic cases, normally we do not view the courts as allocating values. But they do, as we can see in the decision to release some suspects on bail but not others; to put Mrs. Altman on probation and send Mr. Boldt to prison. These are as much allocations of societal values as the decisions to spend tax money or to change the nation's international relations.

Klonoski and Mendelsohn provide a short summary of this essential concept of the courts as allocators of values: "Political considerations, broadly conceived, explain to a large extent who gets—and in what amounts and how—the 'good' (justice) that is produced by the legal system in the setting of the local community." [9] Thus, the law and the courts are not separate from politics. In fact, the legal system is best viewed as a subsystem of the larger political system. The officials who staff the courts are recruited through the political system (by election or appointment by an elected official) and the output of the court system affects society.

In summary, Mrs. Altman's case of driving without a license and Boldt's charge of burglary will be decided not only on the basis of what the formal law states, but also on the basis of the informal application of that law. How the judges, prosecutors, and defense attorneys interpret and apply the law can be just as important as what the law says. These people are the law appliers who translate the lifeless black letter law of statute books, rules of procedure, and appellate court cases into concrete decisions.

The term "law appliers" is not limited to those with legal training—judges, prosecutors and defense attorneys—but also

---

[8] David Easton, *A Systems Analysis of Political Life* (John Wiley, 1965), p. 350.

[9] Klonoski & Mendelsohn, *Politics of Local Justice*, p. xx.

includes the police, whose actions and decisions provide the raw materials for the criminal courts. The law is administered by different actors. Their views and perspectives, wishes and desires, shape the application of that law. Because these people make important decisions, they allocate justice. They place some people in prison and put others on probation; keep some in jail before trial and allow others their freedom until the case is settled, and they decide who is innocent and who is guilty. Thus, if we want to know how justice is administered in Prairie City, we must examine these law appliers.

How Do the Prairie City Courts Allocate Justice?

Attorneys who represent suspects accused of crime are well aware of the importance of the people who apply the law. In representing their clients they need to know not only what the law says, but also something about the people who administer that law. For example, one Prairie City defense attorney recalled an experience he had in another county. His first contact with this county involved a client accused of writing several bad checks. As is normal in such situations, the defense attorney talked to the prosecutor and the two reached the agreement that if the defendant pled guilty to one of the charges, the defendant would be placed on probation. Such deals are fairly common. When the defendant pled guilty, however, the prosecutor refused to honor his part of the bargain. Instead, he urged the court to send the defendant to jail for a year. The judge concurred with the prosecutor, and the suspect spent a year at the penal farm in Vandalia. As the lawyer reflected on his unhappy experience in the small Illinois county, it was obvious that he had misjudged the law appliers. It was obvious also that he did not plan to make such a miscalculation again.

Such a dramatic turnabout is rare, but it does illustrate the importance of the defense attorney knowing how the other law appliers go about their task. As another defense attorney phrased it:

> When I get to a new community on a case, I ask them flat out—
> what's the score here? Who has the power? For example, I need
> to know if the judge will concur with the prosecutor's sentence
> recommendation. I have to have some idea of what sentence the
> judge is likely to hand out.

This defense attorney acts as an amateur sociologist as he tries to plot the social network underlying the formal court system.

In asking how the Prairie City courts allocate justice, it is useful to begin by viewing the courts through the eyes of a defense attorney. He is as interested as we are in understanding how the law appliers go about their tasks. In other words, what kind of questions would a lawyer unfamiliar with Prairie City raise in order to plan the defense of his first client in the community. What would he need to know if he represented either Altman or Boldt? A snapshot of the social terrain would rapidly reveal some important features of the social network underlying the formal law. A lawyer new to Prairie City would soon find out that the chief judge has the reputation of being a hard liner who can be expected to give out long prison sentences. However, the outside observer soon would learn that the judge has relatively little power, for plea bargaining occurs between the defense attorney and the prosecution. The judge *pro forma* approves the agreements they reach. A snapshot of the social terrain would also show that certain crimes are handled differently than he might expect. According to Illinois law, for example, defendants convicted of aggravated battery can be placed on probation. In Prairie City, however, if the defendant used a deadly weapon he will not get probation. The defense attorney, acting as an outside observer, would also discover that if the defendant has a jury trial and is convicted, he will get a much longer prison term than if he had pled guilty.

The observations of our mythical defense attorney working in Prairie City for the first time highlight some important features of how justice is administered. In this way the task of the outside observer and the defense attorney are analogous—both wish to know who has the power and what are the consequences for such an ordering of power. At this point, however, the interests of the defense attorney and the interests of the outside observer diverge. Whereas the defense attorney needs to know enough to represent his client, the outside observer has a broader range of interests. For example, the defense attorney is interested only tangentially in how the judge views the prosecutor, yet the outside observer is likely to find this quite important. In short, our interests are much broader than those of the defense attorney.

We are interested not only in a broader range of questions, but we want to find out why things happen the way they do. For example, a lawyer's knowledge that the judge will approve *pro forma* plea bargaining agreements is sufficient in representing his client. The outside observer, however, wants to know why? Does the judge approve the "deals" of the defense and prosecution

because he does not care? Is it because he agrees with their results? Or, is it perhaps, because he does not have the power to
alter their arrangements?

As outside observers, therefore, we have a broader range of
questions that we wish to answer and we also wish to know why
things happen as they do. And, because the process is a complex
one, it is helpful to start with a set of broad questions. Going
to a community and asking, "How is justice administered?" will
not produce the most useful results. As others have observed,
such barefoot empiricism is not likely to focus on essential questions. Thus, in probing how justice is administered in Prairie
City, it is useful to begin with some questions to which we wish
to find the answers. In this way, our major premise that courts
allocate justice can be translated into more specific questions that
we can answer more easily. Five questions seem particularly important:

1] Who makes the decisions?
2] What standards are employed in making these decisions?
3] How do the decision makers interact?
4] How are the defendant's rights protected?
5] Who benefits from this process?

These questions should be regarded as preliminary. They need
elaboration and may omit some important features of the administration of justice. Nevertheless, they are useful beginnings, especially since past studies often failed to concentrate on such
basic issues.

Who Makes the Decisions?

A basic question in studying any social system is, who makes
the important decisions? At first glance such a question does not
seem too troublesome. After all, the tasks of the legal officials are
specified by law. This is true: but these legal blueprints at times
do not tell us who actually wields the power. An example should
clarify the point. According to the statutes, only the judge can
sentence a defendant. For example, only a circuit court judge can
formally send Boldt to the state prison for from one to ten years,
or place him on probation. But just because the judge has the
formal authority does not mean that he is wielding the power.
In Prairie City, on the contrary, the judge has relatively little to
say about the sentence because the prosecutor, defense attorney,
and probation officer make this important decision. The judge
normally ratifies, but seldom alters, their decision. Thus, in the

very important area of sentencing, the formal authority is not a guide to who makes the decision.[10]

Another situation reveals that formal authority does not provide guidelines for determining who makes the decision, and that the statutes are ambiguous about who should make the decisions. Consider the charging decisions: filing criminal charges is a very important activity of the criminal courts, yet the law does not specify who shall decide whether Boldt should be prosecuted or Altman's case be dismissed. Instead, the statutes merely allow the prosecutor, judge, and the complainant (usually the victim) to have a voice. Obviously, such ambiguous grants of power leave room for interpretation. A basic goal of this study is to determine who makes the decisions in Prairie City.

What Standards Are Employed in Making Decisions?

After one asks who makes the decisions, it is useful to inquire into the basis for those decisions. We wish to know how the judges, prosecutors, defense attorneys (or whoever is the important decision maker in a given issue) make these decisions. For example, what are the criteria for releasing suspects on bail? What factors are considered in deciding between prison and probation? The basis for the decisions has an obvious influence on how justice is allocated.

In examining the standards employed by the decision makers, we will discuss a particularly perplexing question in the administration of justice—how much discretion is involved? As we have already noted, the law is not self-executing; people must make decisions. Does this mean that the law is irrelevant? The answer is no, for several reasons. First, the law provides the context for decision making. It limits the ability of actors to do certain things. The law is not irrelevant for a second, very fundamental reason and that is that most of the law appliers (excluding the police) have been trained in law schools. Law schools teach the importance of the law, and one must assume that lawyers trained in the law are influenced by the formal law. Observing their activities for even an hour reinforces this view.

Thus, the formal law is not irrelevant, but as we have stressed continually, law does not make every decision ahead of time. If the law was so clear and unambiguous that all problems were presolved, then we would not need lawyers to apply that law.

---

[10] A more detailed discussion of these factors will be found in chapters 5 and 9.

The point is that law and discretion interact. The law provides a context for decision making, sets forth certain criteria, and the law appliers must adapt the law to the situations as they find it. One of the goals of this study is to try and determine where law ends and discretion begins.

How Do the Decision Makers Interact?

In asking who makes the decisions and the standards they employ, we will want to pay particular attention to how the law appliers interact. While the police, prosecutor, judge, and defense attorney represent separate institutions, they must work together. In carrying out their assigned tasks, these law appliers interact on an almost daily basis. Such interactions are crucial because no one law applier can make decisions independently. Each must consider the reactions of others. This can be seen by examining the defense attorney. The lawyer representing Boldt in the burglary case will have to decide the best way to defend his client. Would it be best for Boldt to plead guilty, or would it be better to demand a jury trial? The course the lawyer chooses will depend on his assessment of what the judge, the prosecutor, and the jury are likely to do. The prosecutor who is handling the Boldt burglary case also will have to make judgments about what the defense attorney, the judge, and the jury will do. In short, none of these officials are isolated. Instead, they are closely intertwined in the execution of their tasks.

A useful way of conceptualizing these interactions is to view the courts as a social system. Abraham Blumberg, a former defense attorney who is now a sociologist, has suggested that we should view "the criminal courts as a social system, as a community of human beings who are engaged in doing certain things with, to, and for each other." [11] Viewing the courts as a social system highlights the importance not only of the people who administer the law but also the interrelationship of these officials. It is this social network that underlies the formal law.[12]

As in any social system, whether it be Congress, the local PTA or the city council, there are likely to be sources of agreement as well as of disagreement. Let us first consider sources of disagreement in the social system of the courts.

---

11 Abraham Blumberg, *Criminal Justice* (Quadrangle Books, 1967), pp. viii–ix.

12 Others who have employed a somewhat similar approach are George Cole, "The Decision to Prosecute," *Law and Society Review*, 1970, 4: 331–343 and Dallin Oaks & Warren Lehman, *A Criminal Justice System and the Indigent* (University of Chicago Press, 1967).

We would not expect the defense attorney to see eye to eye with the prosecutor or the police. After all, the defense attorney is viewing the situation through the eyes of his client, while the police and prosecutor can be expected to have a different perspective. Such differing perspectives are likely to produce tension. As Skolnick has commented in his study of the police, "The policeman and the judge consequently measure the quality of the policeman's work against inharmonious standards derived from the different responsibilities of each." [13] The police, the prosecutor, the judge, and the defense attorney are tied together in executing their tasks, but at the same time they have differing perspectives on how these tasks should be executed. These organizations have separate and different recruitment patterns, varying reward systems, and sometimes competing clientele. Political scientists should find the study of these competing expectations particularly rewarding, for the disagreements and tensions produced are likely to highlight contrasting views of the courts.

Thus, the courts, like most social institutions, exhibit disagreements among the components. But such disagreements normally must be muted. If the disagreements cannot be moderated, then the institution cannot perform its intended tasks. Consider the U.S. Senate, which, like the courts, is based on competing perspectives. A southern conservative seldom agrees with a northern senator from an industrial state. The Senate, however, has developed a series of unwritten rules designed to moderate these disagreements. During a debate, a senator never addresses his colleagues by name but instead uses his title, as for example, "the junior senator from Alabama." According to the unwritten rules, senators may disagree over bills, but this disagreement may not be carried over to their personal relationships. Thus, senators with such different perspectives as Goldwater and Kennedy may still be friends.[14] The court also develops such personal ties. Indeed, it is expected that lawyers arguing opposite sides of a case will not carry their disagreement to the corridors outside the courtroom. These are cohesive factors that mute possible tensions in the social system.

Thus, when we ask, "How do the decision makers interact?" we are interested not only in analyzing these interactions but also in exploring how these interactions affect the administration

---

[13] Jerome Skolnick, *Justice Without Trial* (John Wiley, 1967), p. 225.

[14] Donald Matthews, *U.S. Senators and Their World* (Random House, 1960), p. 97.

of justice. What consequences flow from the disagreements among the principal actors? How do the close working relationships that mute these tensions affect the allocation of justice?

How Are the Defendant's Rights Protected?

Probably the most distinctive feature of American criminal justice is the protection that it offers the suspect. No other criminal justice system, even the British, which is the forefather of the American system, creates so many rights. Among the numerous institutions designed to minimize abuse in the system and protect the suspect's rights are the preliminary hearing, grand jury, and provisions for release on bail. Nevertheless, the Warren Court still found many abuses in the process and sought to further protect the defendant against illegal police searches, abusive and coercive interrogations by the police, and denial of counsel.

Although these rights exist on paper it depends on the law appliers how and if life is breathed into them. One of the goals of this study is to determine how the social system that underlies the formal law shapes the procedural rights available to the suspect. Two apparent contradictions highlight the importance of studying the social system when discussing procedural rights of the defendant.

The first is the preliminary hearing, which is designed as an independent review of a case by an impartial judge. This can be an important protection for a suspect who is charged with the crime when little if any evidence points to his guilt. Yet in Prairie City the judge seldom fails to agree with the police and the prosecutor. Cases are dismissed only rarely at the preliminary hearing. Does this mean that the judge is not diligently protecting suspects' rights? Only an in-depth examination of how the social system uses and modifies the preliminary hearing can answer this question.

Our second example concerns confessions. The Supreme Court in *Miranda*, and several related cases, sought to protect suspects against coercive police interrogations. Across the nation, these decisions were attacked by some for handcuffing law enforcement. Yet in Prairie City the judge rarely suppresses a confession. If the confession was suppressed, it could not be used as evidence. Again, we wish to know how the law appliers are translating the formal protections derived from Supreme Court decisions into actual decisions that affect the people of Prairie City.

In inquiring how the social system affects the procedural

rights of the defendant, we should note that this orientation differs from most past studies. The traditional emphasis has been to study whether a suspect received all the protections afforded by the law. Several studies, for example, discuss the apparent anomaly that many suspects waive the preliminary hearing. We also are interested in whether these protections are utilized. Our emphasis, however, is different. These past studies adopted an absolutist position. Their unstated premise was that failure to have a preliminary hearing, grand jury, and so on, involved a denial of these rights, a denial that must be corrected.[15] We, on the other hand, are interested in the conditions for utilization or nonutilization of these rights. This orientation allows us to probe a question the absolutists never consider: do these institutions protect the rights they are supposed to shield? Thus, we wish to determine how important these protections are, as well as how the social system affects these procedural protections.

Who Benefits?

A fundamental question in political science is "who gets what?" [16] This question was the guiding light for our earlier discussion of the courts as allocators of justice. In asking who benefits, we are inquiring into the outcomes of the cases, the substance of the decisions reached. While this type of inquiry is a basic one, we should note that most past studies have not seemed interested in examining this aspect of the courts, having centered instead on the procedures and process of the courts. This emphasis is not necessarily misplaced because how the suspect is treated is of vital concern. At a very fundamental level, justice under the law may be reduced to the question of whether the suspect believed he was treated fairly. Thus, we wish to examine procedural protections of a suspect's rights, and at the same time place an equal emphasis on the outcomes of the process. After all, a suspect is probably less interested in whether he receives the full panoply of the law's protections than he is in what will happen to him. Will he be released on bail? Will he go to prison?

We are interested in who benefits from the court process. The underlying concern is that different types of defendants may receive different types of justice. For example, we wish to know whether the rich receive a different type of justice than the poor?

---

[15] See Klonoski & Mendelsohn, pp. 4–5; Jacob, *Justice in America*, p. 206.

[16] Harold Lasswell, *Politics: Who Gets What, When, and How* (Meridian Books, 1958).

Do the young receive different treatment than adults? In examining who benefits from the court process, we hope to answer some of these questions.

Conclusion

Most Americans' mental image of justice centers on the marbled halls of the Supreme Court or some other high tribunal. For Altman and Boldt, and millions like them, though, the reality of justice consists of waiting with numerous other people for a brief encounter with a judge. The decor of their court is just as likely to be peeling paint as marble. Our defendants—Boldt and Altman —are but part of the stream of people the courts handle every year. The large volume of court work is marked by an important interaction between citizen and government—an interaction that is usually negative because the court's primary duty is the enforcement of community norms. In performing this task the courts handle a wide range of social problems. How well the courts perform this task has been the subject of sharp criticism within the last decade.

These problems and contradictions make the lower courts an important political and social institution. We cannot afford to treat them as an institution standing above the ebb and flow of society. The courts are deeply involved in society. The courts allocate justice since the legal officials who apply the black letter law to the actual cases coming before them are called upon to make numerous decisions. To repeat just a few of these important decisions: the courts must decide which suspects will be charged with a crime, which suspects will be released on bail, which suspects are innocent or guilty, and what should be done with the guilty.

In short, we want to know how the courts in Prairie City allocate justice. Hopefully, by studying one community we will have a better understanding of how the courts in general function. As a focus for our analysis we have posed five questions: 1] Who makes the decisions? 2] What standards are employed in making these decisions? 3] How do the decision makers interact? 4] How are defendants' rights protected? 5] Who benefits from this process?

Our analysis of the Prairie City court system will begin with the most crucial factor involved—the officials who are called upon to make the decisions. We will examine the values, preferences, and pressures of judges, prosecutors, defense attorneys, and police in Prairie City. In Part Two the focus shall be on how the courts process cases from the time the police make an arrest until the case is ready for trial. Part Three will examine how the guilt of the suspect is determined and how penalties are imposed.

The Setting of the Research

CHAPTER 2

This chapter answers many of the standard questions raised about research. What type of community was studied? Is it similar (or different) to other cities? Is crime a significant problem? What part do partisan politics play in the administration of justice? What kind of police force does the community have? How are the courts and prosecutors organized? Are there any significant features of the law that need to be considered? Why was this community chosen? And, finally, what types of research techniques were utilized? This chapter is intended to provide background information for the reader who wants to develop a mental image of the type of community under investigation. We should repeat at this point that the city has been given a fictitious name in order to preserve the anonymity of those who were interviewed.

Prairie City

Prairie City is a medium-sized Illinois community and county seat. According to the 1970 census, 90,000 people lived in the city with an additional 30,000 residing in the county. Located in the central part of the state, Prairie City lies within fifty miles of several other communities of similar size.[1] One of these cities, University Towns (another fictitious name), is also mentioned occasionally. University Towns served originally as a pretest site for the interview schedule. Subsequent research showed that, despite their geographical proximity, justice was administered in a decidedly different fashion in the two towns. Therefore illustra-

---

[1] The fictitious name of the city is borrowed from a study by Joel Handler on lawyers in civil practice in Prairie City. Joel Handler, *The Lawyer and His Community* (University of Wisconsin Press, 1967). Much of the background information on the city is taken from this work, pages 6–10. Additional information on Prairie City can be found in Daniel Elazar, *Cities of the Prairie* (Basic Books, 1970).

tions from University Towns have been incorporated to highlight significant features of criminal justice in Prairie City.

The central location of Prairie City is largely responsible for its diversified economy. Originally settled as a railroad service center, Prairie City has become a major manufacturing center. A number of national firms have plants in the city where a variety of goods ranging from construction equipment, electronic components, and plumbing fixtures to processed meat and grain are produced. Prairie City is not a one company town, however. The largest single company, a grain processing firm, employs no more than four thousand workers. Only a handful of firms employ over a thousand workers. Thus the thirty percent of the work force employed in the manufacture of durable and nondurable goods is not tied to any one employer. Because of its proximity to other cities, Prairie City also serves as a regional retail and wholesale center. Roughly twenty percent of the work force is employed in such trade.

Although the size of the community (neither large nor small) and the diversity of the economy might suggest that it has a heterogeneous population, this is not the case. While some cities have an extensive foreign-born population, only five percent of the Prairie City residents were born outside of the United States. Another measure of the heterogeneity of a community is religous pluralism. In Prairie City, however, the population is predominantly Protestant. Only twenty percent of the population belongs to the Roman Catholic Church. Thus in terms of ethnic stock and religious preference, Prairie City is a homogeneous community.[2]

The only significant minority group in Prairie City are the nonwhites (predominantly black). Like most cities, Prairie City has experienced increased black migration. The number of blacks has grown from five percent in 1960 to eleven percent in 1970. Concomitant with the influx of blacks has been increased racial tensions; the racial problems of the sixties did not bypass Prairie City. In 1968 Prairie City had a riot, but little physical damage was done. Besides the riot the only visible measure of racial tension exists in the area of school busing. The blacks live in two or three areas of the city. The school board adopted a school busing

---

[2] Handler also cites a 1950 study of Prairie City that found a general blurring of class differences. While many communites are divided between working class and middle class, the class lines in Prairie City are blurred. The study was originally done by Elazer. See Handler, *The Lawyer and His Community*, p. 160, footnote 9.

plan to alleviate the racial imbalance caused by this residential segregation. A citizens group formed to challenge the busing and, later, sought to defeat incumbent members of the board who sought reelection. The retention of the school board members served to defuse the issue.

Thus Prairie City was not insulated from the racial problems of the sixties but no event has served to intensify racial hostilities. While the influx of blacks somewhat affected the otherwise homogeneous makeup of the city, the racial issue has not fundamentally changed the dominant pattern. For one thing the proportion of the total population that is black is not very large—only eleven percent. For another, jobs in the city are reasonably plentiful and the city has no recent history of job discrimination.

To better place the economic, social and racial attributes of Prairie City in perspective, table 1 provides a social and economic

TABLE 1
A SOCIAL AND ECONOMIC PROFILE OF PRAIRIE CITY AND THE STATE OF ILLINOIS

	Prairie City	Illinois
Population, 1970	90,000	11,109,450
Population growth, 1960–70	15.9%	13.6%
Percent nonwhite	11.0%	13.6%
Percent foreign-born	5.1%	5.7%
Median school years completed	12.1	12.1
Percent employed in manufacturing	31.9%	30.3%
Percent employed in white collar jobs	48.0%	49.1%
Median income	$10,239.	$10,959.
Percent under poverty level	7.7%	7.7%

Sources: U.S. Bureau of the Census, *Census of Population: 1970 General Population Characteristics* (Government Printing Office, 1971); U.S. Bureau of the Census, *1970 General Social and Economic Characteristics* (Government Printing Office, 1972).

profile of both the city and the state. These figures show that Prairie City mirrors Illinois. In terms of education, foreign-born population, white collar and manufacturing employment, median income, and percent under the poverty line, Prairie City deviates no more than two percent from the state as a whole. The only differences are minor—Prairie City has slightly fewer nonwhites and has grown slightly faster than the rest of the state. In short, Prairie City is as representative of Illinois as any community in the state.

Crime

Given the social, economic, and racial attributes of Prairie City, does it have the amount of crime one would expect? To answer this question table 2 reports the 1970 crime rate for Prairie City along with the national average for cities in the same population category. These figures are crimes known to the police. Although the FBI figures have been extensively criticized, they are the only figures available.[3] A matching of the two columns in table 2 shows that on the whole Prairie City closely parallels the national average. Note, however, that for certain offenses (murder, manslaughter, rape, and auto theft) the city falls significantly below the national average. On the other hand aggravated assault and larceny over fifty dollars are higher than the national average. Because of the problems with the FBI crime data, we should not extend our interpretation any further. But the figures do indicate that Prairie City's major crimes fall well within the average for cities of its size.

Although the average citizen is most interested in comparing crime rates, it is equally important to examine the absolute numbers. While the crime rates allow a comparison to other communities, the unstandardized figures indicate the workload of the law enforcement agencies. Again referring to table 2, Prairie City had over 2,000 crimes reported to the police in 1970. By far the largest single category was burglary with over 1,000 offenses. These numbers indicate that even though Prairie City has an average amount of crime, in terms of the actual volume the police and the criminal courts have a large workload.

The problem of crime should not be equated solely with the objective data—the amount of crime known to the police. Subjective assessments made by the police, prosecutors, and judges are just as important. All of those interviewed thought there was more crime than there should be, but none believed that crime in Prairie City had reached crisis proportions. This subjective assessment is critical because one would expect that officials who perceive crime to have reached epidemic levels would be likely to respond in a different manner than officials who consider the crime rate as high but still at manageable levels.

---

[3] The FBI crime figures have been criticized on two accounts: 1] many crimes are never reported to the police and 2] police reporting of crimes can be juggled to show either high or low crime rates. A useful summary of these critiques can be found in Edwin Schur, *Our Criminal Society* (Prentice-Hall, 1969), pp. 27–36.

TABLE 2
CRIME IN PRAIRIE CITY AS COMPARED
TO OTHER CITIES—1970.

FBI Crime Designation	(Rates per 100,000) National Average (Cities 50,000 to 100,000)	Prairie City
Murder	5.2	3.32
Manslaughter	3.2	0
Forcible rape	15.3	3.32
Robbery	110.2	143.8
Aggravated assault	142.8	219
Burglary	1,114.5	1,100.6
Larceny over $50	1,094.0	873.9
Auto theft	477.0	164.8
Crime index	2,959	2,628.3

Source: U.S. Department of Justice, Federal Bureau of Investigation, *Crime in the United States, Uniform Crime Reports—1970* (Government Printing Office, 1971).

In terms of crime in Prairie City, we need to note one important qualification. While Prairie City has the full range of street crimes, it has little vice. Drugs, prostitution, illegal gambling, and public drunkenness are a major concern in many communities, particularly the large urban centers, but such vice problems are absent in Prairie City. For example, Prairie City has only one bordello, a small numbers racket (that the police periodically break up), and only a small (but growing) drug problem. This relative lack of vice is an important qualification to bear in mind when comparing Prairie City to other cities that have been studied. Many past studies draw heavily for their examples and illustrations on vice problems in law enforcement. This is understandable since vice presents the police and the courts with the most difficult legal problems. However, legal problems with vice enforcement are not necessarily the same types of problems faced in other crime areas. Thus the unique problems involving vice enforcement are not discussed in this book, because vice is not a major concern in Prairie City. Rather the problems in Prairie City involve the serious street crimes—murder, robbery, burglary, and so on.

The Police

Since the police force is the public agency most immediately concerned with crime, it is appropriate to begin a discussion of the criminal justice agencies in Prairie City by examining them. Police functions in Prairie City are carried out by two major organizations: the city police department and the county sheriff's office. (Several small departments have equally small police forces, but the number of cases they handle is so negligible they can be safely excluded from the analysis.)

The sheriff in Illinois is an elected county official. He provides police protection for the unincorporated areas of the county and administers the county jail. In Prairie City the sheriff has twenty-two deputies, several of whom are assigned exclusively to managing the jail. The small staff, coupled with the multiple tasks of the sheriff's office, leaves only a small number of deputies available to patrol the unincorporated areas of the county. Since there is relatively little crime in the sheriff's jurisdiction, his office does not provide many cases for the criminal justice system.

Having described the tasks and organization of the sheriff's department, we should note the quality of the services provided. The sheriff's department is not a highly professionalized police force. For example, little training is provided beyond that required by state law. In particular, the state's attorney does not view the sheriff's department as very thorough in their investigations, a point that will be developed in greater detail in chapter 6.

The bulk of the arrests (and subsequent court cases) involve the Prairie City police department, which has one hundred sworn officers and twenty-four civilian employees. The department consists of patrol, detective, juvenile, and administrative divisions. Most notably lacking is a specialized traffic division. Of special interest is the detective division, because these officers have the most contact with the criminal courts and the state's attorney's office. Detectives investigate all cases, both felony and misdemeanor, which require more inquiry than the initial report by the patrolman. The detectives, therefore, perform the tasks most likely to be scrutinized by the courts: police interrogations; police line-ups: search and seizure of evidence; and testimony in court. As a result the beat patrolmen has only occasional contact with the rest of the criminal justice system, but the detectives have a continuous interaction.

Before analyzing the professionalism of the city police department, we should note a recent event that influenced the department. In the early sixties, the city fathers hired a new police chief from outside the department. The chief's tenure produced accelerating controversy. There were serious morale problems in the department as well as a number of resignations. In addition, the character of the chief was not held in high repute. For example, during an early interview a defense attorney was highly critical of the police chief's veracity. At first these comments were interpreted as a defense attorney's expected reaction to the police. But subsequent interviews with other defense attorneys, judges, prosecutors, and police officers revealed the same pattern. In 1968 the police chief was removed from office after being convicted of stealing a television set from the police evidence room. In short, the tenure of the former chief was quite controversial, and this experience served to temper changes within the department.

Assessing the professionalism of a police department is not an easy task because the concept is essentially qualitative. A study by James Q. Wilson, however, provides some categories useful for a discussion of the type of police force in Prairie City. Wilson studied eight communities and categorized them as a watchman style or a legalistic style.[4]

The hallmark of the watchman style department is noninvolvement. Like the watchman of the nineteenth century, the police try to maintain the peace and, in the process, ignore minor violations of the law. The watchman style department makes few arrests for traffic or misdemeanor offenses and treats juveniles informally. Such a police force has several key characteristics: low pay; low educational requirements for joining the force; little training; and promotion based on personal or political ties. Watchman style police forces are found most often in working class towns that have a partisan political system where little emphasis is placed on good government.

A legalistic style police department is an extension of the reformed city with nonpartisan elections and a professional city manager. Such communities place high emphasis on governmental services. The police reflect this orientation. They are paid higher salaries, have higher educational requirements for joining the force, provide training for the force, and promote on the basis of merit. The legalistic style department defines its task not just as maintaining order but as enforcing the law. Thus, the legalistic department does not ignore common minor violations but makes more arrests for traffic and misdemeanor offenses. This kind of department handles juveniles formally through the courts.

The differences between the watchman and legalistic style are

---

4 James Q. Wilson, *Varieties of Police Behavior* (Harvard University Press, 1968).

intended to illuminate two ends of a continuum rather than to provide precise categories for describing every police department. Where does the Prairie City department fit on this continuum? It falls somewhere between the two ends but more closely resembles the legalistic style than the watchman style. For example, the Prairie City department has introduced in-service training programs, is raising the educational requirements for new recruits, and bases promotions on civil service examinations. These developments are fairly recent, however, so the Prairie City police department is best described as moving in the direction of a legalistic style department. That it has not reached this stage is shown by a study of the force by outside consultants who criticized many facets of the department's operations. In terms of arrest behavior, the department also falls between the watchman style and the legalistic style. The emphasis is not on full enforcement of the law, but on the other hand such behavior is not ignored as it would be in a watchman style department. In short, the Prairie City police department is moving in the direction of greater police professionalism.

The State's Attorney's Office

After the police arrest a suspect, the case is forwarded to the state's attorney's office. The state's attorney, an elected county official in Illinois, is the chief prosecutor for the county, equivalent to the district attorney in other states. In Illinois, unlike some states, however, the state's attorney prosecutes both felonies and misdemeanors. The only local arrests not prosecuted by the state's attorney are city ordinance violations, which are the province of the city attorney. The city attorney in Prairie City, however, is not very active. For example, the police can write a traffic offense either as a city ordinance violation or as a violation of the state traffic code. The police prefer to cite the violator under the state code because the state's attorney provides more vigorous prosecution. As a result, city court handles very few cases.

The office of the Prairie City state's attorney consists of the state's attorney, five assistants, and one investigator (who has no legal training). An understanding of the structure of the office is important for our later discussion of the work of the office. The number two man in the state's attorney's office is the first assistant. His primary responsibility is felony cases. The first assistant reviews all cases that might be prosecuted as a felony and prosecutes about half of the felony cases filed. One of the younger assistants prosecutes the less serious felonies. There are three young assistants in the office who handle a variety of tasks. All three are assigned to a specific court (misdemeanor, traffic, or preliminary hearing). They also divide the misdemeanor and traffic cases. Finally, one assistant works exclusively on juvenile cases. Since the handling of juveniles involves a very different process than criminal cases, the work of the juvenile assistant is not discussed in this book.

The state's attorney devotes his time to cases that are appealed and to supervision of the office. Only on rare occasions does he personally conduct a jury trial, perhaps because the assistants are better trial attorneys than their boss. The state's attorney supervises the office in an informal manner. He is available to discuss problems with an assistant, but the bulk of the day-to-day work is performed by the assistants without his direct supervision. The state's attorney's assistants prefer this arrangement. They view themselves as professionals, not bureaucrats, and like working on their own. The opportunity to gain experience is a primary reason most assistants join the office. They view the state's attorney's office as a stepping-stone to private practice, and the more responsibility they are given the greater their experience.

Given the overlapping responsibilities of the assistant state's attorneys, the promise to preserve their anonymity, and the awkwardness of the phrase "assistant state's attorneys," the remainder of the book uses the term "state's attorney" to refer to the office collectively. Where appropriate, however, we will distinguish between the state's attorney and his assistants.

The Courts

Deciphering the structure of American courts is a difficult task because the labels are confusing and contradictory. For example, "supreme court" usually refers to the highest court in the state or nation. In New York, however, the supreme court is the county court—the lowest trial court in the state. Such confusion usually stems from state constitutions that were adopted in the nineteenth century and not altered since. Illinois, however, is one of the few states that reorganized its court system. The 1964 judicial amendment to the Constitution abolished all local courts and replaced them with a single circuit court. Thus Illinois has only three levels of courts: the State Supreme Court; Courts of Appeals; and twenty-one Circuit Courts. This arrangement means the smaller counties have judges who ride circuit, while judges are permanently assigned to large counties.

Prairie City has four circuit judges, but one of them spends two mornings a week in a neighboring county. The circuit court handles the most important cases: felonies, juvenile proceedings, probate, divorce, personal injury, and the like. The minor cases come to the magistrates court, a subdivision of the circuit court. Magistrates court hears misdemeanors, traffic violations, minor civil cases, city ordinance violations, and the preliminary stages of felony cases (arraignment, setting of bail, and preliminary hearing).

The contrasting jurisdictions of the police, state's attorney, and courts produces a confusion we should clarify at this point. Notice that most of the criminal cases begin with an arrest by the *city* police department, and are prosecuted by a *county* official in a *circuit* court. To simplify the nomenclature this book uses one term—Prairie City—to refer to both city officials and county officers. This should cause no confusion if we bear in mind that the criminal courts are effectively organized on a county level.

Partisan Politics

Judges and the state's attorney are elected officials in Illinois. Since elected officials in many communities have close ties to their parties, this section considers the degree to which partisan politics affects the administration of criminal justice in Prairie City.

Historically, central Illinois has been dominated by the Republicans. Prairie City, however, has a functioning two-party system. Although the GOP dominated city politics until 1928, the Depression produced a general shift to the Democrats. Since the thirties the Republicans have been gaining voters and as a result enrollment in the two parties was about evenly divided in the late sixties. The county officials tend to be Democrats, while the county board and the state representatives are Republicans.

The court system and the administration of justice is insulated from party politics, which is unlike many other communities. For example, the President's Commission on Law Enforcement and Administration of Justice commented on "the high political orientation of the prosecutor's office," pointing out that "prosecutors in most cities select a high proportion of their assistants primarily on the basis of party affiliation. . . ." [5] This pattern does not apply to Prairie City. The state's attorney, while

---

[5] The President's Commission on Law Enforcement and Administration of Justice, *Task Force Report: The Courts* (Government Printing Office, 1967), p. 73.

a Democrat, is only nominally involved in party affairs. His assistants are not chosen for their involvement with the local party. Not only are none of the assistants active in party politics, but at least one is a Republican.

The judges in Prairie City are not politically active. Illinois judges are initially elected on a partisan ballot, but once elected they run unopposed on their record. Magistrates, however, are not elected but appointed by the circuit judges. In many cities, the elected office of the judge has made judgeships dependent upon the political party. In Chicago, for example, a lawyer is slated for a judgeship on the basis of loyal work for the party machine. In short, the candidate seeks the party. In Prairie City, on the other hand, the party usually seeks a candidate. As one of the top Democratic leaders described the selection process, most trial attorneys do not want to be a judge. They prefer the more active career of being a trial attorney, which also pays more. When a judgeship becomes vacant the party looks for a qualified lawyer who is willing to run. The competitive two-party system of Prairie City is reflected in the party backgrounds of the judges —two are Republicans and two are Democrats.

Clearly, in Prairie City the court system and partisan politics are distinctly separate. The parties play a nominal role in running people for office but beyond that exert no influence. Interviews and observations also failed to turn up any indication that the party influenced the administration of justice. On occasion a person would request a break from the state's attorney because the person supported him in the last election. Such requests were either ignored or the normal fine increased.

The lack of favoritism for party members also is indicative of the general lack of corruption in the administration of justice. In some cities traffic-ticket fixing, special handling for party members, and general political favoritism has been endemic.[6] During the time of this study there was never even a hint of such favoritism. The state's attorney on several occasions recited a list of party officials and prominent local citizens who had been prosecuted by his office. This evidence is persuasive because some of the persons interviewed were critical of the state's attorney and/or the judges. All agreed, however, that they were too independent for corruption or favoritism even to be considered.

An incident that occurred after the study was completed also corroborates the conclusion that there is no favoritism or corrup-

---

[6] Wilson, *Varieties of Police Behavior*, pp. 101–102.

tion in the administration of justice. The local paper reported that a traffic ticket had been fixed. The defendant had been convicted of speeding. Such convictions are then forwarded to the Secretary of State, who is in charge of drivers' licenses. If this defendant's conviction had been forwarded he would have lost his license under the point system used in Illinois. Instead, the conviction was not forwarded to the Secretary of State. The newspaper's account brought an investigation by the state's attorney that resulted in conviction of the defendant, a state representative, and the clerk of the county court. The minor nature of the event, coupled with the strong official response of the state's attorney, indicates that not only is corruption rare, but even the smallest transgression invokes the ire of the community.

Distinctive Features of Illinois Criminal Law

Although this study focuses on the discretion of the law appliers and how their contacts with other officials shape their decisions, we should not leave the impression that what the law says is insignificant. On the contrary, the formal law is critically important because the law provides categories for decisions, setting forth permissible alternatives and at the same time prohibiting other options. Further, the law appliers (here excluding the police) are lawyers, who have been trained to respect the formal law. In this sense we can speak of the law as providing the setting for the exercise of discretion, and throughout the book we will discuss how the formal law structures decision making.

In this context we should point out that Illinois law has several distinctive features not found in other states. As already noted, Illinois—unlike most states—has unified its court structure. But this alteration in the structure of justice is of less importance than changes made in the substance of justice, the criminal code. In 1961 the Illinois legislature adopted a new criminal code and code of criminal procedure. Criminal codes are always undergoing piecemeal change but Illinois systematically redrafted the entire code.[7] This rewriting produced five significant changes: decriminalization of certain vice offenses; reduction of statutory penalties; alteration of common-law criminal definitions; expanded arrest powers for the police; and reform of the bail system.

---

[7] For an analysis of the revision of the Illinois criminal code by a lawyer and a political scientist see: Robert Salisbury & John Heinz, "A Theory of Policy Analysis and Some Preliminary Applications." In Ira Sharkansky, ed., *Policy Analysis in Political Science* (Markham, 1970), pp. 39–60.

One of the major questions in the administration of criminal justice is whether certain deviant acts should be illegal. The nation is debating whether abortion, gambling, using marijuana, and homosexuality between consenting adults should be prohibited by the law. Critics contend that acts that do not harm others should not be made illegal, citing alleged disrespect for the law and illegal police behavior as major consequences of current laws.[8] On the other hand, defenders of these laws believe they are necessary for the protection of society and that removing the criminal penalties would mean government was sanctioning these activities. The redrafting of the Illinois criminal code decriminalized several areas, particularly homosexuality between consenting adults in private. Sunday blue laws and public drunkenness were removed from the list of societal prohibitions. At the same time statutory rape was reduced from a felony to a misdemeanor. Thus several of the gray areas of the criminal law were decriminalized in Illinois.

The redrafting of the Illinois criminal code also altered the prison sentences that may be imposed upon the guilty. Most criminal codes are historical accumulations of past legislative actions that can result in inconsistencies. For example, horse stealing is still a very serious offense in some states. Illinois removed such inconsistencies and substituted a more contemporary list of penalties. Table 3 provides a summary of the statutory penalties for major offenses. Compared to other states these penalties are less severe than most.

Commensurate with the modification in potential prison sentences, the Illinois legislature also altered the criminal definitions. The criminal codes in most states (Louisiana's civil law tradition excluded) are legislative enactments of the common law. Some states make a distinction between daytime and nighttime burglaries, and the latter are punished more severely. New York's code specifies five degrees of assault. The new Illinois criminal code, however, makes no distinction between daytime and nighttime burglaries. The assault section provides for only two offenses: assault (a misdemeanor) and aggravated assault (a felony). The codification of the definitions of crime has had a major impact on the way plea bargaining is conducted, as we shall see in chapter 9.

---

[8] For an introductory treatment of this topic see: Edwin Schur, *Crimes Without Victims* (Prentice-Hall, 1965). For a more advanced discussion see: Herbert Packer, *The Limits of the Criminal Sanction*.

TABLE 3
STATUTORY PENALTIES IN ILLINOIS
FOR COMMON FELONIES IN YEARS.

| | Penalties | |
Felonies	Minimum	Maximum
Theft	1	10
Burglary	1	indefinite
Robbery, unarmed	1	20
Robbery, armed	2	indefinite
Battery, aggravated	1	10
Rape	4	indefinite
Indecent liberties with a minor	4	20
Murder	14	indefinite
Voluntary manslaughter	1	20
Involuntary manslaughter	1	10

Source: *Illinois Revised Statutes*, Chapter 38, 1971.

In altering the common law traditions, Illinois also expanded police arrest powers. At common law the police can arrest a suspect for a misdemeanor only if the crime has been committed in his presence. This practice is followed in the majority of states. But Illinois now allows its police officers to arrest whenever they have reasonable grounds to believe a crime has been committed, irrespective of whether a felony or misdemeanor is involved. Thus Illinois police have broader arrest powers than in other states.[9]

Finally, the legislature reformed the bail system and indirectly eliminated the bail bondsmen. Bail bondsmen secure a defendant's release by posting bail, in return for which the bondsmen charges a ten percent fee. Historically, the bail bondsmen has been associated with many abuses in the criminal justice system. The Illinois statute eliminated the need for the middleman because the defendant is allowed to post ten percent cash bail with the clerk of the court. Thus if the bail is set at $1,000 the defendant must raise $100, the same fee as the bail bondsmen would charge. The only difference is that when the defendant appears in court as scheduled, he receives a refund of ninety percent of the amount he posted. The law also provided for nonmonetary forms of pretrial release. A court may release a suspect on his own recognizance and the police can release a suspect on a Notice to Appear (which functions like a traffic ticket). The implications of these reforms are discussed in chapter 7.

---

[9] Wilson, *Varieties of Police Behavior*, p. 22.

Criminal Justice in Medium-sized Communities

So far in this chapter we have examined some important features of Prairie City: the diversified economy; the relative homogeneity of the population; the average crime problem; the composition of the police agencies; the organization of the state's attorney's office; the structure of the courts; the lack of partisan involvement in the criminal justice system; and distinctive features of Illinois criminal law and criminal procedure. This information provides general background data so the reader may compare Prairie City to his own community and/or to communities researched by others. In the next section we will discuss how the research was conducted and how the data were gathered. But first we should explain how Prairie City was chosen for research, and why a medium-sized community was selected.

The selection of a medium-sized community was determined primarily by the objectives of the study. Whereas the bulk of past research has analyzed single agencies (police, prosecutor, judges, or defense attorneys), this research focuses on the *interrelationships* of these agencies. A medium-sized community is ideally suited for such a study because the number of persons directly involved in the administration of criminal justice is not large. By contrast, the criminal courts in the large cities involve so many persons that it is more difficult to study how the various parts fit together. At the same time the small volume of cases in rural communities is insufficient for the type of analysis undertaken.

Not only has past research focused on single agencies, it has centered on criminal justice in large urban areas. This concentration on large cities obscures an important aspect of the administration of criminal justice: in the aggregate, the small and medium-sized communities handle a substantial number of cases. Chicago, for example, has fewer felony prosecutions than the rest of the state. Table 4 documents this important consideration. For ease of comparison, Illinois has been divided into Cook County (Chicago and suburbs) and Downstate (the other 101 counties). Although the state's eleven million inhabitants are divided almost equally between Cook and Downstate, table 4 shows that crime is not equally distributed. Cook County has twice as much crime known to the police as the rest of the state. Felony prosecutions, however, show no such imbalance. Downstate prosecutes more felony defendants than Cook County. Similarly, a large proportion of the prison population (forty percent in 1970) come from Downstate. Thus, Cook County has more crime than the rest of the state, but Downstate handles a comparable workload in terms of the criminal courts and the prison system.

Although crime is clearly associated with the larger cities, table 4 shows that if one is interested in how those arrested are

TABLE 4

COMPARISON OF CRIME RATES, COURT CASES, AND PRISON SENTENCES IN DOWNSTATE AND COOK COUNTY, ILLINOIS

	STATE TOTALS	COOK	DOWNSTATE
1970 Population	11,109,450	5,487,845	5,621,605
	(100%)	(49.4%)	(50.6%)
Serious crimes known to the police—1970	260,884	170,398	90,476
	(100%)	(65.3%)	(34.7%)
Felony defendants—1970	12,865	5,049	7,816
	(100%)	(39.2%)	(60.8%)
Cases dismissed—1970— as percent of all cases		40%	47%
Jury trials as percent of all nondismissed cases		10.1%	10.55
Percent convicted by jury		20.9%	34.0%
Percent sentenced to prison of those found guilty		65.0%	44.3%

Sources: Crime Studies Section, Illinois Department of Law Enforcement, *Crime in Illinois 1970* (Springfield, 1971). Administrative Office of the Illinois Courts, *1970 Annual Report to the Supreme Court of Illinois* (Springfield, 1971).

processed by the courts, then medium-sized communities are quite significant. Further, the study of the administration of criminal justice in a medium-sized community can serve as an important counterpoise to the studies done in large cities. Among other things, Prairie City does not have the problems of delay in the courts, overwhelming case loads, and vice problems often found in large cities like Chicago. Table 4 points out some differences between criminal justice in the Chicago area and the rest of the state. For example, Downstate counties dismiss a higher percentage of cases prior to trial, as well as employing jury trials more extensively. On the other hand, Cook County sends a higher proportion of the guilty to prison.[10] Thus, studying a medium-sized

[10] For an analysis of disparities in the administration of criminal justice in downstate Illinois see: David Neubauer, "Policy Outputs of Illinois Trial Courts: An Exploratory Study." Paper presented at the Annual Meeting of the American Political Science Association, Washington D.C., September 5–9, 1972.

community can point out what problems in the administration of criminal justice are unique to the urban areas and which are inherent in the criminal justice process.

The primary factor in selecting a research site was to find a medium-sized community. Prairie City was not chosen on the basis of any particular attributes. In this sense Prairie City does not claim to be representative of a wider universe. Given the sparseness of research in this area, this is not a major drawback. It is better to concentrate on raising critical questions and isolating major variables rather than making a premature attempt to determine how representative these factors are. Such concern with statistical sampling is better left to a later stage of research when one has confidence in the major dimensions under scrutiny.

Research Methods

Field research was conducted in Prairie City from October 1969 to April 1970. Several subsequent trips were made to the city in order to clarify some points and to monitor changes after the basic research was concluded. Three sources of data were collected: interviews, observation, and a court-docket study. Each data source complemented the other by eliciting different types of information. The three types of data yield a more complete picture than any source standing in isolation.

Using past studies of the administration of justice, a tentative interview schedule was drafted, pretested in University Towns, and then extensively modified. Conceptually, the interview schedule is of primary importance for it sought to specify in advance the framework for inquiry. In research with an exploratory thrust and a heuristic goal, these ends are best reached if important questions are specified in advance. A copy of the state's attorney's interview schedule is reprinted in Appendix I.

All major participants, and most of the minor ones, were interviewed. Since those interviewed were viewed as informants, no attempt was made to hold to the interview schedule. Since the participants tended to be specialists, there was no point in probing aspects of the administration of justice about which the respondent knew little. Flexibility in interviewing was also important in creating the proper atmosphere. Respondents were urged to talk about how things were done in their community. Once rapport had been established, the respondents invariably covered the topics envisioned and usually more.

Closely linked to the data obtained from the interview schedule was the information obtained during observation. Extensive time was spent in observing the prosecutor's office and the courts. In addition two weeks were spent with the detectives of Prairie City. The researcher was allowed to observe virtually all aspects of the state's attorney's office: contacts with defendants and victims; discussions with other attorneys; and in-house discussions. Such observation gave a perspective on the work and also allowed the researcher to pose questions at the appropriate time. Observation also extended to the courtroom. During court hours virtually all the participants are in the courtroom, and thus unavailable for interviews. The view from the court's back bench is important especially for the bulk of misdemeanors because defendants seldom hire attorneys. Most plead guilty on the first or second court appearance. During courtroom observation, participants also provided the researcher with background on what they were doing and why—thus adding to the accumulation of data on how justice is administered.

Interviews allow the participants to explain what they do. Observation permits the researcher to examine the decision-making process in action. Each yields valuable information, but it is advisable to supplement these sources with "harder" data. In this study, the disposition of cases was analyzed. Information for all felony cases in 1968 and all police arrests for January 1970 were coded. Methodological notes will be found in Appendix II.

Gathering data through interviews and observation is dependent upon access. Since access is such a concern in social science research, it is helpful to spell out the techniques used, as well as to reflect on the field research experience. Access proved to be a problem during the pretest; permission to interview the prosecutor's staff was denied. After this early setback, techniques were changed to improve chances of access. Whether these changed techniques were the cause or not, we cannot say, but we can report that no additional access problems were encountered.

In certain ways the choice of Prairie City was fortuitous. The state's attorney is best described as bighearted and willing to help anyone. The office is not so swamped with work that research would interfere greatly in the day-to-day activities of the office. More important, however, the research and the researcher were not viewed as a threat. No one felt he had anything to hide. Added to this was the element of flattery. People are glad someone is interested in what they are doing. They regard their task as important and are delighted someone else thinks so.

Once original contacts had been made, further access was no problem. In Prairie City the initial contacts introduced the researcher to other legal participants and so forth. By attending court sessions, etc., the researcher further indicated his interest in what was happening. Given this situation, participants were happy to discuss their work.

This relative ease of access is in sharp contrast to Erlanger's warning that "there may be difficulty gathering data in areas which involve a great amount of discretion, especially with respect to the prosecutor's office." [11] As with the "purple curtain" of the judiciary,[12] approach holds the key to access. What Erlanger fails to realize is that prosecutors do not see that they have that much discretion. During early interviews they stated that they did not consider themselves to have discretion in a sociological sense. Later they modified this to say they did have discretion in certain instances. Chapter 6 is an attempt to examine this discretion systematically. The point is, if one approaches the prosecutor as possessing discretion, and hence unwilling to allow research, then one is involved in a self-fulfilling prophecy. If, however, one shows a tactful interest in what the prosecutors do, the possibilities of access will be maximized.

The corollary of access is confidentiality. Sources were promised anonymity. For this reason we have concealed the city and refer to interviews only by position (state's attorney, defense attorneys, etc.). Divulging any other information would not be in accordance with the promises of confidentiality.

---

11 Howard Erlanger, "Jury Research in America: Its Past and Future," *Law and Society Review*, 1970, 4:359.

12 For another discussion of the problems of obtaining access to judges, see: Ted Becker, "Surveys and Judiciaries, or Who's Afraid of the Purple Curtain," *Law and Society Review*, 1966, 1: 133.

Part One · THE LAW APPLIERS

INTRODUCTION

Prosecutors, police, judges, and defense attorneys are the subject of Part One. In the first chapter we termed these officials law appliers because they must decide what the black letter law of the statute books and courts decisions mean in a specific case. What happens to Mr. Boldt (our hypothetical teen-age burglary suspect) and Mrs. Altman (the middle-class mother charged with not renewing her driver's license) is directly related to how these law appliers perform their jobs. Since the prosecutors, police, judges, and defense attorneys are the central figures in the administration of criminal justice, it is appropriate to begin by investigating how they define their jobs and how they interact with one another.

How the judges, prosecutors, and defense attorneys define their jobs, what they think is important about their tasks, and the goals they seek to achieve, is our first concern in Part One. We can label these factors role orientations, that is, "the actor's own expectations about the kind of behavior he ought to exhibit. . . ." [1] The actor's definition of what he should do is important because each actor may define his tasks in a different way. For example, some defense attorneys believe it is important to maintain

---

[1] John Wahlke et al., *The Legislative System* (John Wiley, 1962), p. 246.

good working relationships with the prosecutor. Others, however, believe they can best represent their clients by fighting the state's attorney on every point. Obviously these defense attorneys define their jobs in very different ways.

The interrelationships of the law appliers is the second concern of Part One. As we stressed earlier, the law appliers are not independent actors for each must be cognizant of the likely reactions of other decision makers. Further they are in almost daily contact with their counterparts. In turn these working ties are influenced by the fact that there are only a small number of actors. In Prairie City only fourteen people (out of the county population of one hundred and twenty thousand) are major participants in the criminal court process. While others operate on the periphery (notably police and jurors), their input is structured by four prosecutors, four judges, five defense attorneys, and one probation officer. The interrelationship of the law appliers thus are very much like a community. George Cole likens the justice system to a small town.[2] In the justice system, as in a small town, a person's reputation is a vital consideration. In Part One we want to determine how these interrelationships among the law appliers influence the administration of justice.

The number of law appliers in Prairie City is limited but this does not mean that analyzing their interrelationships is simple. Even small social systems may be complex. Given such complexity it is useful to have guidance in asking questions about how the system operates and explaining such operations. This study used role theory to structure the analysis and to construct the interview schedule. Role theory is particularly helpful because it suggests a number of factors that might otherwise be overlooked. In addition, role theory has been used

---

[2] George Cole, ed., *Criminal Justice and Politics* (Duxbury Press, 1972), p. 212.

to investigate a wide variety of social settings: schools, legislators, and hospitals.[3] Using role theory facilitates comparison to these other studies. A brief introduction to role theory as well as an explanation of some key terms should prove helpful.

The terminology of role theory is derived from the theater: an actor plays a role. According to the script he is expected to say his lines as would the character he is portraying. The script, however, only provides a framework for the actor, who has some freedom in deciding how he is going to play the part. The role of Hamlet, for example, is structured by the words of the play, but two actors may interpret the part differently. Role theory starts with this rather simple formulation and provides a more sophisticated set of categories for analyzing a wide variety of social behavior. In certain ways social behavior is analogous to the actors in a play. In society we talk of social positions as analogous to the parts of a play.

Let us examine several key points of role theory. The basic concept in role theory is expectations. Expectations are equivalent to the script of the play, for both structure the actor's behavior. Thus persons occupying social positions (roles) of father, judge, church member or college professor are expected to behave in certain ways. They have a framework for their actions (the parts of the play), a concept that is nicely summarized in Goffman's phrase, "bounded action." Thus the core of role theory is expectations: persons occupying certain social positions are expected to behave in certain ways. Closely related to expectations are rewards and deprivations. Those who deviate from the expected pattern are likely to meet with

---

[3] On role theory see Neal Gross, Ward Mason & Alexander McEachern, *Explorations in Role Analysis* (John Wiley, 1967). Other helpful and instructive works are John Wahlke et al., *The Legislative System*; Erving Goffman, *Encounters* (Bobbs-Merrill, 1961).

disapproval (termed sanctions) and those who
conform are likely to receive benefits (rewards).
This is not to say that all judges, fathers, or
college professors behave in the same way.
Obviously they do not. Instead, like actors playing
the part of Hamlet, persons play their societal
roles differently, but their actions are bounded by
the expectations of others. Role theory begins
with an analysis of expectations and sanctions in
order to determine the core of the role and what
differences in interpretation are considered
within the rules.

Given the complexity of society, it is not
possible to investigate all the roles that a person
plays. Instead one must choose those that are most
important. Of the rules listed previously, it is
possible that one person might play all of them as
father, trial court judge, church member, and
(sometimes) college professor. But not all of these
roles are equally important for a particular
analysis. If one were interested in a trial court
judge, his role of father, church member, and
part-time teacher could be excluded. The concept
of role set is employed in role theory to focus
the analysis on key variables. A role set
encompasses the persons or positions who have
expectations about the actions of the incumbent.

In our analysis of Prairie City the role set
of the prosecutor is analyzed. The state's attorney
was chosen as the focal position because his
duties require interactions with all the persons
involved in the administration of criminal justice.
Figure 1 diagrams this role set. We should note
two things. First, we have limited the number of
positions included. We could have added the
state's attorney's colleagues in other counties
or prison officials; however, the complexity of the
social system is so great that we have included
only the most important members of the role
set. Second, the diagram omits lines connecting
the members of the prosecutor's role set.
Although the defense attorney interacts with
jurors, judges, police, and so on, these lines have

been omitted in order to simplify the diagram. Such interrelationships, however, are very important and they will be examined throughout the book.

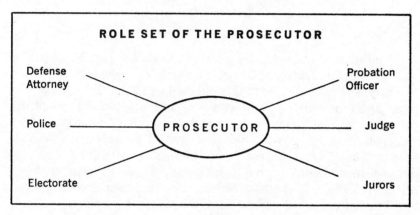

Figure 1

Prosecutors: House Counsel for the State

CHAPTER 3

The most important official in the criminal justice system is the prosecutor. Raymond Moley's comments, although made over forty years ago, are equally applicable today. "The great and constantly increasing significance of the American prosecuting attorney has been strangely neglected . . . it is quite clear that the potentialities of the office are limited by scarcely anything except the skill, intelligence, and the legal and political capacity of the incumbent." [1] The importance of the prosecutor flows directly from his central position, for his duties encompass the entire range of criminal justice. While other law appliers specialize in one area (the police in arrests, for example), the prosecutor must be concerned with all stages of a case. He is the only official who works with all the other law appliers. The prosecutor is dependent upon the police for input into his office. The processing of these cases requires contacts with judges, defense attorneys, and probation officers. Further, he must be conscious of the general public for the public will sit on juries, and if he is an elected official, may vote him out of office.

The centrality of the prosecutor's task is unique. Few political actors have the complex and varied strategic environment of the prosecutor. [2] The diversity of officials with whom the prosecutor must work provides ample opportunities for conflicting expectations to develop. For example, the police may pressure the prosecutor to recommend a lengthy prison sentence for a defendant, while a defense attorney may urge the prosecutor to concur in a recommendation for probation. Given the diversity of the

---

[1] Raymond Moley, *Politics and Criminal Prosecution* (Minton, Balach, 1929), p. 48.

[2] James Eisenstein, "The Federal Prosecutor and His Environment," Unpublished paper delivered at the Annual Meeting of the American Political Science Association, Washington, D.C., September 2–7, 1968.

actors the prosecutors must work with, and the conflicting expectations that develop, we would not expect every prosecutor to behave in the same way because the prosecutor has wide latitude in choosing how to run his office. Some prosecutors follow the advice of the defense attorney more than that of the police; others stress fighting crime and maintaining good relationships with the police.

Wayne LaFave's study of the police suggests four ways a prosecutor may approach his job.[3] Some prosecutors act as trial counsel for the police and reflect the views of the police at trials. Others view their job as house counsel to the police department and provide them legal advice but do not necessarily advance the police viewpoint in court. Still other prosecutors define their job as representatives of the court, which means they enforce rules that control the police. Finally, LaFave observes that still other prosecuting attorneys choose to reflect community opinion. LaFave has summarized the meaning of this diversity:

> Appraisal of the role of the prosecutor is made difficult because the role is inevitably more ambiguous than that of the police or the trial court. . . . A prosecutor, however, may conceive of his principal responsibility in a number of different ways. . . . The uncertainty as to whether the prosecutor is responsible for all these tasks and as to which is his primary responsibility creates difficult problems in current administration.[4]

To see how the Prairie City prosecutor approaches his complex task we shall examine three facets of the state's attorney's role orientation: 1] representational role—the prosecutor's view of the public, 2] purposive role—the major goals of the office, 3] career-orientations. Once we have established the major dimensions of the office, we shall examine how the prosecutor's definition of his job produces tension with the police.

The Representational Role: The Prosecutor and the Public

The most distinctive feature of the American legal system is the influence of the public on its operations. Whereas European courts maintain a distance, almost an aloofness from the public, American courts are relatively close to the people. Such differences are highlighted by contrasting recruitment systems. Euro-

---

[3] Wayne LaFave, *Arrest: The Decision to Take a Suspect into Custody* (Little, Brown, 1965), p. 515.

[4] Ibid.

pean judges and prosecutors are selected, trained, and promoted through a national career civil service, while American judges and prosecutors are locally recruited [5] often without regard to previous experience in the criminal process. In America the majority of legal officials (judges, prosecutors and, in some states, public defenders) are popularly elected. Even in places where popular elections have been replaced by appointments, studies show that the appointed judge is not necessarily removed from politics.[6] Thus Americans ultimately hold legal officials accountable to the people. Richardson and Vines have labeled these influences on the judiciary as the democratic subculture. The democratic subculture provides direct and indirect forms of popular control on the operations of the legal system.[7]

Popular controls on the judiciary, however, are circumscribed by a set of counterexpectations, for we anticipate that a judge will act differently than other elected officials. For example, a judicial candidate usually will not attack his opponent during an election campaign. Judicial candidates find it hard to use the politicians' stock-in-trade: promises. For a potential judge to pledge to vote a given way before hearing a case would strike us as seriously out of place.[8] These are but some examples of the "insulated posture that judges are expected to maintain from pressures and interests. . . ." [9] In short, elected legal officials, as well as candidates for those offices, are expected to reflect and be responsive to legal and professional norms. Richardson and Vines term this the legal subculture. The dominant theme of the legal subculture is that the law is so specialized and complex that only professionally trained lawyers can be expected to have mastered the subject. Like numerous other modern professional groups, the American Bar Association attempts to insulate itself from the larger public. It insists that only lawyers can judge fellow lawyers.

---

[5] See Kenneth Culp Davis, *Discretionary Justice* (Louisiana State University Press, 1969).

[6] Richard Watson & Ronald Downing, *The Politics of the Bench and Bar* (John Wiley, 1969).

[7] Richard Richardson & Kenneth Vines, *The Politics of Federal Courts* (Little, Brown, 1970), p. 7.

[8] Herbert Jacob, "Judicial Insulation—Elections, Direct Participation, and Public Attention to the Courts in Wisconsin," *Wisconsin Law Review*, Summer, 1966: 812.

[9] Richardson & Vines, *The Politics of Federal Courts*, p. 8.

The interactions between the legal and democratic subcultures result in a court system and judicial process that reflects elements of both. In addition the conflicting expectations of the two subcultures leave the prosecutor (or judge) in an ambiguous role. On the one hand the prosecutor is an elected official who is expected to be responsive to the people. LaFave, for example, refers to the prosecutor who "will try primarily to reflect community opinion in the making of the decision whether to prosecute." [10] On the other hand the prosecutor is a professional who is expected to make decisions on the basis of his professional judgment, regardless of the effect on his political popularity. LaFave provides an example of this when he writes of "the prosecutor who may consider himself primarily a representative of the court, with the responsibility of enforcing rules designed to control police practices." [11] These conflicting expectations based on popular versus professional standards relate to a prosecutor's representational role.

How then does the Prairie City prosecutor define his job? Does he reflect the democratic or legal subculture? The Prairie City state's attorney follows the legal subculture, rejecting any thoughts of popular control of his office. The dominant element of the office is independence. He firmly believes that a prosecutor has been elected to run the office the way he sees fit. The work of the prosecutor then is determined by internal standards of the office. This stress on internal standards fits the legal subculture, for as we have noted, the legal subculture stresses the complexity of the law. Because the law is so complex, only professionals (in this case, lawyers) know what should be done.

The Prairie City prosecutor's stress on independence is coupled with his insulation from the public. When asked how he views the public, he replied, "with a jaundiced eye." He believes the public is usually misinformed, but out of deference to his elected position he tries to provide the public with the correct information.

This approach to decision making and the public closely resembles Wahlke's concept of the legislative trustee. The trustee is elected to carry out his own view. "The trustee sees himself as a free agent in that as a premise of his decision making behavior he claims to follow what he considers right or just, his convictions

---

[10] LaFave, *Arrest*, p. 515.

[11] Ibid.

and principles, the dictates of his conscience." [12] Wahlke also sums
up the Prairie City prosecutor's view of the public; "if the people
had the facts, their judgment would be the same as that of the
representative." [13]

It seems reasonable that the majority of prosecutors would
adopt some version of the trustee's view of role definition. In this
way they are reflecting the professional subculture. By contrast
some prosecutors place a greater emphasis on the democratic subculture, choosing to govern their office more on the basis of the
wishes and desires of the electorate. Such a perspective is analogous to a legislative delegate who believes he should vote the way
his constituents want him to vote. In short, the delegate reflects
community opinion more than the trustee. To quote one legislator,
"I want to express their views [the electorate] rather than my
own. On a controversial matter I'll vote the way I think the
majority wants even if I personally disagree." [14] One hypothesizes
that if comparable measures could be constructed, prosecutors
would express the delegate role much less often than legislators.[15]

Purposive Role Orientations: The Major Goals of the Office

In this section we shall explore the yardsticks by which the
Prairie City prosecutor gauges the work of his office. Wahlke's
study of state legislators was interested in a similar question.
Each legislator was asked: "How would you describe the job of
being a legislator—what are the most important things you should
do here?" The answers to these questions were grouped around a
central concept—purposive role orientation.[16] Simply stated, purposive role orientation examines the actor's definition of the most
crucial things he thinks he should do, what he gives top priority
to and what he slights.

James Eisenstein has examined how federal prosecutors define
the major tasks of their jobs. He divided prosecutors into two
ideal types: law enforcement officers and officers of the court. The

---

[12] John Wahlke et al., *The Legislative System* (John Wiley, 1962), p. 272.

[13] Ibid., p. 274.

[14] Ibid., p. 277.

[15] Neal Milner, *The Court and Local Law Enforcement* (Sage, 1971) discusses prosecutors on pp. 87, 114, 168. Some of the prosecutors he examines, particularly the ones in Racine and Kenosha, appear to have a
trustee role orientation.

[16] Wahlke et al., *The Legislative System*, p. 246.

prosecutor as a law enforcement officer sees his primary duty as protecting society and controlling crime through vigorous prosecution. By contrast, the officer of the court stresses the prosecutor's duty to see that justice is done. Eisenstein describes their goals as follows: "Violations of the law must be prosecuted, of course, but in a way that guarantees that the defendant's rights are scrupulously protected." [17] As with any ideal type, however, we do not expect a prosecutor to be either a law enforcement officer or an officer of the court exclusively. Rather, these two concepts are best viewed as two ends of a continuum. We expect most prosecutors to fall somewhere between the two poles. We do not expect prosecutors to hold to all elements of either category.

The law enforcement officer and officer of the court typology of prosecutors is a useful one because it highlights the inherent tensions of an office that is supposed to convict the guilty but at the same time secure those convictions within the American heritage of due process of law. The Prairie City prosecutor reflects these competing expectations. His stress on securing convictions reflects the law enforcement officer. At the same time he does not ignore the dictates of his role as officer of the court. He insists on fairness in the office. Let us look at these dual elements of the prosecutor's definition of his job.

Conviction Counts

In Prairie City the state's attorney measures the success of his office by the number of felony convictions. In the office one heard numerous comments that included the phrase, "So far this year we have obtained X number of convictions." A further illustration of this emphasis on conviction counts is evident in the following press release:

> CONVICTION RATE SOARS 60% IN PRAIRIE CITY
> Criminal convictions in Prairie City during the first four months of the current record-keeping year were at a rate 60% above the prior year. . . . There were 73 convictions between December 1 and March 31. . . .

This emphasis on convictions reflects the Prairie City prosecutor's interpretation of the law enforcement officer part of his job.

But the Prairie City state's attorney's role as a crime fighter does not incorporate other elements. For example, he does not operate as a crusader against crime. He never issues dire warnings

---

[17] Eisenstein, "The Federal Prosecutor and His Environment," p. 11.

about the increase in crime or the dangers of the "criminal element." Notice also that the stress on convictions does not include measuring success in terms of prison sentences. Sending the guilty to prison and/or sentencing the guilty to long prison terms is not a primary concern of the Prairie City prosecutor.

This seemingly straightforward emphasis on securing felony convictions contrasts with yardsticks used by other prosecutors. The most commonly employed measure of success is the batting average: the percentage of defendants found guilty.[18] The ratio of successes to chances is not deemed important in Prairie City. Rather the office only examines the numerator—the absolute number of convictions. Such a yardstick looks only at the successes and excludes the failures (a nonguilty verdict). Stressing convictions, however, does not carry over to misdemeanor prosecutions. Little emphasis is placed on misdemeanor cases. The office must handle them, but they are viewed as time-consuming and petty. The corollary is that the prosecutor does not define his role as vigorously enforcing all prohibitions. Rather, he defines the task as convicting felonies. Misdemeanors are seen as diverting resources from this major job. The effects of this orientation can be seen in the declining number of misdemeanor prosecutions. While most Illinois counties increased the number of misdemeanors prosecuted, Prairie City, despite a population increase, experienced a decline in the prosecution of misdemeanors.

Officer of the Court: Fairness

The stress on felony convictions, then, is the primary way that the Prairie City state's attorney reflects the law enforcement role of the prosecutor. But, as we have noted, this orientation is circumscribed. He does not act as a crusader against crime. The stress on convictions is also circumscribed by considerations stemming from the officer of the court orientation. In Prairie City the job of the prosecutor's office is defined not merely as the securing of convictions but also as seeing that the job is done fairly. For example, during an interview one assistant pointed to a current case and commented that the office would probably be criticized for being too lenient in its handling of the case. Nevertheless, he felt that "undoubtedly we did the right thing." In another case the suspect was accused of a minor driving offense. The prosecu-

---

[18] John Kaplan, "The Prosecutorial Discretion—A Comment," *Northwestern Law Review*, 1965, 60: 180.

tor felt assured that the suspect committed the offense but that the evidence was not sufficient to support the charge. He dismissed the case, even though he knew the judge would have found the suspect guilty. As he explained his actions, "I just wouldn't have felt right to convict somebody without proper evidence."

Notions of fairness also are incorporated in attempts by the assistants to produce equal decisions. The work of the office calls upon them to handle a string of disparate cases. After a while assistants begin to question whether they are actually handing out equal justice or are merely deciding individual cases. Several discussed the problems of arriving at equal penalties in drunk-driving cases. Most drunk-driving cases are reduced to reckless driving in Illinois. One assistant pondered whether his decision to reduce some DWI's (driving while intoxicated) but not others was fair. Eventually he changed his policy in an attempt to produce what he believed was more equal justice.

Notions of fairness also are related to the desire to be impartial, particularly about elites and politicians. The state's attorney scrupulously attempts to avoid even a hint of impropriety or seeming favoritism. For example, the state's attorney mentioned a number of high ranking officials or their offspring who had been prosecuted. Notions of impartiality extend even more deeply. When a known city leader is charged with a crime, he will not be given the usual sentence but a higher one. The reason is that the public might view any other course as favoritism to the "bigwig."

Defining and describing the concept of fairness is difficult. Each assistant has a slightly different emphasis. No two assistants have identical definitions of fairness. However, the most important consideration is that the state's attorney reinforces his assistants' concern with fairness. Although defense attorneys criticize the state's attorney on a number of points, no attorney interviewed ever believed that the state's attorney did not strive for even-handed justice, although their definitions might sometimes vary as to what even-handed meant.

Although the prosecutors in Prairie City seek felony convictions, they do not make this pursuit their exclusive goal. Rather, they believe that as officers of the court (not necessarily their own phrase) they should be concerned with fairness. Their thinking is analogous to that of a group of quasi-legal officials—the claims adjusters. As Ross observed, "the work of the claims man appears to be strongly affected by ideas concerning fairness,

which modify the pursuit of low settlements." [19] This same conclusion applies to prosecutors in Prairie City.

Career Orientations

To round out our discussion of the prosecutors, we need to
examine their career aspirations. Understanding career aspirations is important as they reinforce the role orientations discussed
previously. A politicaɪɪy ambitious prosecutor will not view his
duties in the same way as the prosecutor who envisions going into
civil practice. Prosecutors may view their tenure in office as 1]
a stepping-stone to politics and higher office; 2] a way station on
the road to civil practice; or 3] a permanent position.

Political Ambitions of Prosecutors

For a lawyer interested in a political career, the prosecutor's
office provides a built-in launching pad. Not only does the prosecutor get his name before the public but he also develops his image
as a crusading prosecutor—a powerful vote-getter in later cam-
paigns.[20] Former Senator Wayne Morse of Oregon, for example,
once served as a prosecutor and in every campaign after that he
reminded the voters of his success as a prosecutor. It is not
surprising, therefore, that a study of the career patterns of governmental officials showed that many governors and federal
district court judges had been prosecutors early in their careers.[21]

But before we conclude that all prosecutors are interested in
pursuing a political career, we should note that there are more
openings for prosecutors than vacancies for higher office. Although a number of high-ranking elected officials began as prosecutors, this does not mean most prosecutors plan to enter politics.
For example, a study in Wisconsin showed that "most district
attorneys do not stay in politics or public life." [22] In addition,
prosecutors were found to be more apolitical than judges. Why
then do lawyers seek the prosecutor's office? Another study of
Wisconsin concluded that lawyers ran for the prosecutor's office

---

[19] H. Laurence Ross, *Settled Out of Court* (Aldine, 1971), p. 46.

[20] Herbert Jacob & Kenneth Vines, eds., *Politics in the American States*
(Little, Brown, 1965), p. 249.

[21] Joseph Schlesinger, *Ambition and Politics: Political Careers in the United
States* (Rand McNally, 1966).

[22] Herbert Jacob, "Judicial Insulation . . . ," p. 810.

mainly to aid their civil practice.[23] Since lawyers are not allowed to advertise, running for office is a convenient way young attorneys can make their names known in the community. In another study, over half of the prosecutors in Kentucky reported they had no further political ambitions.[24]

Given this background about prosecutors in general, what are the political orientations of the prosecutors in Prairie City? Unfortunately, the past studies on political ambitions of prosecutors have not employed comparable measures, so, depending on how we interpret the data, we reach differing conclusions. We can report, however, that the Prairie City prosecutor did run for another elected office. In 1969 a judgeship became vacant. The state's attorney ran but was defeated. To some this may indicate interest in running for higher elected office, but a closer examination reveals that the state's attorney was interested in a judgeship, primarily for the security it offers. Other than that, he is not politically ambitious. This orientation is consistent with our earlier discussion that political parties in this part of Illinois are weak and have little, if any, patronage.

Thus, the Prairie City prosecutor fits the Wisconsin pattern—he has only a limited interest in holding another political office. We should also briefly mention the assistant state's attorney's lack of interest in running for elected office. Possibly one assistant could run for the state's attorney's job if it were to become vacant, but other than that, no assistant expressed interest in politics.

Civil Practice

Assistant state's attorneys in Prairie City do not become prosecutors because of political ambitions. Most join the office because they see the assistant's job as a chance to gain experience in the practice of law preparatory to entering civil practice. They want to make a name for themselves, not as a crusader against crime or a political figure, but as a competent attorney. The majority of assistant state's attorneys view their position as a

---

[23] Irvin Bromall, "Wisconsin Lawyers in Politics: An Exploratory Study," Unpublished paper presented at the Midwest Conference of Political Scientists, Purdue University, Lafayette, Indiana, April 27–29, 1967, p. 19. See also Kan Ori, "The Politicized Nature of the County Prosecutor's Office: Fact or Fancy?—The Case in Indiana," Notre Dame Lawyer, 1965, 40: 303.

[24] Richard Engstrom, "Political Ambitions and the Prosecutorial Office," The Journal of Politics 1971, 33: 190.

way station on the road to a professional career. This is how one lawyer phrased the point: "The idea of the young assistant state's attorney is to establish competency so that when you get out you can find a job in private practice that you want. You're trying to demonstrate competency. You're showcasing." Thus assistant prosecutors are lawyers first and state's attorneys second. They plan to join a private law firm in town. As a result their standards are the standards of private practice and are not guidelines specific to criminal practice. This desire to enter civil practice produces an important element of social control in the social network of the criminal justice community. The same lawyer reflected on this point: "When you're a state's attorney, if lawyers can push you around then no one will hire you. But if you're a complete SOB like . . . then no one will hire you either." During his tenure in the state's attorney's office, other lawyers are assessing the assistant, asking what kind of lawyer he will be in private practice. If he is too easy to deal with, then few lawyers will want him in their firm. But if the assistant is too hard to deal with, if he will not negotiate, or is too prosecution-oriented, then he will find it hard to attract the type of position he prefers. It is interesting that the lawyers in Prairie City could point to a former assistant who had not been able to find a job. This desire to enter civil practice therefore sets limits on the behavior of an assistant. He is being assessed against a yardstick of desirable attributes for civil practice: the ability to negotiate and the knowledge of when to compromise. These criteria are at variance with the standards used by an assistant who plans to make the office a career.

The Career Assistant

For most persons, the organization they are associated with (e.g. school district, public welfare agency, corporation) is a major source of expectations about their behavior. As we have just noted, however, such organizational expectations are limited in the case of most assistant state's attorneys. Whereas European prosecutors are recruited, trained, and promoted through a state bureaucracy, their American counterpart is normally locally recruited with little specialized training beyond law school. Further assistant state's attorneys have a short tenure—on the average two years. Such a short association limits the socialization effects of the prosecutor's office.

Although the majority of assistant state's attorneys do not plan to make the office their career, a limited number of lawyers view their positions as permanent. It is likely that such contrasting career aspirations will be associated with different role orientations.[25] While the transitory assistant is most concerned with the assessment of private attorneys, the permanent assistant will be more concerned with expectations of the organization, in this case the state's attorney's office. For example, Skolnick writes that prosecutors in Westville "could to some extent be distinguished by whether or not they saw themselves as 'committed' to a law enforcement career. Those who were, seemed less solicitous of defense attorneys' feelings than those who were 'working for the experience'—which includes the opportunity to meet practicing attorneys in the county." [26]

In Prairie City one assistant can be categorized as a permanent assistant. Not only was his tenure the longest of any assistant, but he maintained the most distance from the defense attorneys. Several defense attorneys singled out this assistant, saying he was the most difficult to deal with. Although they did not go so far as to label him unreasonable during negotiations, clearly they felt he was the least reasonable. The fit, however, is not a perfect one. Sometime after the study was completed, he left the office to join a private law firm. Such a defection is partially the product of scarce resources—salaries in a small state's attorney's office are competitive with private law firms only at the junior level. Although this particular assistant eventually left the office, his behavior otherwise clearly marked him as a permanent assistant.

The Prosecutor's Office as a Law Firm

So far in this chapter we have examined how the Prairie City state's attorney approaches his complex task: what he thinks is important or unimportant; the major goals of the office; and the type of people who staff the organization. These are the perceptual screens that define the work of the office and also structure the relationships with other law appliers—the police, the defense attorneys, the judges, and the juries.

Overall, the office functions much like a standard, medium-size law office. While other law firms represent banks, corporations, plantiffs or defendants in personal injury cases, the Prairie City state's attorney represents the public and to a lesser extent, the police. This analogy to a private law firm is an important con-

---

[25] Peter Blau & W. Richard Scott, *Formal Organizations* (Chandler Publishing, 1962).

[26] Jerome Skolnick, *Justice Without Trial* (John Wiley, 1967), p. 92.

sideration for most discussions view the practice of criminal law as a unique legal speciality. To a certain extent, criminal practice is unique. It involves a whole set of problems absent from civil practice. On the other hand, the practice of criminal law has definite similarities to civil practice. This is particularly true of the Prairie City prosecutor. For him the major task of the office is processing cases.

The analogy to a law firm nicely summarizes the three major dimensions of the prosecutor's role orientation. First, we noted that the prosecutor does not function as an elected official dedicated to representing the people. On the contrary, he sees his job as similar to a legislative trustee. The hallmark of the trustee is that he sees his job as making decisions on the basis of his own standards. The office is run on the basis of internal standards, not on the basis of what constituents might want to see done. Secondly, we explored the internal standards actually used. In Prairie City a great stress is placed on convictions in felony cases. In addition, fairness is a consideration in how these cases are processed. This view stresses procedure (the processing of cases) much more than the substantive results (prison sentences, guilty verdicts and so on). Finally, we explored the career orientations of the prosecutors in Prairie City. Most assistants do not view the position as assistant state's attorney as a steppingstone to higher political office or as a permanent position. Rather, the goal of the assistant is to enter private legal practice in a few years. This general orientation to private legal practice is an important ingredient in the social control network of the Prairie City legal system.

Police and Prosecutors

The police and prosecutor are commonly viewed as members of the same crime-fighting team. Newspapers often refer to police-prosecutor spokesmen, particularly when they are reporting on negative reactions to Supreme Court decisions. TV shows project the image of the prosecutor working with the police to fight crime. Such a linkage appears to be a natural one since both the police and the prosecutor are dedicated to the same overall goal—the sanctioning of criminal activity. Not only are the two organizations tied together by this general goal, but they also must work together on a day-to-day basis. The prosecutor's office is dependent upon the police in a number of ways. The police supply the prosecutor his raw materials—arrests and investigations of crimes. How the police conduct these investigations affects the prosecutor's processing of these cases. If the investigation is a good one and if the officer makes a good witness in court, then the prosecutor's chances of securing a conviction are enhanced. Similarly, the police are dependent upon the prosecutor. The police are not satisfied with simply arresting an offender, they also want sanctions applied. The prosecutor is directly involved in securing the convictions and setting the sentence. Changes in the law also have increased the police need for legal advice, and the prosecutor can provide such advice. In turn, the better the police understand the law and the more closely their activities conform with its requirements, the better the prosecutor's chance of using confessions and evidence the police obtained.

Thus, police and prosecutors are dependent upon one another. But embedded in this relationship are the potentials for conflict. Although the two organizations pursue a common goal—the sanctioning of criminal activity—they are still distinct organizations with sharply contrasting recruitment systems, differing perspectives on the law, and different work environments. Let us examine how these potentials for conflict may produce tension in the working relationship of police and prosecutors.[27]

Police and prosecutors usually come from different social backgrounds.[28] Most policemen are recruited from the working class; prosecutors are likely to have middle- or even upper-middle-class backgrounds. These differences in social background are magnified by differences in educational attainment. While the police seldom have worked beyond a high school diploma, prosecutors are college graduates who have graduated from a professional school. Police and prosecutors also approach their law enforcement jobs from decidedly different vantage points. Police officers, and particularly detectives, see their job as a permanent career. Prosecutors, as we have seen, view law enforcement as a way station on the road to private legal practice. Studies of the police show they are best described as conventional personalities. We have no comparable studies of prosecutors, but one expects that the prosecutors' generally higher social status and greater educa-

---

[27] Role theory provides a more formal definition, using the concept of potentials for conflict. See Neal Gross, Ward Mason, and Alexander McEachern, *Explorations in Role Analysis* (John Wiley, 1958), pp. 252–256.

[28] On social backgrounds of the police, as well as social attitudes see Jerome Skolnick, *Justice Without Trial*; Arthur Niederhoffer, *Behind the Shield* (Anchor, 1969); and John McNamara, "Uncertainties in Police Work . . ." in David Bordua, ed., *The Police: Six Sociological Essays* (John Wiley, 1967), pp. 163–252.

tion may be related to less conventional social attitudes than those of the police. Such differences in social attitudes are likely to come into conflict on sentencing. We would expect the police to be more punitive in their views of sentencing than prosecutors.[29]

These differences in social background, in education, and in career commitments, as well as the possible differences in general social attitudes, produce markedly different perspectives on the law. Skolnick explored police reactions to the law in great depth and showed how the police are hostile to the formal law, especially procedural restrictions on the police officer. For example, the police officer views himself as an expert, but the courts refuse to recognize such expertise, a refusal the police regard as unjustified.[30] Thus, there can be conflicting standards as to what the police should do—one set of standards based on norms of the police organization and another set based on the law. As Bordua and Reiss comment, the courts often find fault with an officer's conduct which may have been "well within the reasonable limits of departmental policy or regulation." [31] Thus, police often view the procedural restrictions of the law as unreasonable. Prosecutors, however, can be expected to view the law from a different perspective. To be sure, prosecutors may be critical of some restrictions on the police. Nevertheless, the prosecutor has been trained and socialized in the law and the law's dedication to protecting individual rights. He is more likely to understand the reasons for such restrictions and to not be as critical of procedural restrictions on the police.

Finally, the work environments of the police and the prosecutor produce different perspectives. The police officer views his primary task as solving crimes by locating and arresting a suspect, while prosecutors are primarily interested in convicting. For the police the most relevant area is the scene of the crime; for the prosecutor the arena is the courtroom. The prosecutor spends most of his time in court or talking with defense attorneys and judges outside of court. In short, the prosecutor finds himself in the middle. The police view the prosecutor as their spokesman in court. However, the prosecutor must work with the judges and

---

29 We should treat this paragraph as a hypothesis. We do not have the type of information on the prosecutor needed to test the hypothesis at present.

30 Skolnick, *Justice Without Trial*, pp. 196–199.

31 Albert Reiss & David Bordua, "Environment and Organization. . . ." in David Bordua, ed., *The Police: Six Sociological Essays* (John Wiley, 1967), p. 39.

defense attorneys and is subject to their pressures. One major pressure is the need to dispose of cases. The prosecutor has many more cases than he can try. As a result, most cases are disposed of by bargaining with the defendant and reaching a compromise. Not surprisingly, the police can view such compromises as selling them out.

Although the police and the prosecutors are dedicated to the same general goal of sanctioning criminal activity, the subgoals are not necessarily in harmony. Three primary factors produce potentials for conflict between the police and the prosecutor. Their social backgrounds are different, their views of the law are different, and their work environments produce different pressures and goals. We have no reliable studies that definitely point out that such potentials for conflict do produce such tension. Some studies, however, indicate this direction. Milner's study of four Wisconsin cities points out the strained relations in several cities. Bordua and Reiss quote a police official, whose statement is worth reproducing in full.

> Police get conditioned to the idea that we are the only people with our finger in the criminal dike in this country. They feel that everyone else "lets him go." Police differ from the D.A. The D.A. is satisfied with the conviction, finding him guilty. But police want him punished. They become outraged when the result of their work is ignored. "What if they let him off, I get him tomorrow: those bastards kiss him on the cheek and let 'em go," is their attitude of how the D.A. and the judge handle their cases.[32]

Prairie City manifests such tension between the police and prosecutor. The two organizations do not work together except in the most formal ways. Contact between the two organizations is minimal and confined almost exclusively to the necessary appearances of police officers in court. Each organization is critical of the other, although the prosecutors are less critical of the police than the police are of the state's attorney. The flavor of this tension is captured by an outside observer who is knowledgable not only about the Prairie City situation but also the rest of the state. He commented that "the tension between police and prosecutor in Prairie City is the worst I've seen in the state." This comment may be an overstatement, however, for antagonism between the police and prosecutor in one upstate county has become so intense that each makes public statements about the shortcomings of the other. This antagonism escalated so that the police chief arrested

---

[32] Ibid., p. 37. See also Milner, *Court and Local Law Enforcement*, p. 88.

the state's attorney. Later the prosecutor arrested the police chief. The tension between police and prosecutor in Prairie City is neither as public nor as heightened as in this upstate county, but it is nevertheless a permanent feature of the social network involved in the administration of justice. This tension cannot be explained by the personalities of the incumbents; rather, it flows from the competing perspectives of the two organizations. Let us examine these competing perspectives by exploring how the prosecutor views the police, and in turn, how the police perceive the prosecutor.

Prosecutor's Perspectives on the Police

To understand how the state's attorney in Prairie City views the police we need only recall our earlier discussion about the role orientation of the prosecutor. As we noted, the state's attorney's office functions much like a law office. This perspective stresses the independence of the lawyer-prosecutor, for only the lawyer-prosecutor is knowledgable in these areas. Such a law firm orientation does not incorporate working with the client, in this case the police. The prosecutor separates the functions of the police and prosecutor. For the Prairie City state's attorney, the sole responsibility of the police is the investigation of crime. After an investigation has been completed, police concern should end. The prosecutor then must execute his independent judgment about what should be done. Since this law firm orientation looks to the court, it does not incorporate working with the police. Maintaining a close working liaison with the police is deemed neither important nor relevant to the workings of the prosecutor's office. This is in contrast to the prototype prosecutor whom LaFave discusses—the prosecutor who defines his task as "representing police views in court" or "providing legal advice to the police." [33] In Prairie City, these concerns simply are not important.

The prosecutor's lack of interest in working with the police is reflected in the lack of communication between the two organizations. Here communication does not mean the daily exchange of routine information such as police arrest sheets and reports of investigations that tie the two organizations together. Rather, communication refers to the interchange of information about policies of the two organizations, changes in the law, or mutual problems.

During six months of observation the prosecutor or his as-

---

[33] LaFave, *Arrest*, p. 515.

sistants went to the police station only once. There were no conferences between command personnel. On only one occasion was there a conference between police officials and the state's attorney and his first assistant. There were no meetings about changes in the law. A year or so before the study, one assistant state's attorney prepared a handbook on the law for the police. This effort, however, was the product of the assistant's own interest, rather than a desire on the part of the office to systematically help the police understand the law. Thus, there is a marked lack of communication between the police and prosecutors in areas of mutual interest.

What communication there is reflects the gulf between the two organizations. The primary means for prosecutors to communicate with the police is a memo system. If an investigation is incomplete or the prosecutor thinks additional evidence is required, a memo is sent to the police. Such communications are generally negative comments on the police officer's work. The memo system is occasionally used to inform the police of major policy decisions. For example, in husband and wife fights, the police seldom made an arrest, preferring instead to send the victim (usually the wife) to the prosecutor's office so that the state's attorney could decide if charges should be filed. Prosecutors grew tired of hearing these tales of woe and, therefore, altered the policy. A memo instructed the police to make the decision as to whether to arrest or not. If an arrest was not deemed appropriate, the complainant was not to be directed to the prosecutor's office. This alteration in procedure had major consequences for the police. Citizens became irate with the police officer when told that no arrest would be made and the person could not discuss the case with the prosecutor. As one officer commented, "A citizen should have the right to talk to a lawyer about why charges are not being filed. Yet our prosecutor won't talk to these people, so they just get mad at the officer." Despite such implications for the police, the prosecutor unilaterally altered the policy. Since the policy change was made on the basis of the office's desire to maximize the efficiency of processing cases, it may be taken as another example of the fact that the prosecutor's office in Prairie City is run like a law office, and that its operation is marked by a definite barrier between the lawyer (the prosecutor) and his nominal client (the police officer).

The law firm orientation of the prosecutor's office also sets the standards by which the police are judged. The office sees its primary duty as processing cases, and the most important ingredient for processing cases is evidence. A complete and thorough investigation, along with a good police report, greatly aids the office's efficiency. However, the prosecutor's office sees police investigations as inadequate. For example, one assistant commented: "In many cases the police don't complete their investigation. So, we return the case to the detective bureau to get the additional evidence. The police figure they have the case done and go on to the next case. We need evidence in court, but they don't deliver." The police and prosecutors have different criteria for viewing cases. The police feel the case is solved with an arrest, but the prosecutor believes he needs more evidence if the case is to go to court.

The prosecutor's perceptions of the inadequacies of police investigation also surfaced during observation. On several occasions an assistant would hand the author a police report with the comment, "See, this is what I mean about a police report that is incomplete." One such police report was a seven-line description of a shoplifting arrest. The seven lines, however, conveyed little of the essential information the prosecutor required: what was stolen, how it was removed from the store, where the arrest had taken place, and names of witnesses. As a result, the assistant had to phone both the store manager and the arresting officer to find out what the case was all about. On other occasions assistants would ask the author, "Would you read this police report and tell me what it's about—I can't figure it out."

The proportion of police investigations prosecutors found inadequate would be a useful piece of information, but unfortunately no such statistical data was gathered. To place our comments in perspective, therefore, we should report that the prosecutors believe the quality of police investigations and report writing has improved in the last few years. But each time an incomplete investigation came to the office or a badly written arrest report was forwarded, assistants commented, "How many times have we told them not to do it that way."

Police Perspectives on the Prosecutor

While the prosecutor is critical of some police investigations, the police are critical of a good deal more of the prosecutor's operations. In particular, the police would like a say in the operation, but the prosecutor's stress on his independence denies the police a stake in the outcome of cases. The prosecutor's denial of police input to decision making runs counter to police expectations. As Bordua and Reiss point out, "the police want an outcome (from the courts) that signifies for them that their effort has been appreciated and that morality has been upheld. This, for them, is what is meant by justice being done." [34] The Prairie City police do not believe the prosecutor delivers on this count. As one detective said, expressing the views of most detectives: "The state's attorney doesn't prosecute when he has the goods. I don't care to know the reasons. They don't back us up when they should." Another voiced a more specific complaint: "When we arrest them, they should be found guilty on that charge, not some lesser charge. I don't believe in reduced charges, they should be made to answer." The police then voice strong objections to plea bargaining. The prosecutor in disposing of cases regularly reduces the seriousness of some charges, dismisses multiple counts and/or makes concessions on sentencing. The police object to such practices.

One particular case illustrates the police dissatisfaction with the prosecutor, but just as importantly, it illustrates the contrasting perspectives of each organization. The case involved a holiday break-in. From the police perspective, the case was a simple one —they arrested the suspect in a tavern, after hours, with what was to them overwhelming evidence of a burglary. They were shocked several months later to hear that the defendant had been allowed to plead guilty to a misdemeanor. As one detective commented, "Did you hear that, they let X off. See, we get somebody dead to rights, and the prosecutor lets him off." This case merely reinforced the police's image of the prosecutor.

From the state's attorneys' perspective, however, the case was not as simple as it first appeared. Their initial assessment of the case agreed with that made by the police—this was a burglary with good evidence to support the charge. As the case neared trial, however, the evidence looked less convincing. The defense attorney argued that his client had not intended to burglarize the tavern. To convict a person for burglary the state must prove that the suspect entered the building "with intent to commit therein a felony or theft." (Illinois Revised Statutes, 1971, Chapter 38, Section 19–1). The attorney claimed that the state could not prove felonious intent because the suspect had been drinking, was clearly drunk, and broke in because he was drunk, but had no intention of stealing. Since the suspect was in his mid-forties and had no previous felony record, the story appeared plausible. The prosecutor wavered and then personally examined the scene of the crime. He concluded that burglary could not be proven. He reasoned that the suspect had ample time and opportunity to flee

---

[34] Bordua & Reiss, "Environment and Organization," p. 37.

after the first police car appeared but he did not. The layout of the tavern and the location of the police car left several escape routes open, none of which were used. These appeared to be the actions of a drunk, not a burglar. Other details convinced the prosecutor that a conviction for criminal damage to property (a misdemeanor) was an equitable judgment.

This case is somewhat atypical because most burglary cases end with a plea by the defendant to the charge of burglary. However, it does illustrate the contrasting perspectives of the police and prosecutor. The prosecutor is oriented to the court, jury trials, and what must be proven in court to secure a conviction. Here the law demands innumerable details and considerations, details and considerations often lost on the police. The police make a decision that this is a burglary and cannot understand how the lawyers could disagree with their assessment.

The prosecutor is unable to understand the police view. As we noted earlier, success of the prosecutor's office is measured by "conviction counts." The police know of this emphasis on convictions but deem it irrelevant. For one thing, they do not regard a plea to a lesser offense (plea bargaining) as a true conviction. Second, and just as important, the police stress the prosecutor's failures, while the prosecutor stresses his successes. As we commented, the prosecutor does not use a batting average. He looks to the successes, while the police look at the ones that got away. Indeed, given the poor communications between police and prosecutor, the police are much more likely to know when the prosecutor did not handle a case the way they thought he should than when he secures a "proper" conviction.

Thus, the police voice strong objections to the way the prosecutor handles cases. They are particularly critical of the spinoffs of plea bargaining—a failure to secure enough convictions. Yet, when we examine data for the state of Illinois, we find that the Prairie City prosecutor secures more convictions per thousand population than any Downstate county. Further, Prairie City has more people in prison (both in absolute numbers and in population standardization) than any other Downstate county.[35] Both of these hard indicators of the prosecutors' success should meet with police approval, but they do not.

---

[35] For data on Illinois, see David Neubauer, "Policy Outputs of Illinois Trial Courts: An Exploratory Examination," Paper presented at the Annual Meeting of the American Political Science Association, Washington, D.C., September 5–9, 1972.

Prairie City then presents a striking contradiction—the police criticize the prosecutor for not securing enough convictions and for not sending enough defendants to jail. Yet, the empirical data suggest that on this criterion the Prairie City prosecutor is at least as successful as anyone in the state. This anomaly highlights an important aspect of the tension between police and prosecutor in Prairie City. The police assess the prosecutor not only quantitatively (convictions secured) but also qualitatively (image). For the police, the Prairie City state's attorney does not convey the image that a prosecutor should. The detective quoted earlier stated that the prosecutor "Doesn't back us up when he should." Another detective made a similar comment—"X is the only friend we have in the prosecutor's office," referring to one assistant state's attorney. What the police expect of the prosecutor is that he project the image of a law-and-order man. To use LaFave's phrase, "the police expect the prosecutor to act as their spokesman." [36] Such is not the case in Prairie City. The prosecutor represents his own views, and the police are denied even the symbolic quality of being viewed as equal partners in the crime-fighting endeavor. The prosecutor's lack of a law-and-order image magnifies his failures in the police officer's mind; he takes it as further proof that not only are the courts and the defense attorneys hostile to them (as they normally expect), but that the prosecutor also is hostile.

Conclusion

In this section we examined the working relationships of two principal organizations in the criminal justice system—the police and the prosecutor. As we suggested earlier, the term "system" is somewhat of a misnomer, for there is no overall coordination. As Bordua and Reiss note: "The legal system is not a seamless web of tightly articulated rules and roles, however, but a loose-jointed system held together at many points by microsystems of antagonistic cooperation and discretionary decisions." [37] Unfortunately, the relationships between the principal organizations in criminal justice rarely have been studied. In particular, the relationship between the police and prosecutor seldom has been scrutinized, although the nature of this working relationship is a crucial consideration. For example, the President's Commission on Law En-

---

[36] LaFave, *Arrest*, p. 515.

[37] Bordua & Reiss, "Environment and Organization," p. 26.

forcement and Administration of Justice calls for improving the relations between police and prosecutor.[38] This is especially vital in a period when the courts are changing the law rapidly, and the prosecutor seems to be the only law enforcement official who can communicate these rules to the police.

Although the police and prosecutor share points in common— they must work together in the processing of cases and both pursue a general common goal (the sanctioning of criminal activity) —beyond this, the two organizations diverge. Structurally, three major factors provide potentials for conflict: varying social backgrounds; divergent perspectives on the law; and sharply different working environments. Skolnick describes how these potentials for conflict are overcome somewhat in Westville. There the prosecutor acts as a quasi-magistrate. The prosecutor explains the law to the police and also interprets the police to his fellow members in the legal fraternity, including the judge.[39] The concept of quasi-magistrate obviously needs greater specification, for it also poses two crucial questions. First, what are the consequences of the prosecutor acting as a quasi-magistrate? Do the police develop a different perspective on the law? Alternatively, how does this function affect the prosecutor's work? We cannot answer this question, just suggest it. We can, however, suggest and also provide a partial answer to the second question: under what conditions do prosecutors act as quasi-magistrates?

In Prairie City the prosecutor does not act in such a fashion. He does not view working with the police as a vital aspect of his job. The Prairie City prosecutor functions as a law firm—processing cases that come into the office. The inherent tension in the police-prosecutor relationships seems to be magnified by this prosecutor role orientation. First, the prosecutor becomes critical of the police. In Prairie City, as we suggested, the prosecutors view police investigations as inadequate. Second, the lack of police involvement in the prosecutor's decisions makes the police critical. Not only do they perceive shortcomings in how cases are handled, but just as importantly they dispute the image the prosecutor projects. They want a law-and-order image, or at least the image of a prosecutor who works with the police. We hypothesize that where prosecutors adopt a role orientation similar to the

---

[38] The President's Commission on Law Enforcement and Administration of Justice, *Task Force Report: The Police* (Government Printing Office, 1967), p. 65.

[39] Skolnick, *Justice Without Trial*, p. 199.

Prairie City prosecutor, and particularly a self-definition of job that does not incorporate working with the police, there will be tension with the police. This tension basically will be unrelated to any quantitative aspects of how many convictions the prosecutor secures.

Defense Attorneys: Men in the Middle

<u>CHAPTER 4</u>

Mention defense attorneys to most Americans and their first thought will be of Perry Mason. The weekly "courtroom dramas" starring this skilled lawyer (whose clients nearly always were innocent) projected the image of the defense attorney as a true adversary. A person's highly positive image of the Mason-like defense attorney may give way to less complimentary assessments. The general public usually does not see the defense attorney as Perry Mason freeing the innocent but as the defense attorney letting the guilty go free. I have heard more than one citizen ask a lawyer, "How can you defend the guilty? Doesn't your conscience bother you to let these crooks go back to the streets?" Americans tend to equate lawyers and their clients, and defense lawyers are often perceived to be about as shady as their clients. Defendants do not often give high marks to their lawyers either. Letters from disgruntled clients about the inadequacies of their defense attorneys are legion in the criminal justice system. Judges, and others in similar positions, receive a fairly large volume of complaints that their lawyer "sold them out." The public defender is especially prone to such complaints. In some prisons PD is an abbreviation, not for public defender, but for "prison deliverer."

Several academic studies of the defense attorneys also have painted a less than complimentary portrayal of criminal lawyers. To use the near poetry of Cole, the defense attorney is usually an older man forced to haunt the corridors of the courtroom for scraps of legal criminal justice.[1] The most detailed study of defense attorneys to date, contends that lawyers have closer ties to the prosecution than to their client. As a result, clients feel a sense of betrayal because their lawyer is more interested in going along

---

[1] George Cole, "The Decision to Prosecute," *Law and Society Review,* 1970, 4: 339.

with the prosecution on a guilty plea than in fighting the charge.[2] Sudnow's examination of public defenders reports similar findings. The public defender from the very beginning seeks to obtain a plea. He is not geared to gaining acquittals. Furthermore, public defenders seldom cause "serious trouble for the routine motion of the court conviction process." [3]

Thus, the general public, the lawyers' clients, and scholarly studies seem agreed on one point: the defense bar is less than exemplary. The only difference is that the public thinks too many crooks are let loose and the client and the academic studies believe the lawyer does not fight hard enough for his client. All three perspectives, however, share an important point in common —all have an idealized picture of what lawyers do. As Friedman and Macaulay observe, Blumberg and others are "contrasting some sort of idealized picture of the legal system with some sort of operational reality." [4] The idealized pattern for the defense lawyer is the adversary, the lawyer who fights for his client in court.

In this chapter we will examine the defense lawyers in Prairie City to see what type of defense they provide for their clients. However, we will not follow the tact of Sudnow, Blumberg, and others of comparing idealized notions to reality. In such an endeavor reality always comes out second best. We want to look instead at the working environment of the defense lawyer. In particular, we want to examine the pressures upon the defense attorney. Although we usually think that all the defense attorney has to do is defend his client, the working situation is more complicated. The lawyer's task is not easy, because he must mediate between the demands of his client, the dictates of the law, and the working realities of the prosecutor and the rest of the court community. Seldom are the choices as simple or clear-cut as the defense attorney's critics contend. The idealized view that the lawyer is solely an adversary for his client fails to take account of the other aspects of the lawyer's job.

In assessing defense attorneys in Prairie City, we will ex-

---

[2] Abraham Blumberg, *Criminal Justice* (Quadrangle Books, 1967), and Abraham Blumberg, "The Practice of Law as a Confidence Game," *Law and Society Review*, 1967, 1: 15–40.

[3] David Sudnow, "Normal Crimes: Sociological Features of the Penal Code in a Public Defender Office," *Social Problems*, 1965, 12: 255–283.

[4] Lawrence Friedman & Stewart Macaulay, *Law and the Behavioral Sciences* (Bobbs-Merrill, 1969), p. 140.

amine three major areas. 1] How do the lawyers who do criminal work fit into legal practice in the community? Are defense attorneys as low status as past studies have suggested? 2] What are the defense lawyer's ties to his client and how does the lawyer conceive of representing the client's interest? (Critics contend that the defense lawyer has minimal ties to his client.) 3] How does the defense attorney interact with the other members of the criminal justice system? The defense lawyer works with judges and prosecutors on a daily basis, and we wish to assess how these working relationships influence the role of the defense attorney. Critics consistently point to such ties with the court system and contend that the lawyer's ties to the courts are so extensive that they are not properly defending their clients.

The Structure of the Prairie City Bar

The type of lawyers who handle criminal cases is somewhat dependent upon the general structure of the bar in that community. In particular, law practice in medium-sized cities like Prairie City differs greatly from law practice in large cities. This is an important consideration, because past studies usually examined defense attorneys in large, metropolitan areas. These cities are characterized by a highly stratified legal community.[5] Ladinsky categorizes law practice in large urban areas into three rings. The first, or inner ring, handles corporate work, the legal business of large corporations, banks, and insurance companies. These lawyers are the elite of the bar. The second ring represents plaintiffs whose interests are opposed to the inner circle. For example, this group represents plaintiffs in personal injury cases, persons who are suing the insurance companies. The outer ring is composed largely of solo practitioners who may be found "haunting the courts in hopes of picking up crumbs from the judicial table." [6]

Legal practice in medium-sized communities, however, is less stratified. There are seldom large law firms and the bar is more homogeneous. The task of analyzing the structure of the Prairie City bar is simplified by an earlier study of Prairie City by Joel Handler. Handler studied law practice in this community and

---

[5] Exceptions are Neal Milner, *The Court and Local Law Enforcement* (Sage, 1971); Bertram Wilcox & Edward Bloustein, "Accounts of a Field Study in a Rural Area of the Representation of Indigents Accused of Crime," *Columbia Law Review*, 1959, 56: 551–574.

[6] Jack Ladinsky, "The Impact of Social Backgrounds of Lawyers on Law Practice and the Law," *Journal of Legal Education*, 1965, 16: 128.

concluded that it was not specialized. Most lawyers have a general practice, and the bar is fairly homogeneous. This homogeneity is reflected in the distribution of poor clients among members of the bar. When compared to New York City, the lawyers in Prairie City have more poor clients (incomes under $5,000) than their brethren in the large city.[7] This dispersion of poor clients among the members of the bar is reflected in the large number of lawyers who do some criminal work. Whereas few New York City lawyers handled criminal matters, a fairly high proportion of lawyers in Prairie City did. Although criminal work was not an important source of employment for most lawyers, thirty-six out of seventy-five lawyers surveyed did some criminal work.[8] Thus, roughly a third of the lawyers have at least minimal contact with the criminal courts. On the basis of the type of criminal practice and the number of cases handled, Prairie City attorneys may be divided into three categories: the occasionals, the regulars, and the dominants.

The vast majority of attorneys who do some criminal work actually do very little. We can label them *occasional participants* because they handle only a few criminal cases, generally for their regular clients or teen-age offspring of their regular clients. The bulk of such cases are traffic. Although the occasional participants derive a very small part of their living from criminal practice, they do have minimal contact with how things are done in criminal court.

Regulars handle more criminal cases than the occasionals. Fees from criminal cases constitute a part of their economic livelihood. While occasionals handle only a couple of cases a year, regulars average two to four cases a month. The distinction between occasionals is based not only on the number of cases handled but also on the type of cases. Besides traffic cases, the regular handles misdemeanors but only an occasional felony. Felonies are not handled normally because of the time involved in case preparation. Preparing an occasional felony case requires much greater time per case than if one handled them routinely.

---

[7] Joel Handler, *The Lawyer and His Community* (University of Wisconsin Press, 1967). See Edwin Schur, *Law and Society* (Random House, 1968), p. 171 for a general discussion of law practice in medium-sized communities.

[8] The author made a rough estimate of the number of lawyers who were engaged in criminal work. During the period of this study, thirty-four lawyers handled one or more criminal cases. Thus, Handler's findings have persisted over time.

The rest of the criminal cases are represented by the five *dominant* attorneys in Prairie City. These five lawyers handle over ninety percent of the felony cases and about two-thirds of all the traffic and misdemeanor cases. These five lawyers do not practice individually. They are partners in two law firms: the public defender firm and a private law firm. The public defender firm consists of two lawyers. Besides handling all indigent defendants in the county, they also accept fee-paying criminal cases. The private firm consists of three lawyers, and they do the bulk of the fee-paying business in town. The two firms handle roughly similar numbers of cases. Each has about half of the total felony cases and each individual deals with about a third of the total traffic and misdemeanor work.

It is important to stress that each of these firms also handles a goodly amount of non-criminal work. The private firm takes divorces, small claims, and probate but specializes in personal injury cases. The public defender firm has a more general practice. Criminal cases are considered part of the firm's business along with wills, contracts, divorces, and so forth. Thus, criminal law practice is handled in the setting of a general firm. This setting differs greatly from published reports in other communities where criminal lawyers tend to be solo practitioners.

The nature of the non-criminal work load of these two law firms provides a fairly accurate measure of their general status within the bar. Recalling our earlier discussion of Ladinsky's three categories of lawyers, we can safely say that defense attorneys in Prairie City belong to the middle ring. Thus, the criminal lawyers are not the outcasts of the bar as was found in Seattle.[9] Impressionistic data from interviews with the general bar reinforce this conclusion. All of the *dominant* criminal lawyers are viewed as competent attorneys by their peers. None have a reputation for "shady deals." The relatively high status of the defense lawyers (high as compared to other studies) is partially explained by two features of law practice in Prairie City: the nature of law firm specialization and the fee structure.

Compared to large urban areas, law practices in Prairie City are not specialized in terms of concentration in specific areas of the law. Rather, the specialization is one of task. Several of the dominant attorneys, as well as several attorneys who practiced criminal law in the past, are known as good trial attorneys. In larger communities, trial attorneys specialize in personal injury.

---

9 Cole, "The Decision to Prosecute," p. 339.

But in Prairie City the supply of such cases is not sufficient to support an entire practice. Therefore, the lawyers are specialists in trial, whether of personal injury cases or felonies.

Any discussion of lawyers must examine the economic aspects of law practice. Lawyers must be able to make a living. Practicing attorneys are philanthropic only in their spare time. As mentioned in chapter 2, Prairie City is a working man's town with high-paying factory jobs. The job structure means that a good portion of those involved with traffic or misdemeanor cases, and a proportion of those in felony cases, have the economic resources to hire an attorney.

Lawyers' fees varied with attorneys, and they are secretive about them with other attorneys (but not with researchers). In misdemeanor cases, the fees range from $200 to $400. This fee covers only representation if a plea is arranged. If there is a trial, the lawyer's fee is approximately double. This two-stage fee arrangement generates additional money, although clients sometimes cannot raise the additional cash and get a trial anyway. In felony cases the fee varies. Estimates range from $1,500 to $2,500, although some unconfirmed reports indicate the public defender might charge less, depending on the economic resources of the client. The aggregate of these sums can produce a fairly substantial monthly income for the law firms. The private firm handles anywhere from ten to fifteen cases monthly, plus felony cases, so its income is not small. The two public defenders are paid a yearly sum of $23,000 to cover salary and overhead expenses for the office. The public defender understandably felt he should get more, but Prairie City does far better than other cities. In University Towns, for example, the two public defenders in 1969 received $18,900, which was a substantial increase over earlier years. Thus, the fee structure and the money paid the public defenders is not great enough to make them the highest paid attorneys in town but enough to place them within the middle ring of lawyers

The Lawyer and His Client

In criminal law the relationship between the lawyer and the defendant is a complicated one. Obviously, the lawyer's job is to defend his client, but what is involved in defense is not a simple matter. We can best assess the relationship of the criminal lawyer to his client by first examining generally the relationship of lawyers and clients. The lawyer in civil practice and the lawyer in criminal practice share common problems, although in differing degrees.

Normally we think of the lawyer in terms of the courtroom. The lawyer's responsibility is to advocate his client's cause, whether in court, governmental bodies, or to other lawyers. But the lawyer's time spent in defending his client is quite small. Rather, most of his time goes into keeping his client out of court. If you have to go to court, then the lawyer has been less than successful. Lawyers try to keep their clients out of trouble by advising them on how to have their actions conform as much as possible to the law. In short, the lawyer is a counselor and stands between his client and the law.[10] The multiple responsibilities this entails are captured nicely by Talcott Parsons. Lawyers stand "between two major aspects of our social structure; in the case of the law, between public authority and its norms, and the private individual or group whose conduct or intentions may or may not be in accord with the law." [11] Thus, the lawyer is a mediator, an agent of social control, who stands between the dictates of the law and the plans of the client.

Discussions of criminal lawyers, however, stress the traditional role of the advocate (courtroom defender) to the neglect of the lawyer's role as counselor and legal advisor. But a criminal lawyer must not only advocate his client's case and present the client's cause to the legal structure. The lawyer must also be an advisor, interpreting the legal system to the client and explaining what can be expected. This process is fundamental to a lawyer in either civil or criminal practice. In criminal practice, however, the tension between the two roles is likely to be greater. Normally in civil practice one is dealing with people who are familiar with the law and have minimal opportunity or desire to tell less than the truth. In criminal justice these conditions simply do not hold.[12]

Thus, lawyers in discussing their relationships with the client (they are never defendants) talked about these dual considerations—the need to be an advocate for the client and, at the same time, being a counselor on the law. One lawyer gave a particularly helpful and detailed account of how he approaches his client. Other lawyers in the community handle clients a little differently (lawyer's personalities and theories of practice vary) but this

---

[10] Martin Mayer, *The Lawyers* (Dell Publishing, 1966), pp. 37–76.

[11] Talcott Parsons, "The Law and Social Control." In William Evan, ed., *Law and Sociology* (The Free Press, 1962), p. 66.

[12] For a discussion of the lawyer's role as counselor see Mayer, *The Lawyers*, pp. 60–61.

account is essentially similar to interviews with the other defense attorney.

During the first discussion with the client, I try and get his background. What type of individual am I dealing with? This helps me to form an opinion on his chances for probation. I also inquire into what happened: you've been charged with so and so, tell me about it. He can admit it or deny it, but I never argue with his story the first time.

Once I have his story, I discuss the case with the prosecutor to see what position they are taking on the case. Do they see it as a felony or a misdemeanor? I also ask what they can tell me about their evidence. After this, I talk to the client again. If he admits guilt, then I tell him of any gain in the case and may or may not interview witnesses. I tell him my opinion of the evidence. If the defendant admits guilt but I feel the evidence is weak, then it's my duty to tell the client that, and I will recommend a trial. I also discuss the state's recommendations and tell the client whether I think it is fair or not. After that, we can dicker more on sentence.

If the defendant denies his guilt, then I tell him what type of case the state has and the discrepancies in the stories. Sometimes the defendant admits the crime. If the story has merit or corroboration or if there is considerable doubt, then I will recommend a trial. *But where the evidence is contrary to the client, then I interrogate him closely to determine if he actually did it. If the defendant's story is unreasonable and the jury will reject it, you tell him that, too.* I also say that if he wants a trial, I will give him one, but the prosecution's evidence is very strong against him. It's the defendant's decision whether to plead or have a trial [emphasis added].

This lawyer, as all of those interviewed, made repeated references to the lawyer's responsibility to his client. As one put it, "I'm the only friend the defendant has in the criminal justice system; all other officials are either opposed to his interests or at best neutral." As another lawyer phrased it, "If the attorney does not appear to be taking the side of the defendant, then no one will." These ties to the clients impose important restraints on the lawyer's relationship with other court officials. This is particularly the case in bargaining with the prosecution. To paraphrase one lawyer, plea bargaining is analogous to negotiating in civil cases. One must talk to the opposition. Yet, the client must never think that this cooperation "puts him up against it."

No lawyer talked to, or observed, took lightly the responsibility of representing their clients. But representation of the client should not be confused with the acceptance of a defendant's story and the defendant's own definition of his best interests. Rather, lawyers also function as counselors. This role of counselor means, especially in criminal law, that the lawyer will sometimes tell his client things the client might not appreciate. At times clients tell their attorneys stories that are less than true. (This is not unique to the defense side; prosecutors sometimes believe that the complainant's version is somewhat remiss.) A distinguishing feature of civil practice and criminal practice is that in civil practice clients are honest with their lawyers most of the time. This is not necessarily the case in criminal law. The lawyers in Prairie City did not seem to be as cynical about clients' lying as defense attorneys in large cities,[13] but nevertheless their role as counselor requires them to be neutral and detached in the appraisal of the evidence. As the respondent, quoted earlier, put it, "Where the evidence is contrary to my client, then I examine his story closely."

Prairie City lawyers balance the competing demands of representing the client to the law and interpreting the law to the client by asking: "Given the situation, what is the best that can be done for my client?" To answer this question the lawyer must be familiar with the options the system considers reasonable. The system creates parameters, and attorneys must be familiar with them. To use Reissman's much beleaguered concept, the lawyer is operating as an "inside dopester." [14] Only a lawyer has access to the prosecutor's chambers. Few defendants know what to expect from the legal system. A prime attribute of the lawyer is that he knows his way around the courthouse and can render an opinion to the client on what to expect from the law.

Thus, the lawyer is charging a fee not only for his knowledge of the formal law but also for his ability to interpret to the client what the law means to his case, and therefore what the client can expect. Where possible, he will try and get his client's case dismissed if the evidence is weak. Otherwise, he sees his task as getting his client what other, similarly situated defendants receive. Given the charge, the type of defendant and the evidence, the lawyer knows the possible range of penalties. He sees his job

---

[13] Compare, for example, the cynical approach of Connie Xinos, a public defender in Chicago in "Justice on Trial," *Newsweek*, March 8, 1971, p. 28.

[14] David Reissman, *The Lonely Crowd* (Yale University Press, abridged edition, 1961), p. 180.

as getting his client's penalty set at the lowest end of the range. A later chapter will discuss the concept of normal penalty for a given charge. For now, we can say that for most crimes there is an accepted penalty applied, and the lawyer functions to see that his client gets this normal penalty. The lawyer's fee, then, is an insurance payment to ensure that the client gets no worse than what everybody else gets.

Our discussion of the lawyer's role in securing for his client what similarly situated defendants receive may clarify a criticism of defense attorneys as shady operators. Cole, for example, states that "Respondents hold the belief that clients are attracted partially on the basis of the attorney's reputation as a fixer, or as a shrewd bargainer." [15] A state's attorney in Prairie City told the following story, based on private practice, on how such erroneous impressions can develop.

> The greatest boon to the defense bar is the first arraignment, where the defendant is told what the maximum penalty is. In many misdemeanors it can be six months or a year in jail. All the defendant can think of is that he might go to jail for a year, so he hotfoots it to an attorney. . . . The defense attorney then basically gets for his client what everyone else gets, but the client thought his attorney did all sorts of wonderful things. If the lawyer is sharp, he will let the public defender go first and the guy might get six months. When the client gets much less, he thinks his attorney must really have a connection, not knowing that the public defender's client has a long record and is poor.

The lawyer's fee is money charged for getting his client the normal penalty, which is substantially less than the maximum penalty under the law. Clients have no way of knowing what to expect from the system and one imagines attorneys do not go overboard in stressing "I did what any attorney could do."

Any discussion of the multiple roles of the attorney vis-à-vis his client should not omit the client's views. Unfortunately our knowledge of the client's perceptions of his attorney is sparse and for this study we did not interview defendants.[16] It is equally im-

---

[15] Cole, "The Decision to Prosecute," p. 339.

[16] The only systematic study of defendants' views of their lawyers was made by Jonathan Casper. Casper interviewed seventy-one former defendants in Connecticut and found they expressed reservations about their attorneys. This was particularly the case with clients of the public defender who viewed him as an extension of the prosecutor, who did not listen to their story and was only interested in the defendant pleading guilty. Defendants with private

portant, however, to assess the lawyer's perceptions of their clients' views. Interviews with defense attorneys turned up examples of defendants that were suspicious if not hostile to their attorney. However, the lawyers believed that the overwhelming majority of defendants accepted the advice of their attorney. For example, when the lawyers were probed about defendants who might be reluctant to plead guilty, the lawyers replied that the defendants usually deferred to their attorney. According to the defense attorneys, typical comments were: "You know best," or "Whatever you think."

In discussing their clients' reactions, lawyers also stressed their pragmatic concern with what was going to happen. Questions of rights and jury trials are assigned a secondary position. The client wants to know if he is going to jail (if he has been accused of committing a felony). The lawyers in criminal cases function like civil attorneys. They render an opinion on the likely outcome, which is hedged, of course, by the lawyer's inability to make definite promises. A lawyer can only say that, on the basis of past experience, this is the likely outcome.

In summary, lawyers mediate between the law and their clients by presenting their clients' cases to the law as the *advocate*, while at the same time interpreting the law to the clients as the *counselor*. The defense attorneys in Prairie City are conscious of both requirements and the conflicts that arise in mediating these two roles. The lawyer attempts to balance these competing demands by asking, "Given the situation what is the best that can be done for my client?" This requires knowledge of the parameters of the system. The clients' views on the representation they receive are not known but defense attorneys report that clients generally accept the advice of their attorney.

The Defense and Prosecution

The environment of the defense lawyer, however, extends beyond the client. The practice of law involves the lawyer in constant interactions with other lawyers. Defense attorneys, for example, continually interact with other members of the criminal court community—the prosecutors and the judges. To a certain extent, these other lawyers are a more permanent feature of the lawyer's working environment than the client. While clients come

---

lawyers gave them higher marks, but still expressed some dissatisfaction. Jonathan Casper, *Criminal Justice—The Consumer's Perspective* (Government Printing Office, 1972).

and go (repeat business is generally discouraged), the defense attorney is likely to work with the same prosecutor for several years. In short, relations with other lawyers are continuous, while ties to clients are transitory. Given such repeated personal interactions, we expect patterns to develop in these interrelationships. After a while, the informal social network imposes considerations upon its members. In his discussion of the criminal courts, Blumberg was referring to just such a dimension when he commented: "the variable of the court organizations . . . possesses a thrust, purpose and direction of its own." [17] In this section we want to examine this point. In particular we shall explore the relations between the defense and the prosecution.

Defense and prosecution in Prairie City are adversaries, but friendly adversaries. The relationship is cordial and, in some cases, amiable. In some communities lawyers from defense and prosecution are mutually suspicious of one another, but in Prairie City they view their counterparts with respect. While in some communities prosecution and defense views are so far apart that the relations between the two are tense at best, no such pattern is found in Prairie City. To be sure, the two do not see eye to eye. Defense attorneys are critical of certain prosecution practices, but in general, the relationship between defense and prosecution is good. Most attorneys have a good working relationship with the prosecution. Skolnick categorizes such attorneys as "cooperative." In contrast, some lawyers he studied were "gamblers." They had a small but active criminal practice and "rather hostile relations with the prosecutor's office." [18] These lawyers probably represent an "ideal" version of the lawyer as advocate for his client. In the remainder of this section we want to analyze why all the dominant lawyers in Prairie City and most of the lawyers were "cooperative" rather than "gamblers." Cooperative, however, is a slightly misleading word. It is better to replace it with the concept of the attorney who works within the system.

In examining and explaining the working liaison between defense and prosecution in Prairie City, we need to explore three factors: 1] general expectations about how lawyers should deal with their opponents, 2] some more specific considerations flowing from law practice in Prairie City, and 3] specific sanctions

---

[17] Blumberg, "The Practice of Law as a Confidence Game," p. 19.

[18] Jerome Skolnick, "Social Control in the Adversary System," *The Journal of Conflict Resolution*, 1967, 11: 59.

that serve to maintain the social network of the criminal courts in Prairie City.

Follow-up of Legal Practice

Commenting on the relationship between opposing counsel is a difficult task. Normally we assume that opponents are just that. If they are friendly adversaries, as they are in Prairie City, then we begin to suspect something is amiss. For example, if one visits most courtrooms one will see the prosecution and defense exchange pleasantries before, after, and during the court appearance. He may even see two lawyers strenuously arguing their case in court, and then having lunch together. Some commentators interpret such actions to mean that the defense has ties closer to the prosecution than to his client, and his client suffers.[19] This is not necessarily true.

In any profession or occupation involving controversy, norms develop to channel this controversy into manageable directions. Unless such rules of the game develop, controversy is likely to prevent the execution of necessary work. As we noted earlier, the U.S. Senate is built around political controversy, but norms of conduct, which are largely unwritten, have been developed that serve to keep conflict within reasonable bounds.[20]

Law practice involves unwritten norms of conduct very similar to those of the Senate, which serve the same purpose. In a profession based on conflict in court, rules have developed to keep the conflict confined to court. There is enough disagreement without adding bad personal relations among the attorneys. For this reason lawyers are expected to confine their disputes to the courtroom. As one judge commented, "Yesterday two lawyers started arguing about their case in the corridor after the hearing. That just shouldn't happen. Lawyers have to know how to channel disagreement." Thus, if defense and prosecution are on good terms, this does not mean that the adversary process has broken down. It may be only a reflection of the normal rules of conduct expected of lawyers. The "cooperation" of defense and prosecution is a product of such general expectations about how lawyers should conduct themselves. We should not equate effective advocacy with hostility.

---

19 Blumberg, *Criminal Justice*, p. 226.

20 Donald Matthews, *U.S. Senators and Their World* (Random House, 1960), p. 97.

Law Practice in a Small Community

The working relationship of the prosecutor and defense is also a reflection of the type of law practice in Prairie City. As indicated in the last chapter, assistant state's attorneys are interested in entering private civil practice. As pointed out earlier in this chapter, the defense bar in Prairie City is well integrated into the general legal community. The working relationships of prosecutors and defense is an extension of the general working relationships of lawyers in the community.

Law practice is based not only on the legal technicalities that laymen normally associate with the law and lawyers but also on the ethics and stability of the legal profession.

Karl Llewellyn once wrote that law practice is premised on

> a town of twenty-five thousand (or more dubiously, fifty thousand)—a town with a single high school, where reputation speaks itself from mouth to mouth, even on the other side of the railroad track; and reputation not only of the oldster, but of the youngster. The youngster is watched when he hangs out his shingle; watched if he be a home-town boy, watched doubly if he be not.[21]

Prairie City fits this pattern well. The number of practicing lawyers in Prairie City is small (between seventy-five and one hundred), small enough so that one knows what the others are doing, just as in a small town. Courts are an even smaller town. Within such small towns respect is a crucial commodity.

In Prairie City the defense attorneys and the prosecutors respect their opposite number as competent counsel. For example, one state's attorney made an offhand comment about a case that illustrated this point. He said, "Now I know this defendant's attorney, and before I file charges I know I'll have to have a good case." The defense assessments were similar. All of the state's attorneys were viewed as competent attorneys who were effective in court.

This crucial ingredient of mutual respect for one's opponent is reinforced by the continuity in personnel between defense and prosecution. Three of the five dominant attorneys served as assistants to the present state's attorney. The two dominants who have not been prosecutors practiced criminal law for about fifteen years. Given the exchange in personnel and the long terms of several of the defense attorneys, it is obvious that working relations

---

[21] As quoted in Mayer, *The Lawyers*, p. 59.

have developed. There are very few secrets. Each knows the other and knows what to expect from him. It is equally obvious that such continuing relationships can be premised only on respect and credability. A lawyer can pull a fast one on his opponent once, but this would jeopardize his entire standing with the community. Thus, the defense and prosecution in Prairie City are tied together in a fashion similar to the ties of lawyers in small communities. In such relationships integrity is an overriding concern. The cooperation of the defense attorneys is a product of these considerations stemming from the general practice of law in Prairie City.

Sanctions

In any social system, sanctions develop to maintain the social network. For those who go along, there are rewards, and for those who do not, there are penalties. For example, not all U.S. senators work within the social system of the U.S. Senate; some are outsiders or mavericks, and as a result they are not as effective as the senators who work within the system.[22] The same applies to the social network of the court system. Lawyers who work within the system (and appear to be cooperative, to refer again to Skolnick's phrase) can expect some benefits. Those lawyers who choose to work outside of the system pay a price for such activities.

Lawyers who work within the system and have good working relations with the prosecutor can expect some positive rewards in the form of lower than normal sentences in certain instances. For example, a prosecutor described the following situation that occurred just prior to the interview. The case involved a second offense shoplifting, which is a possible felony under Illinois law. The prosecutor recommended a sixty-day jail term if the suspect pled to a misdemeanor. The dominant attorney countered, however, by saying that this case did not fit the normal pattern and a thirty-day jail term would be more appropriate. The State found the arguments reasonable and agreed to the thirty-day recommendation. The state's attorney stressed, however, that he could not deal with other attorneys on the same basis. He respected this lawyer's judgment, had worked with him a long time, and knew he did not make such particularistic appeals in every case.

Lawyers who work within the system in Prairie City also have

---

22 Matthews, *U.S. Senators*, pp. 114–116. For a more technical treatment of sanctions and role theory see Neal Gross, Ward Mason, & Alexander Mc-Eachern, *Explorations in Role Analysis* (John Wiley, 1958), pp. 65–67.

a vantage point for raising questions about its operation. Although we usually think of challenges to police practices, and so forth, in terms of courtroom motions, some dominant attorneys believe it is much more effective to work informally. Let us summarize such an example, which will be expanded upon in greater detail in chapter 8. One of the dominant attorneys believed that a detective was using improper means of interrogation. He could have filed pretrial motions and fought each confession in court. His first response, however, was to challenge these practices informally. He talked to the judge and prosecutor about the situation, and the detective changed his practices. Such an informal challenge was possible, however, only because he worked within the system. Again, the respect in which the lawyer was held by members of the local court community allowed him the vantage point to informally challenge police practices, a vantage point not available to attorneys who work outside of the system. At the same time we should also note that these actions were protective of the police, because they were raised in private. The social network of the Prairie City courts, thus, creates positive rewards for the attorneys who work within the system. The social network also embodies negative sanctions for those who do not. These punishments are subtle and sometimes subconscious, but a feature of the court system nonetheless.

Sanctions may also take the form of the absence of rewards. The absence of rewards differs from the negative sanctions discussed above. Attorneys who push cases have sanctions applied because they put the system to extra work. The absence of rewards does not involve such an overt use of sanctions. Rather, certain attorneys do not know how to manipulate the system to secure the lowest possible penalty. Earlier we examined the lawyer as a counselor, as one who could advise his client on what would happen to him in court. Obviously, lawyers who are not familiar with the system cannot perform such a task as effectively as lawyers familiar with the system.

Lawyers could point to a specific illustration that buttressed their argument that outside lawyers were not as effective as lawyers who "knew the ropes." The public defender had been criticized by several civil rights leaders for "selling black defendants out." To counter what they thought was inadequate representation, a lawyer was hired from Northern Illinois. He represented several defendants (some of them white), but his services are no longer requested by the local citizens. As the lawyers explained it, this outside lawyer ended up by getting his clients higher penalties than the public defender obtained. They said he was not familiar with the way things were done. This example reinforced their opinion that outside attorneys work to the disadvantage of their client.

Limits on Cooperation

Most defense attorneys, but particularly the dominants, work within the system in Prairie City. Such seeming "cooperation" must be assessed against the background of legal practice. As we have noted, lawyers are expected to maintain friendly relations with their opponents, and the type of legal practice in Prairie City fosters good relations among attorneys. This is a small, face-to-face community, where respect and credibility are major commodities. Finally, we noted that those who work within the system are rewarded, while sanctions are available to be applied against those who do not work within the system. The continuing nature of the legal community, coupled with the exchange of personnel from prosecution to defense, means that the defense bar in Prairie City has no major quarrel with the parameters of the system of justice. In general, they agree with how things are done. As one lawyer phrased it, "When a fellow gets in trouble as he did (referring to an armed robbery), he has to expect to pay some price. Society isn't just going to ignore what he did." To this extent the lawyers have been co-opted,[23] but this co-optation proceeds from how lawyers in general go about practicing law. Defense lawyers agree with the major outlines of criminal laws to the same degree that they agree with the general outlines of the law on divorce, personal injury, probate, etc. Law school and law practice emphasize lawyers working within the existing body of the law. Neither the law schools nor the bar are often breeding grounds for revolutionaries who want to reexamine the way society proceeds in a given area.

But the good working relations of the defense and the prosecution, as well as the defense attorney's general agreement with the way justice is handed out, should not be interpreted to mean that lawyers agree with all specific practices. The Sudnow and Blumberg studies contend that lawyers are not critical of the court system, and that they personally or professionally do not criticize how justice is administered.[24] Such is not the case in Prairie City.

---

23 Blumberg, *Criminal Justice*, p. 223.

24 Sudnow, "Normal Crimes," p. 273; Blumberg, "The Practice of Law . . . ," pp. 15–40.

The defense attorneys are critical of some practices. They are particularly critical of the chief judge, a point that will be developed in the next chapter. They are also critical of the prison system, and some of the specific rules of sentencing in Prairie City. Although the lawyers respected the state's attorney, they were critical of some of his policies. In particular, they felt the state's attorney put too great a stress on obtaining convictions, and the emphasis on conviction counts obscured broader considerations of justice.

Thus, the cooperation between defense and prosecution has not muted defense criticisms of the administration of justice, and through the rest of this study we will have occasion to highlight in greater detail these criticisms. Nor do defense attorneys believe that their "cooperation" with the prosecution jeopardizes their role as advocate for their clients. As one lawyer put it, "I cooperate with the prosecution only to the extent I cooperate with an opposing attorney in a civil case. To go beyond that, the client will feel he is up against it." For lawyers in Prairie City, such cooperation is a logical extension of how law is practiced, so they seldom think about the criticisms of Sudnow and Blumberg. If they had thought about this, though, I am sure their response would be similar to that of the lawyer whom Skolnick quotes.

> Our office is on very good terms with the prosecutor's office, because they trust us. . . . But don't get the idea that we don't represent our clients well. If we didn't do that, we wouldn't get all the criminal business that we now have. . . . When we settle cases, we get a reduction of the original charge in virtually every case.[25]

Thus, most defense attorneys believe they can represent their clients best by keeping on good terms with the prosecutor. Prairie City defense attorneys take steps to insure that such cooperation is placed in context. Each side values its independence. Defense and prosecution are engaged in virtually continuous negotiations, and since bargaining is best accomplished from a position of strength, each side tries to keep an upper hand. For example, one prosecutor commented to a lawyer in the hall, "I hope you don't think you got the best of me on that deal yesterday." To regulate contacts with the defense, the assistant divides up the misdemeanor and traffic calendar so that no one assistant will deal continually with the same group of defense attorneys. As the

---

[25] Skolnick, *Justice Without Trial*, p. 61.

prosecutors phrased it, they want to prevent any defense attorney from "developing an in" with the prosecutor's office. Defense attorneys likewise take steps to maintain their independence. Again, the competitive nature of bargaining places limits on "cooperation." Defense lawyers naturally like to bargain from a position of strength, and for them strength involves winning jury trials. The better they are at winning jury trials, the better they can bargain.

Conclusion

The studies of defense attorneys in criminal cases generally portrayed the lawyer in a negative fashion. The deficiencies of the lawyer and the way he conducts the defense have been spelled out by numerous authors. Such studies, however, relied upon ideal notions of the role of the defense attorney. As such, they did not specify adequately the multiple dimensions of the lawyer's role. The studies have been heavily value-oriented. Facts and the author's values are so intertwined that it is hard to distinguish one from another. We suggested that such concern (indeed overconcern) with values must give way to an analysis of the social structure of the defense attorney.

On the basis of the experience in Prairie City, we can say that the defense attorney occupies a multifaceted social network. He is expected to be an advocate of his client's case. As such, he is the only friend the defendant has in court. While he must side with the defendant, this does not mean that he can accept the defendant's definition of his self-interest. The defense attorney is like any attorney; he must interpret the law to the client and render an opinion on what to expect. Within this network the lawyer also has ties to the larger criminal justice system. While clients come and go, the lawyer and the court system remain. The lawyer must maintain his credibility. He cannot cry wolf when there is none, lest he jeopardize his ability to help other clients.

It is fair to say that past studies approached this social framework from a one-dimensional point of view. The value components of past studies clouded the issue. Given the heavy value orientation, it is extremely difficult to compare Prairie City to past studies. One does, however, perceive common ground. Blumberg's charge that lawyers are "agent mediators" is best interpreted in terms of this study as an empirical statement that lawyers work within the existing criminal justice system. Blumberg interprets this relationship negatively. We stressed, however, that the lawyer empirically balances these ties with his ties to the client. He does work within the system, and we suggested that there are negative sanctions for those who do not and positive rewards for those who do. One can interject here that the lawyer's ties to the client may prevent him from challenging certain parts of the system. The lawyer is well aware, however, that he does not face a jail term; his client does. The price for challenging the system may be a long jail term for his client. Positive rewards also accrue in terms of lesser sentences in certain instances, a greater knowledge of the weakness of the police prosecution process, and greater acceptability when challenges are raised. The value-free concept of rewards and sanctions for working within the system should provide a better avenue for future studies assessing the work of the defense attorney.

CHAPTER 5 Judges: Conservatives in Black Robes

For most Americans the judge is *the* symbol of justice. The black robes and gavel symbolize the fairness and impartiality we expect from our courts. "The quality of justice depends in large measure on the quality of judges," is how the President's Commission on Law Enforcement and Administration of Justice phrased it.[1] But beyond these symbols and trappings of office we know relatively little about what trial court judges do. Indeed, of all the actors in the criminal justice system, the least studied has been the trial court judge.

By contrast appellate judges have been extensively studied and scrutinized. An extensive popular and scholarly literature exists on the decision-making process of appellate courts, as well as on the backgrounds and personal values of the judges.[2] Rarely, however, are trial court judges examined in such a fashion. This absence of attention is an extension of the "upper court bias." The assumption was that appellate courts set policy and lower court judges executed this policy. Missing was the realization that trial court judges exercise discretion as much as their upper court colleagues do.[3]

The importance of the trial court judge flows directly from the legal powers and responsibilities of the office. The judge is the one who informs the subject of the charges against him and explains his rights. The judge sets bail, conducts the trial, and imposes the sentence. In addition to his direct duties of trying cases the judge

---

[1] The President's Commission on Law Enforcement and Administration of Justice, *Task Force Report: The Courts* (Government Printing Office, 1967), p. 65.

[2] For example see Glendon Schubert, ed., *Judicial Behavior* (Rand McNally, 1964) ; Thomas Jahnige & Sheldon Goldman, eds., *The Federal Judicial System* (Holt, Rinehart and Winston, 1968). For a critique of the literature see Ted Becker, *Comparative Judicial Politics* (Rand McNally, 1970).

[3] Herbert Jacob, *Justice in America* (Little, Brown, 1965), pp. 26–27.

has administrative responsibilities as well. The judge is expected to see that cases are disposed of and no backlog of cases developed. The corollary of these legal duties is the discretion inherent in the judge's exercise of these powers. Trial court judges differ in their criteria for setting bail, the sentences they impose, and how they interpret appellate court decisions.

But a listing of the judge's powers and responsibilities can be misleading, for the legal blueprint may not be a guide to who actually exercises these powers and responsibilities. As we indicated earlier, many of the tasks traditionally associated with judges are powers actually shared with others. For example, the prosecutor often has more to say about bail and sentencing than the judge does. The position of the trial court judge then is somewhat anomalous. While no one doubts his influence on criminal justice, it is not at all clear why he does not exercise many of the powers that he might.

In this chapter we will investigate the anomalous position of the trial court judge in Prairie City. First we will examine the values that the judges hold and see how these influence the administration of criminal justice. At the same time we want to specify what powers judges exercise as well as explain why judges share some of their powers and responsibilities with others. Most important, we want to see what position the judges hold in the informal social system of the criminal justice community.

The influence of judges on the criminal justice process is somewhat determined by the organizational structure of the court system. Illinois, unlike most states, operates under a unified court system of one court per county. By contrast most states have a number of courts in each county—small claims, justice of the peace, county court, circuit court, probate court. The Illinois judicial reform amendment consolidated all of these courts into one court—the circuit court, which has two divisions: magistrate and circuit.

Magistrate's court replaced the justice of the peace courts. The magistrates are appointed by the circuit court judges and hear minor cases: traffic, misdemeanor, and city ordinance violations. In addition magistrates are responsible for the preliminary stages of felony cases and conduct the arraignment; set bail; hold the preliminary hearing and appoint counsel for indigents. The influence of the magistrates on these processes will be discussed in detail in chapter 7. For now we will concentrate on the role of the circuit court judges.

Circuit court judges, unlike magistrates, are elected. The elected nature of the office often means that political parties play a major role in judicial selection. In many large cities like Chicago, New York, and Pittsburgh the judges are intimately intertwined with the political party system. Lawyers are slated for judicial vacancies on the basis of faithful work and, in some cases, large financial contributions to the party. In addition, judges often maintain their political ties after being elevated to the bench.[4] This pattern does not apply to Prairie City. Rather, political parties play only a tangential role in judicial recruitment, for the party structure in the community is weak. Party involvement in judicial selection is confined to seeking out a qualified lawyer who is willing to run for a vacant judgeship. The party seeks the candidate rather than the candidate seeking the party.[5] As a result none of the judges in Prairie City had more than nominal ties to their party before running for office and none were involved in party work after being elected.

All four of the circuit court judges in Prairie City handle felony cases. However, the degree of involvement is not equal. One judge handles the bulk of the felony cases while the other three handle only an occasional case. This pattern is similar to that found in other communities, for judges tend to specialize in certain types of cases.[6] In Prairie City one judge dealt almost exclusively with probate work, another concentrated on divorce, and a third judge specialized in juvenile work, among other things. This specialization of judicial tasks is routinized in the assignment of cases. Felony cases are automatically assigned to the chief judge. As a result of this assignment process the chief judge influences the processing of felony cases considerably more than the other three judges.

The chief judge is the dominant judge in the felony process not only because of the assignment system but also because of his views on criminal justice. The chief judge is the product of a small rural Ilinois community. He represents an upper-middle-

---

[4] Martin Levin, "Urban Politics and Judicial Behavior," *The Journal of Legal Studies*, 1972, 1: 193–196; Alexander Smith & Abraham Blumberg, "The Problem of Objectivity," *Social Forces*, 1967, 46: 98.

[5] Irvin Bromall, "Lawyers in Politics: An Exploratory Study of the Wisconsin Bar." *Wisconsin Law Review*, 1968: 760–763.

[6] Lief Carter, "The Limits of Order: The Influence of Professional Autonomy, Uncertainty, and Interpersonal Trust on Prosecutorial Behavior," Paper presented at the Annual Meeting of the American Political Science Association, Washington, D.C., September 5–9, 1972.

class perspective that has little understanding of or empathy with the defendants who appear in court. In particular the chief judge believes that long prison terms are the best answer to the crime problem. Given this set of attitudes, we would expect the judge to have a major say in the sentences handed out. Such is not the case, however, for the responsibilities of a judge impose constraints. To understand why the criminal court system imposes constraints upon the judge and operates to insulate and isolate him, let us begin by discussing the judge's viewpoints on sentencing.

The Chief Judge's Attitudes on Sentencing

Variations in sentencing is one of the most critical issues in the administration of justice. Although the equal application of the laws is a major value in the legal system (and Americans tend, therefore, to assume that the law *is* applied equally), the sentences handed out are often markedly unequal. A good working definition of equality is that likes should be treated alike, that is, persons convicted of the same crime and having the same background should receive identical treatment.[7] We would not expect every defendant to be treated identically because a complementary goal of criminal justice is the individualization of justice; that is, the sentence should be based on the character of the offender.[8] But even if we make allowance for this factor, individualization of justice alone can not account for the widespread variations in sentences. For example, federal judges in Western Texas sentence forgers to an average forty-three months in prison while federal judges in Southern Texas, applying the same law, impose an average prison term of twenty-seven months.[9] Studies in other communities that examined a wide variety of crimes highlighted similar variations, not only in length of prison terms but also in the propensity of judges to place suspects on probation.[10]

---

[7] Klonoski and Mendelsohn suggest this empirical yardstick to avoid possible confusion with normative concerns. James Klonoski & Robert Mendelsohn, eds., *The Politics of Local Justice* (Little, Brown, 1971), p. xvi.

[8] Julian D'Esposito, Jr. "Sentencing Disparity: Causes and Cures," *Journal of Criminal Law, Criminology, and Police Science*, 1969, 60: 182.

[9] U.S. Department of Justice, Federal Bureau of Prisons, *Statistical Report* (Government Printing Office, 1966), pp. 46–47.

[10] Henry Bullock, "Significance of the Racial Factor in the Length of Prison Sentences," *Journal of Criminal Law, Criminology and Police Science*, 1961, 52: 411–417; Albert Somit, Joseph Tanenhaus & Walter Wilke.

Such variations in sentencing are the product of numerous factors—some legally relevant and others not. For example, the nature of the community, the type of crime, the sex, age, economic status, and race of the defendant relate in various fashions to differences in sentences.[11] More importantly for our purposes, sentencing is also related to the judge. Simply put, judges vary in the sentences they hand out. This is most readily seen in large jurisdictions where multiple judges make it possible to compare judges' sentencing behavior. An in-depth study of Philadelphia showed that the personality of the judge, coupled with differing perceptions of what factors should be considered in passing sentence, accounted for disparities in sentencing.[12] Such findings confirm the practical knowledge of defense attorneys who maneuver to have their client's case assigned to a lenient judge.[13]

What then are the Prairie City chief judge's attitudes about sentencing? A logical starting point is the judge's own statements. The chief judge assigns a high priority to sentencing. Whereas the prosecutor is primarily interested in securing convictions, the chief justice focuses on sentencing. He expresses his views often to defendants, prosecutors, and defense attorneys. Typical of his attitude is the following statement made during a probation hearing. The defendant through her attorney had requested probation. The case involved shoplifting but since it was her second offense for shoplifting the case was a felony. The judge responded to the defense attorney's arguments for probation.

> There are a number of fallacies in defense counsel's argument. For one the nature of the crime. Obvious from the case record this is more than just a theft. When apprehended she assaulted the man. Defense counsel says the fight is unclear but she still is acting illegally. This is an anti-social act. The second point is to ask, was rehabilitation successful before? What in the record contributing rather than parasite on society? Nothing positive in the

---

"Aspects of Judicial Sentencing Behavior," *University of Pittsburgh Law Review*, 1960, 21: 613–621.

[11] For a critical review of the studies on race see Michael Hindelan, "Equality under the Law," in Charles Reasons & Jack Kuykendall, eds., *Race, Crime and Justice* (Goodyear Publishing, 1972), pp. 312–323.

[12] Edward Green, *Judicial Attitudes in Sentencing* (St. Martins' Press, 1961).

[13] Lynn Mather, "To Plead Guilty or Go to Trial?" Paper presented at the Annual Meeting of the American Political Science Association, Washington, D.C., September 5–9, 1972, p. 10.

record. (sic) I reject the idea that sentence is pure punishment. Sentencing is constructive. Need something to straighten out when on the wrong track. (sic) [To the defendant] When something is seriously wrong a slap on the wrist won't work. Not a case for probation. Can't ignore charges which indicate how the defendant lives. I agree with the recommendation of the probation officer [that probation be denied]. Any other recommendation not based on reasonable grounds. Just probation won't work.

This statement is representative of the judge's views. Although the exact details might vary, the same points were made on numerous occasions. The judge's attitudes on sentencing involve three major elements: 1] prison sentences are positive, not merely negative, 2] can correct the wayward lives of the defendants and, 3] deter future wrongdoers. In considering these three elements it is helpful to incorporate a recent study of Minneapolis and Pittsburgh judges because the chief judge's attitudes on sentencing are remarkably parallel to the viewpoints expressed by the Minneapolis judges.

Minneapolis and Pittsburgh were selected for study because of major differences in the political systems and consequent differences in judges. In Pittsburgh judges are selected via the political machine. Almost all of them held government positions prior to becoming judges and were active in party work. Pittsburgh then represents the traditional political system, while Minneapolis represents the good government or reformed city. In Minneapolis the machine was much weaker. Judges were not recruited through the party. Instead the local bar association played a major role. Prior to becoming judges most of the incumbents in Minneapolis were not active in the party but maintained private legal practices. Sentencing varied between the two cities. Minneapolis gave more uniform sentences than Pittsburgh, but the decisions were more lenient in Pittsburgh. Based on this synopsis of the Levin study,[14] let us simultaneously consider the viewpoints of the chief justice in Prairie City and the Minneapolis judges.

The chief justice believes prison sentences are positive, not merely negative. His verbiage, at least, rejects a purely punitive approach to sentencing. Prison terms are constructive, according to the judge, in that they can "straighten defendants out." The penitentiary provides "activities, education, training in trades and crafts" that can correct the life style of the defendant. Minneapolis judges voiced a parallel opinion. For example, "I know that

---

[14] Levin, "Urban Politics and Judicial Behavior," pp. 193–196.

I am considered a tough judge here, but that doesn't bother me because punishment works. You won't sit on a hot stove if you have been burned." [15] In both communities the stress on positive aspects of prison does not incorporate criticisms of the penal system. Prisons have been marked by a high rate of recidivism, as well as severely criticized for not providing the training cited by the chief judge. Yet the chief judge never incorporates these negative aspects of the prison system into his thinking. Similarly in Minneapolis "Few of these judges are critical of the penal system." [16]

Closely tied to the positive comments on prison are the chief judge's negative views of the defendants. During sentencing hearings the judge often commented on the wayward lives of the defendants. This term was heard on more than one occasion in the chief justice's courtroom. More than one defense attorney either directly mentioned or subtly indicated their belief that the judge was prejudiced. By prejudice they did not necessarily mean racial but prejudiced against certain types of people. According to one lawyer the chief judge is "prejudiced against psychiatrists, psychologists, sociologists, clergy, trailer courts, small loans, small claims cases and, of course, people on welfare." The words may be different but the emphasis is the same among Minneapolis judges. When asked to describe the defendants these judges used terms like "coming from low intelligence groups," "crummy people," "not learning from their mistakes." [17] In both Prairie City and Minneapolis the judges come from middle to upper-middle-class backgrounds, backgrounds not noted for their familiarity with the poor. By contrast, Pittsburgh judges came from predominantly lower-middle-class backgrounds and had grown up in some of the neighborhoods from which the defendants were coming. The Pittsburgh judges had a better understanding of the defendants and were more inclined to give them a break.

The third major category in sentencing viewpoints in the two cities are similar stresses on deterrence. To quote again from a remark made by the chief judge during a probation hearing, "I don't accept the fact that sentences don't deter." In his view the court needs to make examples of the people convicted so that others will not commit similar acts. Defense attorneys' comments

---

[15] Ibid., p. 208.

[16] Ibid., p. 208.

[17] Ibid., p. 206.

reinforced this theme. As one phrased it, "Judge ———— believes that he is single-handedly keeping crime down." Much the same point is made in Minneapolis where the judges were more oriented to "society" and its protection than toward the defendant.[18]

The chief judge believes such corrective action is needed because of the bad class of people with whom the courts must deal. Not only will prison straighten out the wayward lives of defendants but the examples set will deter others. The chief judge and the Minneapolis judges share a number of viewpoints. In both cases the image of justice is very much a reformed one. Emphasis is placed on maintaining the formality of the law, as well as a stress on applying abstract concepts of law and justice. What it does not incorporate is an empathy with the defendant.

Constraints on the Judge

The chief judge's attitudes on sentencing are, however, only an imperfect guide to actual sentencing behavior. In general the sentences are lower than the judge would prefer. Why then does the judge not impose higher sentences? After all the judge is the only one with formal power to impose a sentence. The prosecutor, defense attorney and probation officer operate only in an advisory capacity. Why does the judge heed their advice even when he disagrees? The answer to this seeming paradox is found in an analysis of the social system of the Prairie City courts. The judge, like the other actors, is not totally free to act solely on the basis of his personal views. Rather he must consider the expectations of others. For example, we have shown that the prosecutor must consider the expectations of the defense attorney in deciding upon a course of action. In the same manner the defense attorney must consider the expectations of both his client and the prosecution. A set of similar expectations acts upon judges in Prairie City, particularly the chief judge. These expectations are best termed constraints on the judges.

The operations of plea bargaining impose major restraints on judges. The norm is quite strong in Prairie City that a judge should accept an agreement negotiated by opposing attorneys. To fully understand this norm we need a brief overview of the plea bargaining system in Prairie City.[19] Most criminal cases are settled not at trial but by negotiations between defense and prose-

---

[18] Ibid., p. 202.

[19] Chapter 9 analyzes the plea bargaining process in greater detail.

cution. After they have agreed upon the defendant's guilty plea to a given charge and the likely penalty, they appear in court. The judge need not accept the sentence agreed upon by the two attorneys but he almost invariably does. Why? One factor is that the judge knows relatively little about the case. The judges uniformly mentioned that they know very little about a case except the minimal information recorded on the indictment and on the court docket. By contrast the attorneys have a full set of facts. Given this limited knowledge of a case, judges believe they should defer to the judgment of the experts—the two opposing attorneys.

This predisposition to accept the results of plea bargaining in criminal cases is reinforced by the judge's experiences in civil cases. In the typical civil case, whether it be divorce, personal injury, or probate, the attorneys normally work out a mutually acceptable settlement. They then approach the bench and request that the judge provide the legal imprimatur. Thus, in civil cases, the judge respects the agreement negotiated between two lawyers and only provides the formal seal to finalize the agreement. The judge treats criminal cases like civil disputes. If two attorneys reach a mutually acceptable settlement based on a full set of facts then the judge should defer to that decision.

The second role constraint is the necessity of disposing of cases. Judges recognize that the county functions on a plea basis. About eighty percent of the cases do not go to trial but are settled with a plea of guilty. It is obvious that a change in that situation would mean that cases are not being disposed of. Judges fully recognize that if they were to interject their own views into plea bargaining then the plea process would be destroyed. If one side felt he could reach a better settlement by going directly to the judge, then there would be no need to deal with the opposition. Thus a judge's rejection of previous agreements would mean that plea bargaining would be destroyed and a backlog of cases would likely develop. It is thus much easier for the judge to accept the lawyers' agreement.

Efficient administration of the court system is a particularly strong influence on the chief judge. The last section stressed the conservative views of the judge. But any one attitude does not exist in isolation and must be balanced with other and sometimes competing interests. The chief judge is especially proud that his county does not have a backlog of cases. The corollary of this is if he rejected the pleas arranged by counsel in favor of a higher sentence then cases would not move along efficiently. The tenor of these views is captured in comments the judge made to the prosecutor. Trials were set to begin on Monday and the judge informally commented on Thursday, "There are a lot of cases that have to be disposed of by Monday." The judge strongly desires to keep cases moving and thus does not want to alter the plea bargaining process.

The first two role constraints operate on all judges in the county whether full judges or magistrates. A third role constraint, desire to avoid appellate court reversal, operates primarily on the chief judge. Other judges, of course, do not want to be reversed, but the chief judge is particularly concerned with making an impeccable record. No matter what else attorneys say about the chief judge, they do say he is a very able lawyer who strives for an impeccable record. He makes a very clear trial record. For example, he intensively questions defendants when they plead guilty. This intensive questioning is designed to prevent a defendant from later claiming he was pressured into a plea.

A trial judge's concern with following the existing law and thus avoiding a reversal usually applies only to the actual trial of a case. Appellate courts normally reverse lower courts only if there is an error in the conduct of the trial. As a result, sentences usually are immune from appellate court scrutiny.[20] This does not apply to the intermediate appellate court for Prairie City, however. One of the appellate judges formerly served as head of the state pardon and parole board. His background and interest in sentencing are reflected in the court's appellate decisions. The appellate court has ruled the sentences must not be excessive and furthermore the trial record must justify any higher than normal sentence. Thus the court will affirm the trial judge's record on guilt of the defendant but on occasion will lower the sentence because it is excessive. This means that the trial record must justify the sentence imposed; if it is longer than normal the appellate court is likely to modify it. During the interview with the chief judge he referred to two recent cases where this happened. The appellate court found no fault with the conduct of the trial, thus sustaining the finding of guilt, but ruled that the sentences were excessive. The chief judge felt the appellate court was meddling where it should not.

The exact legal ramifications of the appellate court position

---

[20] For a discussion of appellate court review of sentencing see The President's Commission on Law Enforcement and Administration of Justice, *Task Force Reports: The Courts*, p. 25.

need not detain us here because the crucial dimension is the participants' expectations surrounding the court's position. Informants interpreted the appellate court position to mean that if the chief judge (or any judge for that matter) denied probation when probation had been recommended, or if the judge imposed a higher sentence than the prosecutor recommended, then the appellate court probably would lower the sentence. According to the participants the record must justify the sentence handed out. Notice this assessment is not necessarily based on hard law but rather on the perceptions of the court's position. The possibility that the court will lower sentences adds a further role constraint on the ability of the trial judge to interpose his own views in sentencing.

In summary, the duties and responsibilities of a judge impose constraints on his behavior. The judge is not isolated. As a member of a role set he is conscious that his decisions have wider ramifications. Further, there are alternative considerations that the judge must balance in his own mind. He may want to see higher penalties but at the same time he does not want a backlog of cases. We suggested three primary role constraints on Prairie City judges: 1] pressures are strong for the judge to accept agreements negotiated by attorneys; 2] the need to "move cases" means that the plea system can not be altered and 3] all judges, but particularly the chief judges, are conscious of appellate court reversal on sentencing.

Judges and the Communications Network

The judges' views on sentencing and the constraints imposed on judges are not written down nor do the participants refer to them directly. Rather these factors come into operation in the interactions among members of the role set. In this section we want to consider the nature of the communication process.

In considering judges' interactions with other members of the criminal justice community we must be cognizant of broader norms involving judges. A good amount of contemporary work considers what part he should play in the plea bargaining process. The dominant viewpoint is that judges should not actively take part in negotiations. Because the role of the judge is to decide conflicting issues in court, legal reformers stress that the judge must maintain a posture above the fray.[21] Typical of this viewpoint is the opinion of a federal court that stated: "We disapprove

---

[21] Edward Fisher, "Plea Bargaining in Traffic Cases," *The Prosecutor*, 1969, 5: 96.

the judicial plea bargaining disclosed in the present record. The trial judge should not participate in plea discussions." [22] These judicial norms, however, do not take into account an equally compelling consideration—the needs of the social system. The traditional role assigned to the judge—one of almost splendid isolation—fails to comprehend that all members of the social network require information on the likely actions of other participants. There exists, then, a tension between judicial ethics and the realities of the administration of justice.

In some communities this tension is resolved by ignoring the ethical prohibitions on participation in plea bargaining. For example, studies in Oakland, Chicago, and New York show that judicial isolation is a myth, because the judge is a full participant in plea bargaining.[23] Plea bargaining in these cities is a triangular arrangement involving prosecutor, defense attorney, and the judge.

Downstate Illinois judges know of the Chicago practice and during interviews spontaneously mentioned the practice. However, Downstate judges uniformly expressed their dislike for the practice. As one phrased it, "None of the judges wants anything to do with participating in plea bargaining." In Prairie City, therefore, plea bargaining does not incorporate the judge. However, other arrangements work to fulfill the same function of communication of judicial views.

In Prairie City the main vehicle for communication of judicial views on sentencing is the probation hearing. Probation hearings are held in most felony cases. After the defendant is found guilty, he will request probation, and a probation report is prepared. At the probation hearing the report is formally submitted in court together with the probation officer's recommendations as to whether to grant probation or not. Probation hearings, like most formal court proceedings, are mainly routine, with the report being accepted and the recommendations likewise accepted. In some cases, however, there is a dispute. In such a situation the state gives reasons why the probation officer's recommendation of no probation is a reasonable recommendation. Defense counters with its viewpoint. At the conclusion of arguments the judge responds and presents his own views. Thus the probation hearing functions as an auction block for varying sides to express opinions

---

[22] Brown v. Beto, 5 Cir., 377 F. 2d 950, 956–957. Quoted in Ibid., p. 96.

[23] Abraham Blumberg, *Criminal Justice* (Quadrangle, 1967) ; Jerome Skolnick, *Justice Without Trial* (John Wiley, 1966), pp. 191–196.

over the propriety of sentencing. It is in this open forum of ideas that the participants, but especially the judge, have an opportunity to make their views known. Most of the quotes from the chief judge, which were used earlier, come from such remarks from the bench during probation hearings.

The judge also has informal means of communicating his viewpoints. Identifying these informal procedures is important. As Arnold Enker writes: "Presumably a judge has other unofficial ways of expressing his displeasure with a reduced charge, but I have never heard of such judicial expressions." [24] One form of informal communications in Prairie City is a discussion with the probation officer. For example, in a burglary case the probation officer had recommended probation. At the probation hearing the judge commented: "We discussed this case yesterday and I indicated that this was not a case for probation. For once I disagree with his recommendation." This statement is significant first of all for its acknowledgment that cases are discussed by the judge in private with the probation officer. Informants in the community indicated that such discussions were not confined to isolated cases. This statement is significant also because the judge is publicly expressing his displeasure with the work of another official. It is one thing to express one's views in private but quite another to repeat them in open court. Thus the above statement can be interpreted as a judicial rebuke of the probation officer.

Another form of informal communications is a discussion with the judge in private by defense and/or prosecution. Such informal discussions are atypical however. As we have already indicated, judges do not participate in the plea bargaining process, but on occasion an unusual situation arises. A prosecutor provided the following illustration. A defendant was convicted of a minor felony. On the basis of his past record he normally would not qualify for probation. However, the defendant had cooperated with the police in clearing up other offenses in which he had not been involved. Therefore the prosecutor believed probation was in order and went to the judge's chambers to explain the situation. The tone of such a conversation was: rather than surprise you in open court we will tell you the reasons for our recommendation. The judge gave no indication whether he would go along but was advised of the situation. A second example involved multiple defen-

---

[24] Arnold Enker, "Perspectives on Plea Bargaining," *Task Force Reports: The Courts*, p. 109.

dants in a murder case. The state decided several were less culpable than the others and recommended a much lighter sentence for these defendants. The judge was advised before the court hearing, and independent sources said he was quite upset that the sentence recommendation was so low. In court, however, the judge accepted the state's recommendation. In another case involving a probation violation, the attorneys agreed on an extension of probation rather than a jail term. According to the defense attorney the state went to see if the judge would follow the recommendation. During the seven months of studying the Prairie City courts, the three examples cited above were the only indications of informal discussions with the judge prior to the court appearance.

Judicial Role and Tension in the Social System

The probation hearing and informal discussions in chambers serve to tie the judge into the broader criminal justice community. Through these communication channels, information is transmitted covering the other members of the community and what they would like to see done. Such communications often produce disagreement over specific policies. But more fundamental than these specific disagreements are the tensions apparent in the relationships of prosecutors and defense attorneys to the judges, particularly the chief judge. We pointed out the tension between police and prosecutor. While both organizations share similar concerns—the apprehension, conviction and sanctioning of wrongdoers—they also disagree on how these goals should be pursued. At the heart of the tensions are contrasting views of what the prosecutor should do—the police believe that the prosecutor should represent their views in court while the prosecutor believes he should be independent. In the same way, the tensions between defense and prosecutor, and the judge stem from a basic disagreement on the proper role of the judge.

The most fundamental expectation of a judge is that he should be impartial. For example, when a sample of Kansas citizens were asked to name the most important attributes a judge should have, they mentioned honesty, impartiality and objectivity in deciding cases.[25] In capsule form these are the norms by which attorneys assessed judges in Prairie City. Furthermore, many felt that the judge was not impartial. Typical was the response of a defense

---

[25] Gene Mason, "Judges, and Their Public: Role Perceptions and Role Expectations," (Ph.D. dissertation, Department of Political Science, University of Kansas, 1967), p. 147.

attorney to the question: what improvements would you like to see in the administration of justice? "The defendant is entitled to trial before a judge, not another prosecutor—a judge who doesn't care which way the case comes out. Judge ——— wants to see convictions." In the same vein, another lawyer stated, "If we had an impartial judge, the prosecutor would deal better. There would be more acquittals and more probation." In one form or another most of those interviewed (both defense and prosecution) either directly or indirectly indicated that the chief judge violated this norm of impartiality and objectivity in deciding cases.

Not only do many perceive that the chief judge lacks objectivity and impartiality; their expectations of what a judge should do also clashed with their perceptions of judicial activism.[26] Although defense and prosecution were never asked about their concepts of what a judge should do, their standards were similar to those of Eville Younger, then state's attorney for Los Angeles. "A judge who is performing his proper role should simply decide conflicting issues of fact or conflicting arguments of law. He should not be the aggressive intervener in any piece of litigation." [27] In contrast to this normative expectation that judges should be neutral, attorneys saw the judge as an "aggressive intervener." When a prosecutor was asked about the chief judge's interest in seeing that cases were disposed of, he replied that the judge was interested but it was none of his business. Defense attorneys used more colorful language to convey the same point. For example the prosecutor was talking to the judge and the attorney commented "he's seeing if the judge will 'take the bit in his mouth.' " The judge's interest in seeing that no delays developed, as well as concern over proper degree of the sentence, often

---

[26] Discussions of judicial activism and its supposed opposite, judicial self-restraint, form a substantial part of the literature on the Supreme Court. The dispute centers on the court's power of judicial review. The terms are, however, far from unambiguous. Contemporary political dialogue has equated judicial activism with liberalism and particularly Warren court decisions. A theme of President Nixon's 1968 campaign was the activism of the court and his promises to appoint strict constructionists. Such a simple equation of judicial activism and a liberal position beclouds the issue for prior to 1936 judicial activism was a conservative practice. Joel Grossman & Richard Wells, *Constitutional Law and Judicial Policy Making* (John Wiley, 1972), pp. 53–58. While the term judicial activism is usually applied to the Supreme Court and is somewhat ambiguous we are using the term here because it seems to have applicability to the lower courts as well.

[27] Eville Younger, "The Challenge of the Prosecutor's Office." *The Prosecutor*, 1968, 4: 208.

conflicted with defense and prosecution views that once the lawyers reached a decision the judge should defer to their decisions
and not "meddle."

Tensions between the judge and other members of the criminal justice community stem from a fundamental disagreement
over the proper role of the judge. According to defense and prosecution a judge should be objective, impartial, and neutral. On
these points they find the judge's behavior does not conform to
their expectations. Such tension is not normally on the surface,
for defense and prosecution have few, if any, sanctions to apply.
As a result the tension involving the judge becomes focused on
specific policy-sentencing.

The judge's views on sentencing are more hard-line than those
of the prosecutor and defense attorney. That defense attorneys
believe in lighter penalties should come as no surprise. In particular, defense attorneys singled out the judge's positive views of
sentencing for criticism. Whereas the chief judge stresses the
rehabilitation possible in prisons, defense attorneys view prisons
as failures, citing as evidence the high recidivism rates. Further,
they believe the judge should visit the prisons to see if the training
and education actually do occur. In a like manner defense attorneys believe the chief judge's emphasis on deterrence is misplaced because of the nature of certain offenses. Assaults, for example, are the least deterrable because most assaults occur between acquaintances as a result of some triggering event. Not only
are defense attorneys critical of the chief judge's views on sentencing, but prosecutors are also somewhat critical although their
remarks are more subdued. The prosecutors' views are shaped
by the desire to see convictions–sentencing is strictly secondary.
The judge reverses this emphasis and, as a result, can jeopardize
the securing of convictions. But even beyond the prosecutor's emphasis on convictions, the prosecutors in general are not as hard-
line in sentencing as the chief judge.

The tension over sentencing was evident not only during interviews but also in remarks made by the judge. The judge is often
critical of the prosecutor and probation officer for being too
lenient. For example, during a probation hearing the chief judge
commented that the sentence recommendation was "most, most
lenient and generous under the circumstances. The court will not
recommend a heavier sentence but the sentence is a most lenient
one." On other occasions, both in open court and in comments in
chambers, the judge indicated that some sentences were too light.

The tension over sentencing that involves members of the

criminal justice community stands in sharp contrast, however, to the views on sentencing expressed by people outside the day-to-day activities of the criminal courts. While defense and prosecution generally see the judge as being too harsh, others view sentences as too lenient. The police are such critics. When talking to detectives they were asked to comment on things they liked or did not like about the court system. Several detectives mentioned the lenient sentences handed out by the chief judge. Similar public comment occasionally followed the sentencing of a defendant. Referring back to the example involving multiple defendants in a well publicized murder case, several letters to the editor, as well as comments on the local radio talk show, expressed displeasure with the light sentence. These external criticisms point up an important aspect of the court system—the judge was being criticized for policies he took only reluctantly. Neither the police nor the general public could know that the judge objected to the "light" sentence in the murder case.

Tension between the judge and attorneys practicing before him is a basic aspect of the social system of the Prairie City courts. This tension translates not only into specific conflict over sentencing but also into a subdued lack of goodwill between the judge and defense attorneys. For example, the private law firm that does the bulk of the criminal work routinely files a motion for change of judge on *every* felony case, because they believe the judge is not impartial. Such actions and the reasons for them cannot escape the judge's notice. Moreover there is an element of personal animosity between at least one defense attorney and the chief judge. Several years ago the chief judge initiated disbarment proceedings based not on what a lawyer had done in his court but on what the judge heard the attorney had done in another court. This fact was known by all participants and mentioned by several. In turn the lack of goodwill between judges and attorneys was heightened by attorneys' experiences with another judge. The former chief judge was respected by the entire legal community as a fair and dedicated jurist. In talking about judges lawyers often mentioned positively incidents involving practice before him. Such positive references were notably absent when discussion turned to the incumbent.

Conclusion: Judicial Power

The position of the judge in Prairie City is an anomalous one. To paraphrase from Dickens: the judge has all the power but none of it. While legally the judge is the only one who can formally pronounce guilt (excluding, for now, jury trials) and impose the sentence, the social system delegates these tasks to the prosecutors, defense attorneys, and the probation officer. The norms surrounding the judge in criminal cases are very close to the norms associated with civil cases. In the vast majority of cases the attorneys reach an acceptable agreement that they then request the judge to ratify formally. Participants believe a judge should be neutral—reactive rather than proactive. The chief judge is seen by most informants as deviating from the pattern of expected behavior. The judge is portrayed as encroaching on the proper domain of the defense and prosecution and interfering in areas that are none of his business. Rather than being neutral, the chief judge attempts to insert his attitudes, but his ability to do so is sharply limited by role constraints. The judge is expressing a version of judicial activism and defense attorneys see this as a violation of the judge's duty to be impartial. As one commented, "You can't respect a man who isn't fair."

Thus, in operation, the norms of Prairie City sharply limit the judge's power. The judge's main source of power in sentencing is anticipation by others. Reduced to its basic dimension, the judge in most cases can only reject agreements reached by opposing counsel. Interviews uncovered only one example (which was unconfirmed) where the judge actually rejected such an agreement. In a child-beating case, the state was reported to have recommended the minimum jail term, one year. According to the informant the judge replied, "You're out of your mind," and raised the penalty to from seven to ten years. A solitary example from University Towns illustrates the same point. In an armed robbery case the state agreed to a recommendation of probation. The judge publicly stated he felt the recommendation was out of line, especially since the defendant had been involved in two armed robberies, not one. The judge further stated that this type of conduct must not go unpunished and therefore imposed a penitentiary sentence. A judge's rejection of prior agreements is rare but has influence beyond the particular case. Defense and prosecution in the bargaining session must be somewhat conscious of whether the judge will accept or not. Thus, by rejecting isolated settlements, the judge influences future cases. The judge, in rare instances, is then setting the boundaries for acceptable penalties in future cases. Judicial power involves not only direct action but anticipation as well.

Part Two · PRETRIAL

INTRODUCTION

Let us briefly reunite with our hypothetical defendants: Mrs. Altman—accused of not having a driver's license; and Mr. Boldt—charged with burglary. We indicated in Chapter 1 that how their cases are handled and the punishment they receive (if any) are dependent not only on the formal law but also on the people who administer that law. Prosecutors, judges, defense counsel, and the police shape the law. While these organizations are separate, they are not unrelated. Rather, they comprise a "criminal justice community" [1] of interrelated positions. The formal law is undergirded by an informal social network. The importance of understanding this social network is emphasized by Edwin Schur, who states the social network "must be examined in its entirety by the researcher if the constituent elements are to be fully understood." [2]

In Part One we provided an analysis of the criminal justice community. Basically, we adopted the outlook of a lawyer new to Prairie City who wanted to know "What's the score here?" (to quote again from our defense attorney respondent). Our investigation produced some important answers to the questions we raised in chapter 1. By concentrating on the first three

[1] Jerome Skolnick, *Justice Without Trial* (John Wiley, 1967), p. 28

[2] Edwin Schur, *Law and Society* (Random House, 1968), p. 159.

of these five questions, we can summarize the major findings so far.

Who Makes the Decisions? It is obvious that the prosecutor is the most important member of the criminal justice community in Prairie City. Not only does his position (both legal and structural) provide him with a great potential for power, but also he has the ability and desire to exercise this power. This domination by the prosecutor largely eclipsed the powers normally associated with judges. The social network operates to restrict the power of the judge. A series of role constraints (most notably the judge's lack of information), normal expectations that judges go along with arrangements agreed to by counsel, the desire to keep cases moving, and the fear of appellate court reversal combine to make the judge less of a decision maker than legal theory assumes.

What Standards are Employed in Making these Decisions? In Parts Two and Three we shall examine this question in greater depth. But our examination of the social network of the Prairie City courts already revealed one factor—the importance of general legal practice. Criminal law practice in Prairie City exists within the framework of general legal practice. Defense lawyers maintain an active civil practice, and the prosecutors want to enter civil practice. This orientation to civil practice should lead us to believe that the law will be an important source of standards. These are people trained, bred, and practicing in the law. We, therefore, expect they will approach decision making as primarily a legal matter. Our latter discussions of the charging decision (chapter 6) and plea bargaining (chapter 9) will reinforce these first impressions.

How Do the Decision Makers Interact? The premise of our analysis is that the courts are not

simply a legal entity but also consist of a group
of human beings doing certain things to
other people. As we noted throughout Part One,
all the actors are required to work with other
actors. No one actor is an isolated decision maker.
The nature of these interactions is important
first for what it reveals about the nature of the
decision-making process (see particularly
chapter 6) and also for understanding the
dynamic elements of the criminal justice
system. We can summarize Part One by
concentrating on the important match-ups.

The Police-Prosecutor relationship is packed
with tension and bad relations on both sides. The
prosecutor's stress on independence has
aggravated and magnified the normal police
suspicions of, and hostilities to, the criminal law.

Prosecutor-Defense maintain good working
relations. Most attorneys work "within the
system" to the same degree they negotiate,
compromise, and discuss with their opponents
in civil cases. Since the prosecution and defense
have been working together for a number of
years, each side has a good idea of what the
other side will do in a given situation.

Judges and Prosecutors: Judges and Defense.
The dominant element of the judge's relations to
the other attorneys in the community is the chief
judge's conservative outlook. Just as the police
expect the prosecutor to project the image of a
law-and-order man, we normally expect the judge
to project an image of an impartial man who is
above the fray. Defense attorneys and, to a lesser
extent, prosecutors believe the chief judge does
not live up to this ideal. As we will see later, the
prosecutor is often more lenient and liberal on
sentences than the judges. An additional element
affecting the relationship of the judge and
prosecutor is the autonomy of the prosecutor. The
judge, however, takes an active interest, an
interest not always appreciated by the prosecutor.

In Part Two we will be interested primarily
in answering the fourth question: *How are*

defendant's rights protected? As we will show,
the protection offered to defendant's rights is a
direct product of the social network of the court
system. A number of factors tend to encourage
protection of the defendant's rights, while other
influences tend to move the system in the direction
of less protection and more expediency. But
before we discuss how the defendant's rights are
protected in Prairie City, we need a working
knowledge of the major steps in the history of a
case. After an arrest, the law provides a number
of stages: a legal blueprint of what should
happen. It is upon this stage that the principal
actors—judge, prosecutor, and defense—play
their parts and make their decisions. At the risk
of oversimplifying some technical legal points,
we can divide the time from police arrest to the
plea bargaining-trial stage into the following:

1] *Charging decision.* After the police make
an arrest someone must decide if the arrested
person should be charged with violating the law.
As we shall see in Chapter 6, this stage is a
formality in many communities, but not in
Prairie City.

2] *Arraignment.* Assuming a charge has been
filed, arraignment is the next step. This is the
suspect's first appearance in court. The arraigning
magistrate provides the defendant with a copy
of the charge, states the maximum penalty for the
offense, explains the right to bail, trial,
appointment of counsel for indigents, and
preliminary hearing (in a felony case). How the
magistrate handles the administrative task of
advising the defendant varies among the
magistrates and, perhaps, is an indicator of how
scrupulous the judge is in protecting the
defendant's rights. In Prairie City the arraigning
magistrate gives a full and thorough explanation
to the defendant and makes an effort to see that
the defendant understands what is happening
(not always with success, however). By way of
contrast, the magistrates in University Towns and
the traffic judge in Prairie City spend less time

informing each defendant of his rights. Simply
put, they are more cryptic in explaining the
defendant's rights. They will omit certain features
of the warnings, dispensing with the maximum
penalty for the offense, for example.

3] *Bail.* The purpose of bail is to insure that
the person shows up in court when he should.
In Illinois defendants have the right to bail,
except in a murder case. If the charge is speeding,
bail may be nothing more than giving the officer
your driver's license, but if the charge is a
misdemeanor or a felony, you may have to post
money with the court as a guarantee that you
will appear in court. The requirement of money
for bail obviously involves an important allocation
of justice that we analyzed in chapter 1. If
bail is dependent upon money, it is likely to mean
that the rich await trial at home with their
families and maintain their jobs, while the poor
await trial in jail, away from families and jobs.

4] *Counsel.* A suspect has the right to a
lawyer in Anglo-American justice, but the right
to a lawyer can be different from having a lawyer.
The difference is money. The Supreme Court has
ruled that indigent defendents in felony cases
must be provided with a lawyer. We will examine
how lawyers are provided for the indigent in
Prairie City.

5] *Preliminary hearing.* 6] *Grand jury.* If the
case is a felony, the defendant's next encounter
with the courts can be a preliminary hearing.
At the preliminary hearing the judge hears
evidence to determine if there is probable cause
to hold the suspect for a grand jury. The grand
jury performs a similar screening function. This
time, however, instead of a judge reviewing a
case, twenty-three citizens with no connection with
the court examine the evidence. If they think
the case is without merit, they have the power
to vote a "No True Bill," which means the suspect
cannot be held accountable for a felony. Grand
jury and preliminary hearings, however, are not
required by law. Rather they are allowed, which

means that defendants can decide to waive the
preliminary hearing and/or the grand jury.

7] *Pretrial motions.* Pretrial motions provide
the transition from procedural aspects of a
criminal case (the first six steps) and the
disposition of the case (jury trial or plea
bargaining). We will examine pretrial motions in
Part Two, because pretrial motions are the vehicle
for enforcing the procedural rights the Supreme
Court has provided in cases such as *Mapp* and
Miranda. If a lawyer believes his client was
improperly searched, or the police improperly
interrogated their client, then the lawyer can file
a pretrial motion to suppress the evidence.

Thus, analytically, there are seven distinct
stages between the arrest and trial. These seven
stages do not have to occur in the order given.
For example, the majority of defendants in Prairie
City hire a lawyer after the preliminary hearing,
not before it. Nonetheless, these are the steps in
the case and provide the framework for decision
making.

The most notable attribute of Prairie City is
the steady and regular processing of criminal
cases from first appearance to trial. Regularity
is the hallmark of the process. Officials are
conscious of the possibility of a backlog of cases
developing and strive to keep the cases moving.
At the same time every effort is made to allow the
defendant to take advantage of his rights.

The most crucial element for regularity in the
flow of cases is the absence of a backlog of
cases. Whereas delay poses a major concern in
many other jurisdictions, it is absent in Prairie
City. As mentioned earlier, the chief judge is
responsible for moving the court docket and wants
to prevent a backlog from developing. One
informant commented the judge is "very
meticulous about the expeditious disposition of
the docket." Prior to jury week he continually
asks how the schedule is going and examines the
trial setting with the prosecutor. In short, the
pressure is on to settle cases.

The concern lest a backlog of cases develop is more than a Prairie City malaise. It is reinforced by the experience in University Towns, where the press reported the backlog reached 5,000 cases, roughly equivalent to two years of normal work for the criminal courts. The widespread publicity about this backlog reached Prairie City and the responsible officials wanted to prevent any such problem from developing in their community. The pressure to move cases, however, is not warmly embraced by all participants. Some defense attorneys believe the pressure is too intense and the short period of time for case preparation is a hardship on them.

The regularity in the flow of cases can be seen in the amount of time that elapses from arrest to final disposition of the case. In Prairie City the preliminary hearing usually is held within three days of the filing of charges. The grand jury meets the first Monday of each month, and a trial date is set for six weeks after the indictment. Thus cases are regularly disposed of between six to ten weeks after arrest. Some cases take longer but usually these cases involve some complex matter that lawyers believe requires extra preparation time. Other than that, ten weeks is the maximum time between arrest and disposition. When compared to many other jurisdictions, Prairie City is a model of speedy justice.

Part Two examines the seven steps from arrest to trial. Rather than treating these stages individually, however, it is best to group them, because such a grouping better focuses on important political dimensions of the criminal court process. The genesis of a case from arrest to just prior to trial can be divided into three categories:

Chapter 6 concerns the transition from a police arrest to a court charge, what we have termed the charging decision. Chapter 6 also will examine how the prosecutor handles the charging decision and how his procedures have eclipsed the functions normally associated with the preliminary hearing and the grand jury.

Chapter 7 examines the economics of justice. Posting bail and hiring a lawyer, by definition, indicate the importance of money in the criminal justice process. Since it is presumptive that defendants with some money will be treated differently than defendants without any, we want to investigate the importance of economics on justice. As we shall see, local courts may seek to mute economic inequities or magnify these differences.

Finally in chapter 8 the impact of the Supreme Court is examined. The Supreme Court has made controversial decisions involving police interrogations and the police ability to search and seize. The impact, if any, of these decisions on the local administration of justice ultimately involves a defense attorney's pretrial motion challenging the police conduct in a given case. We will examine how the social network of the Prairie City courts influences the bringing of allegations of police irregularity to the courts, and how the social network shapes the application of the Supreme Court decisions to these alleged infractions.

After the Arrest— the Filing of Charges

CHAPTER 6

One of the most hallowed and often repeated phrases of Anglo-American jurisprudence is "innocent until proven guilty." This is strikingly different from civil law countries where the filing of charges involves a presumption of guilt and the defendant must prove his innocence. In the common law countries the defendant is presumed innocent. The state must prove him guilty. This concern with the presumption of innocence is also apparent in court proceedings prior to trial. Shortly after the filing of a felony charge, the preliminary hearing provides for judicial review of the case to establish whether "probable cause" exists. Similarly many states allow for a grand jury, twenty-three men and women, who as laymen review the work of the legal officials to determine whether the case merits further prosecution. Both the preliminary hearing and grand jury may result in the case being dismissed. The underlying philosophy of both is that in cases without merit the defendant should not be forced to bear the costs of a trial.

But this concentration on formal court proceedings neglects an important consideration—the filing of charges carries important consequences even if the defendant is later acquitted. Consider the following examples. In midseason, the quarterback of the Atlanta Falcons was arrested at a party for resisting arrest. It was also reported that marijuana was found at the party. During the annual session of the Florida legislature, a state senator was arrested for immoral conduct. A nineteen-year-old Florida State coed complained that the senator had asked her to pose for lewd pictures and had offered her liquor. The senator asked to be excused from legislative duties. Finally the state's attorney in Gainesville, Florida, with a well deserved reputation as a law-and-order man, was arrested for assault. The complainant was characterized by the local paper as a local hippie entrepreneur—his store sold waterbeds. These three examples have several points in common. All involved fairly newsworthy subjects, and the press is quick to report any alleged infractions of the law by celebrities. A further point that the cases had in common is that each of the charges was later dismissed, either for lack of sufficient evidence, or in the case of the state senator, because the complainant changed her story. Even though all three charges were dropped, we can ask whether these charges might negatively have affected individual reputations. Obviously each person in question can fall back upon the American ideal—innocent until proven guilty. Still, the consequences of being charged with a crime are not likely to be undone so easily. The general public often is less interested in the lofty premise of "innocent until proven guilty" than in the better known aphorism, "Where there's smoke, there's fire."

For the average citizen, however, the potential damage to one's reputation is of less immediate importance than other consequences of being charged with a criminal offense. Consider what might happen if you were charged with something more serious than a traffic ticket. You would have to post bail or await trial in jail. In March, 1970, 78,000 persons were being held prior to trial.[1] Other economic burdens are also involved. If the charge is a serious one, you will probably have to hire a lawyer. Even if the charges are minor, you will have to take time off from work to appear in court.

The charging decision is important, not only because of the consequences it has for the people involved, but also because it may be a significant stage in the criminal process. Each year a significant number of cases are "dismissed" before charges are filed. In St. Louis County, for example, fifty percent of the police requests for a warrant are denied by the prosecutor. The figures for California indicate roughly the same pattern. In 1962 over one-fourth of all felony arrests resulted in the suspect's release. In addition twenty percent of the California felony arrests resulted in misdemeanor charges.[2] Thus the decision to file formal charges in court may produce a major alteration in the nature of the case. Why is it that some cases are "dismissed" before charges are filed, other arrests result in a reduction from felony to misdemeanor, and in still other cases the arrest and the charge are

---

[1] U.S. Law Enforcement Assistance Administration and U.S. Bureau of the Census, *1970 National Jail Census* (Government Printing Office, 1970), p. 2.

[2] Gene McNarry, *1971 Annual Report, St. Louis County Prosecutor's Office* (Clayton, Mo., 1972), p. 17; Jerome Skolnick, *Justice Without Trial* (John Wiley, 1967), p. 114, table 2.

the same? These are important decisions, but unlike the results of the preliminary hearing and grand jury, they are seldom made public. Instead, these decisions are made behind closed doors without any court records.

This chapter investigates the charging decision in Prairie City. Our discussion will focus on four topics. First: who controls the charging decision? In Prairie City the prosecutor exercises this power. The absence of police influence will also be examined. Second: what standards does the prosecutor use in deciding to file charges? Here we will look at the scope of the prosecutor's discretion. Third: what are the consequences of the charging decision? What factors lead to no charges being filed, or the change to misdemeanor charges rather than felonies? Fourth: How has the prosecutor's handling of the charging decision eclipsed the traditional functions associated with the preliminary hearing and the grand jury?

The Charging Process in Prairie City

State statutes provide no guidelines on how the charging decisions should be handled or who is responsible. As a result each community may adopt different procedures, procedures that allow certain actors more influence than others. Four actors may exert influence over who will be charged with a criminal offense: the policeman, the prosecutor, the judge, and the complainant. Which actor, or which combination of actors, is allowed to make the charging decision has a great influence on the results. For example, if the police dominate they are likely to employ different standards than a prosecutor or judge. If, on the other hand, the complainant is allowed a major role, it is possible that the criminal courts might be used as a forum for personal vendettas or family fights. Viewed from this perspective, asking who controls the charging decision involves asking who is the gatekeeper to the powers of the criminal courts, that is, who regulates inputs to the courts.[3]

Although in some communities the police, the judges, or the "victim" may play important roles, in Prairie City the prosecutor dominates the charging decision. Every weekday morning the police arrest sheet, which lists all arrests for the previous day, along with the police arrest reports are brought to the state's attorney's office. The assistant who is handling the charging deci-

---

[3] Sheldon Goldman & Thomas Jahnige, *The Federal Courts as a Political System* (Harper & Row, 1971), p. 114.

sion for that day reviews each case to determine what, if any, charges will be filed. He has three options to chose from: 1] An information may be filed. This is a formal charge detailing the defendant's conduct and the sections of law alleged to have been violated. 2] The assistant may refuse to file charges, in which case he sends the arraigning magistrate a slip indicating that no charges will be filed. 3] The assistant may try to hold the suspect in jail while the police attempt to gather additional evidence. The third option is used only rarely.

The overriding feature of the charging process in Prairie City is the dominance of the prosecutor. In other communities the police, and sometimes the complainant, have some say in who will be prosecuted; in Prairie City they have virtually none. The prosecutorial dominance relates to our earlier discussion of the role orientation of the Prairie City prosecutor. As we noted, the office is run much like any law firm. The prosecutor makes the charging decision because this is viewed as the most efficient procedure. By carefully reviewing cases before charges are filed, he eliminates any weak cases and sees what additional evidence may be required. The state's attorney is quite proud of this procedure. He believes his office functions more closely to the federal model than any other office in the state. (The federal model refers to the practices of assistant U.S. attorneys general who do not file charges until they are virtually certain that they will obtain a conviction.) In Prairie City the state's attorney believes this is the only efficient way to operate the office because it saves a lot of work.

This office norm of efficiency results in the absence of police influence on the charging decision. The absence of police influence in Prairie City stands in sharp contrast to previous research. McIntyre's study of Chicago, for example, reports that the prosecutor makes no attempt to review cases before charges are filed.[4] Instead, the police file charges, and the prosecutor learns about the case at the preliminary hearing. Frank Miller observes, "In many cases prosecutors agree with the police assessment, but in others they simply defer to it." [5] In these communities the police can be said to dominate the charging decision.

---

[4] Donald McIntyre, "A Study of Judicial Dominance of the Charging Process," *The Journal of Criminal Law, Criminology, and Police Science*, 1968, 59: 470.

[5] Frank Miller, *Prosecution: The Decision to Charge a Suspect With a Crime* (Little, Brown, 1969), p. 195.

What seems to be a more widespread pattern is a sharing of power between the police and prosecutor. Studies of Oakland, Seattle, and assistant U.S. attorneys general indicate that the two agencies jointly discuss cases before charges are filed.[6] In such a situation the police have an opportunity to influence the outcome by providing additional information that is not contained in the police report or extralegal information, such as the suspect's reputation as a bad actor. The influence of the police in such a situation is reported by Skolnick. He found that some defendants were initially overcharged—that is, charged with a more serious offense than the evidence would warrant, or charged on the basis of weak evidence—because of police pressure.[7]

In contrast, the police in Prairie City have little if any impact upon the charging decision. The state's attorney reviews the case without the police being present. Indeed, the arresting officer is never contacted by the prosecutor, except in a situation where the police report is hopelessly confused. In fact, police influence would not be allowed because the state's attorney believes the police and prosecutor are separate organizations. As he phrases it, "The police book and we charge." [8] To be sure, the police, and to a certain extent the complainant, have a limited influence on the charging decision by virtue of their role as suppliers of information. However, they are granted no formal power to make these decisions, as they are in some other jurisdictions. Further, there seemed to be little, if any, attempt by the police to slant police reports if the person in question was one whom they particularly felt should be dealt with officially.

Standards: The Prosecutable Case

Having identified the prosecutor as the dominant official in the charging decision in Prairie City, we can now inquire into the standards employed in making that decision. The basic criterion is the legal strength of the cases. In this way, prosecutor and civil lawyers are very similar in Prairie City. A private attorney

---

6 Skolnick, *Justice Without Trial*, pp. 199–202; George Cole, "The Decision to Prosecute," *Law and Society Review*, 1970, 4: 334–337; and James Eisenstein, "The Federal Prosecutor and His Environment," unpublished paper delivered at the Annual Meeting of the American Political Science Association, Washington D.C., September 2–7, 1968, pp. 8–9.

7 Skolnick, *Justice Without Trial*, p. 200.

8 Neal Milner found similar views expressed by prosecutors in Green Bay and Kenosha, Wisconsin. Neal Milner, *The Courts and Local Law Enforcement* (Sage Publications, 1971), pp. 89 & 114.

considering accepting a personal injury case, or the prosecutor deciding whether to file charges, wants to know if the case can be proven in court. If the civil attorney does not think that the case is likely to win at trial he probably will not take it because he would be spending time on an unprofitable cause. Many of the same concerns are voiced by the Prairie City prosecutor. George Cole's study of Seattle labeled this a "question of evidence." [9] While he treats it as one of several factors involved in the prosecutor's charging decision, in Prairie City it is the dominant factor.

When presented with a case, the Prairie City prosecutor asks: "Is this case prosecutable?" As one assistant commented, "When I examine the police report I have to feel that I could go to trial with the case tomorrow. All the elements of prosecution must be present before I file charges." A prosecutable case differs from the more familiar legal benchmark, probable cause. For example, at the preliminary hearing the judge determines if there is probable cause, that is if a crime has been committed and if there are reasonable grounds to believe the suspect committed the offense. From the prosecutor's perspective, however, probable cause is too gross a yardstick; it may be present but a case still may be weak legally. Thus the concept of a prosecutable case is not the same as the standard of probable cause, which is used by the police when they arrest, or by a judge when he conducts a preliminary hearing. Rather it is the standard of trial—what must be proven in order to secure a conviction. The state's attorney's office in Prairie City sees no advantage to filing charges on a legally weak case that will survive a preliminary hearing but will lose at trial. They prefer to weed out such weak cases as soon as possible, before the arrest even becomes an official case.

Employing a trial standard—does the case have a good chance of winning at trial?—produces an important transformation in the history of a case, a transformation highlighted by Skolnick's distinction between factual guilt and legal guilt. Factual guilt focuses on the suspect's action—did he do it? By contrast legal guilt looks at what can be proven about the suspect's activities. [10] The perspective of legal guilt and factual guilt are very different, a difference that can produce tension in the working relationships of the police and prosecutor. For example, the police might be convinced that a suspect committed an illegal act but the prosecutor may be equally convinced that there is not enough evidence to

---

[9] Cole, "The Decision to Prosecute," p. 334.

[10] Skolnick, *Justice Without Trial*, p. 182.

justify filing charges. In Prairie City the prosecutor chooses to confront the difference between factual and legal guilt at the earliest possible moment by judging cases against a standard of winning at trial.

The seeming simplicity of the concept of the prosecutor's assessing cases to see if they are prosecutable should not, however, obscure the broader empirical question—to what extent do prosecutors perform this task? This question is suggested by a former state's attorney in another county who commented, "If a prosecutor is not objective he develops what I call a 'police complex'— that is he ignores the legal aspects of what makes a case." In terms of Skolnick's distinction between factual and legal guilt the prosecutor may come to use the former. This qualitative assessment finds statistical support in a study of deputy prosecutors in Los Angeles. Of those interviewed twenty percent felt prosecutors should file charges even if the case "will probably not get past the preliminary hearing stage." Thirty percent stated charges should be filed if the case would survive the preliminary hearing but probably lose at trial. Only one-half agreed with the Prairie City practice of filing charges only "if the case will probably win at trial." [11] Obviously, prosecutors employ varying standards in making judgments on evidence. The consequences of these varying standards require greater study.

Discretion

The charging decision involves more than just examining the police report to see if legal guilt can be established. As the prosecutors in Prairie City acknowledge, discretion also plays a role. Discretion is one of the most important dimensions of criminal justice. Unfortunately the meaning of "discretion" is ambiguous. A standard text on crime and the criminal process states: "Since legal formulations do not provide specific instructions for interpreting law, the administration of law is largely a matter of discretion on the part of *legal actors*." [12] Another study that focuses directly on prosecutors takes a similarly broad view of discretion. "The American legal system seems to be shot through with many excessive and uncontrolled discretionary powers but the one that stands out above all others is the power to prosecute or

---

[11] "Prosecutorial Discretion in the Initiation of Criminal Complaints," *Southern California Law Review*, 1969, 42: 526.

[12] Richard Quinney, *The Social Reality of Crime* (Little, Brown, 1970), p. 40.

not to prosecute." [13] These formulations are useful because they alert us that the administration of justice is not a mechanical process. However, their definitions of discretion are so broad that the concept is robbed of any utility. These works seems to suggest that virtually all that prosecutors do is discretionary. To clarify this point let us consider two hypothetical examples. A suspect has been arrested for armed robbery. The police reports indicate that the victim has identified the suspect in custody and that the stolen goods were found in his possession at the time of the arrest. Is this the same situation as the arrest of a high school senior for statutory rape? The "victim" is alleged to be his girl friend. If the prosecutor files an armed robbery charge in the former case we would be hard pressed to term that decision discretionary. By contrast, if no charges are filed in the latter case, it appears closer to our intuitive notions of discretion.

In order to confine the concept of discretion to a more restrictive use, we can say that *discretion* exists when an official is free to select his own grounds for a decision. Alternatively, we can say that discretion exists when there are no standards to guide a decision maker. By contrast *judgments* on law and evidence (the prosecutable case standard in Prairie City) are based on fairly clear but imprecise guidelines—the statute books and court standards. In practice it may be difficult to distinguish between judgments and discretion but, despite such measurement problems, it is helpful and necessary to maintain a conceptual distinction.

The working environment of the prosecutor's office supports such a distinction between judgments and discretion. As the Prairie City prosecutors verbalize it, discretion operates in the gray areas, on the borderline, where the law fails to provide guidelines or where the guidelines are ambiguous. The major use of such discretion is in deciding whether a suspect should be charged with a misdemeanor or a felony. As one assistant overstated the point, "We could charge as many felonies as misdemeanors if we wanted to." Normally the decision to file a misdemeanor or a felony possesses no problem because the applicable law is fairly explicit. Armed robbery, murder, and burglary leave little room for discretion; it is mainly judgments that are involved. In some areas, however, the law's guidance falters and the prosecutor must

---

[13] Kenneth Culp Davis, *Discretionary Justice: A Preliminary Inquiry* (University of Illinois Press, 1971), p. 188. Similar discussions of discretion are found in: Miller, *Prosecution*, p. 152; and Joseph Goldstein, "Police Discretion Not to Invoke the Criminal Process: Low-Visibility Decisions in the Administration of Justice," *The Yale Law Journal*, 1960, 69: 543–594.

decide on a basis other than the formal standards of law and evidence.

The most typical offenses that involve a high degree of discretion are vice crimes. However, since there are very few of these in Prairie City, vice cannot serve as a vehicle for discussing discretion. In Prairie City aggravated battery is the crime that invokes the most prosecutorial discretion. Battery involves bodily harm to the victim. Illinois law provides for two categories of battery: simple battery (a misdemeanor); and aggravated battery (a felony). An offense becomes aggravated battery if one of the following criteria is involved: a deadly weapon is used; a police officer is injured (no matter how slight his injury), or "great bodily harm" results. The last standard is the most ambiguous. At either extreme—a victim with a bruise versus a victim near death—prosecutors have no difficulty deciding to charge the first suspect with simple battery and the second with aggravated battery. Borderline cases, however, require the prosecutor to make a discretionary decision.

Prosecutors mention two primary factors that are involved in the exercise of discretion: the nature of the defendant and the nature of the event. One assistant commented that he tends to charge a misdemeanor if the defendant is a little down-and-out, a little stupid, a first-time offender, or the case is unclear. The nature of the event also plays a part. An attempt is made to interpret the cold law in light of what happened. A prosecutor pointed to a recent aggravated battery case stemming from a barroom brawl. While the evidence could have established a felony, the office chose to file a misdemeanor because the victim had provoked the defendant. A special example of the prosecutor looking at the nature of the event rather than the sterile law involves aggravated battery charges involving police officers. While it is a felony to cause bodily harm to a police officer, the state's attorney does not treat this protection as sacrosanct. Instead, he inquires into the nature of the event. Did the defendant take a good swing at the cop with an evil intent? Or, did he just struggle a little? Was he too drunk to know what he was doing? As one assistant stated it, the police want an aggravated battery charge every time a drunk lurches at them. But the more dispassionate prosecutor tends to examine the events from a broader perspective.

The law as a dispute-settling device provides guidelines for settling disputes but at times these guidelines are lacking or ambiguous, which then involves the discretion of the legal actor. In the context of the prosecutor's office in Prairie City, the prime example of such discretion is the borderline aggravated battery arrest. Conceptually this decision is of a different order than the usual judgment on the law and evidence. While discretion and judgments are conceptually distinct, methodologically it may be difficult to specify precisely which factor is operating, or both may be operating simultaneously. Returning to the barroom brawl illustration, a second factor was involved—barroom brawls are hard cases to sell juries. Middle-class juries have little sympathy for working-class barroom brawls (believing both parties are culpable) and tend not to convict. Thus, the assistant prosecutor appeared to be exercising discretion—deciding to examine the victim's activity—as well as making a judgment that the case was not a strong one.

In this discussion of the exercise of discretion in the charging decision in Prairie City, we have employed a more limited definition of discretion than past studies have utilized. We have suggested particularly that some of what has been termed "discretion" is better viewed as judgments on evidence. Beyond this conceptual clarification, what can we say about how much discretion the prosecutors in Prairie City exercise? Obviously, it is imperative for future research to move in the direction of developing empirical measures of discretion so that prosecutors' offices can be compared. Without such empirical measures we must rely on qualitative assessments. Three different sources of information on Prairie City point in the same direction: relatively little discretion is used in felony cases.

This qualitative assessment is supported first by state's attorney's comments on discretion. While acknowledging that the office could not exist without it, they do not believe they exercise general sociological discretion. In the majority of cases the evidence is the crucial determinant and the assistant does not know the defendant's race, income, education, etc. This assessment is consistent with the earlier comments that the orientation of the office is one of a law firm. Such an orientation places little, if any, emphasis on getting beyond legal analysis. After all this is not an office staffed by social workers but an office made up of apprentice lawyers. A third source of support for our overall assessment is the defense bar. The defense attorney approaches the subject with the bias of the client and some comments must be discounted. Nevertheless, the impression of the defense bar was that the state's attorney failed to use discretion when he should have done so. They offered as support for this statement the prosecutor's great stress on felony convictions, a stress that obscures the need for discretionary judgments. While each of these sources of data may individually be suspect, their triangulation points to the overall assessment that the office exercises relatively little discretion in felony cases.

Notice that in discussing the amount of discretion, an internal definition has been used. It is the definition of discretion that the actors employ in their day-to-day activities. Such an internal definition may be at variance with an external definition of discretion, such as a researcher might impose. This is an important consideration, for the researcher's definition of discretion may not coincide with the one used by the persons under investigation. The most likely ramification of contrasting definitions of discretion is that the researcher may label a decision as discretionary, while the participants may not view it as such.

Effects of Prosecutorial Screening

We have isolated three key characteristics of the charging decision in Prairie City. First, the prosecutor dominates. While police, judges, and victims have a major influence on who is charged with a crime in other communities, they have very little influence in Prairie City. Second, the state's attorney's office evaluates cases primarily on the basis of whether the evidence is sufficient to give the prosecutor a good chance of winning at trial. Third, relatively little discretion is involved, although discretion is important in borderline cases, like aggravated battery. What many authors label discretion, we have divided into judgment and discretion. This section examines the consequences of this arrangement.

Other studies have shown that the charging decision has a major effect on the way criminal cases are processed. In Seattle, Cole found that a large number of felony arrests were reduced to misdemeanors at the charging stage. Miller also cites examples of cases that were dismissed or reduced. In Oakland prosecutors tend to over charge—due somewhat to police influence—which results in charge reductions at a later stage.[14] These assessments of the consequences of the charging decision, based on interview and observation data, yield valuable information. However, they are largely impressionistic. Without a sampling of cases, we have no way to test the validity of the insights offered or to judge the representativeness of the examples presented. Therefore this

---

[14] Skolnick, *Justice Without Trial*, p. 200; Cole, "The Decision to Prosecute," p. 333; Miller, *Prosecution*, p. 39.

study analyzed all adult nontraffic arrests in Prairie City for January 1970.

Table 5 shows the impact of prosecutorial screening of cases in Prairie City. In roughly two-thirds of the arrests, the prosecu-

TABLE 5
COMPARISON OF POLICE ARRESTS
TO CHARGES FILED, JANUARY 1970

	Misdemeanors	Felonies	Total
Prosecutor filed same charge as police booking	76 (62%)	20 (66%)	96 (63%)
Prosecutor filed less serious charge	12 (10%)	7 (24%)	19 (13%)
Prosecutor filed more serious charge	5 (4%)	0	5 (3%)
No charges filed	29 (24%)	3 (10%)	32 (21%)
Total arrests for month	122 = 100%	30 = 100%	152 = 100%

tor agreed with the police assessment of the offense and filed the same charge as the one for which the police booked the suspect. In thirteen percent of the cases, however, the prosecutor filed a less serious charge. Notice, though, that this pattern was particularly pronounced in felony cases. Of the twenty-nine felony arrests for the month, the prosecutor filed misdemeanor charges in seven cases, or almost one-fourth. Examples include police arrest for grand larceny (theft of over $150) for which the prosecutor charged only petty larceny, a misdemeanor. Another prime example was aggravated battery, which we discussed earlier. The data in table 5 show that the prosecutor had a third option—not filing any charges. In twenty percent of the arrests, no charges were filed, but we should note that this was more likely in misdemeanor arrests. Finally, the prosecutor occasionally filed a more serious charge than the police envisioned, but this happened so rarely (five percent of the time) that we included those cases with the ones on which the police and prosecutor agreed.

Another feature of the charging decision in Prairie City is the absence of multiple charges. A common practice in some areas is to file several charges against the defendant. Where a single act technically violates several sections of the criminal code, the prosecutor will charge the defendant with all possible violations. Such multiple charges give the prosecution leverage in securing a guilty plea because the prosecutor can offer a plea to one charge in return for the dismissal of the other counts.[15] The Prairie City prosecutor, however, rarely files such multiple counts, unless the defendant has committed several offenses on different days, or the events are truly seperate.

Charging is one of the most important decision-making stages in the Prairie City criminal process. During the charging decision the prosecutor decides which cases he wishes to prosecute and on what charges. The effects have been shown in table 5: some arrests were dismissed before they became charges and others were reduced. These alterations, however, were neither random nor uniform. They were related directly to 1] the police department making the arrest and 2] the nature of the case.

TABLE 6

COMPARISON OF MISDEMEANOR ARRESTS TO CHARGES FILED: SHERIFF'S DEPARTMENT, JANUARY, 1970

Reason for Arrest	Same Charges Filed	Reduced Charges Filed	No Charges Filed	Total
Order maintenance	2	0	0	
Disorderly conduct	2	0	0	2
Property crimes	1	0	0	
Criminal trespass to a vehicle	1	0	0	1
Youth related				
Contributing to the delinquency of a minor	0	1	2	
Illegal possession of alcohol	3	0	7	
Investigation	0	0	7	
	3	1	16	20
Overall Total	6 (26%)	1 (4%)	16 (70%)	23

Contrast Between the Police and Sheriff

Tables 6 and 7 show the prosecutor's handling of misdemeanor arrests for the sheriff's department and the city police. A comparison of these tables indicates that the state's attorney's charging decision dramatically altered arrests by the sheriff, but had less of an impact on city police arrests. Whereas prosecutors

---

[15] Miller, *Prosecution*, p. 7.

TABLE 7

COMPARISON OF MISDEMEANOR ARRESTS TO CHARGES FILED: CITY POLICE DEPARTMENT, JANUARY, 1970

Reason for Arrest	Same Charges Filed		Reduced Charges Filed		No Charges Filed		Total
Order maintenance							
Disorderly conduct	22		0		4		
Criminal damage to property	1		3		0		
Public indecency	1		0		0		
Reckless conduct	0		1		0		
	24	75%	4	12%	4	12%	32
Crimes against persons							
Battery	12*		3		2		
Resisting arrest or obstructing justice	2		1		1		
Weapons offense	3		1		1		
	17	65%	5	19%	4		26
Property crimes							
Larceny	16		0		1		
Deceptive practices (bad checks)	3		0		0		
	19	95%	0		1		20
Youth related							
Illegal possession of liquor	3		0		3		
Curfew violation	5		0		0		
Contributing to the delinquency of a minor	6		0		0		
	14	82%	0		3		17
Miscellaneous							
Illegal possession of a drug	1		0		0		
Aiding a fugitive	0		2		1		
	1		2		1		4
Overall Total	75	75%	11	11%	13	13%	99

* Includes the five arrests from table 1 where the prosecutor filed more serious charges than the police reason for the arrest.

agreed seventy-five percent with the city police, they *disagreed seventy-five percent* of the time with the sheriff's arrest designation. Why was there such a sharp contrast between two departments in the same area? A partial answer is found in the perceptual screens prosecutors use in evaluating the sheriff's department. In general, the state's attorney's office does not view the sheriff's office as efficient and they do not think it conducts thorough investigations. They also consider the sheriff's deputies to be inordinately interested in teen-agers. The concentration on teen-agers is in part a product of the sheriff's rural jurisdiction, which produces little criminal activity, but provides a number of deserted roads ("lover's lanes"). Perhaps because of the lack of work, the deputies seem to pay particular attention to teen-agers' choice of beverages and their sexual proclivities. As the prosecutors portray it, however, investigations of such suspicious activity only rarely reveal any actual wrongdoing. The prosecutor's perceptions of the sheriff's department find statistical support in our data. Ninety-one percent of the sheriff's department's arrests are tied to teen-age activity. Further these "crimes" are dismissed or reduced eighty-five percent of the time. Thus prosecutors approach the sheriff's department with a bias based on past experience that deputies are too concerned with teen-agers. Such activity is often hard to prove and as a result the prosecutor dismisses or reduces most of these cases.

The prosecutor's explanation, however, must be considered only a partial one as table 7 suggests. The police department makes arrests in teen-age-related areas but the prosecutor agrees with their assessment roughly eighty percent of the time. It is not only the type of crime the sheriff handles, but also the internal processing of these cases that explains the high alteration rate. When the sheriff's department makes an arrest, the reports are forwarded to the state's attorney for his evaluation. By contrast, the police department does not routinely forward all reports to the prosecutor. It reviews the case first. The arresting officer and, later, his commanding officer both make an assessment as to whether charges should be filed. Through talking with the victim and/or the suspect, the police determine that some complaints are either unfounded, or that the suspect did not do it, or that the cases cannot be proven.

The police claim (and the author's observations confirm) that they weed out the obviously weak cases. However, the police do forward to the prosecutor what they consider borderline cases, or cases that they do not think they can evaluate fully. Thus, the prosecutor's review of a case is affected by prior police assessment. Prairie City shows the contrast between a department that makes little attempt to thoroughly review cases (the sheriff's) and a department that makes some efforts to do so (the police). One can speculate that if there were no prosecutorial review of police reports many more Prairie City teen-agers would be appearing in court.

The Nature of the Case

The nature of the crime also is related to the output of the charging decision. Table 7 shows that city police arrests for property crimes are seldom altered by the prosecutor. Out of twenty arrests for petty theft and bad checks, only one was not followed by the same charge and this arrest involved an atypical shoplifting case. The case was atypical because the store manager requested that no charges be filed since he believed that the suspect (a minister's wife) needed professional counseling. Otherwise, the prosecutor usually agrees with the police assessment of property crimes. One hypothesizes that such agreement stems from the lack of evidence problems. It is relatively easy to decide if one has a sound case when property is involved.

TABLE 8
COMPARISON OF FELONY ARRESTS
TO CHARGES FILED, JANUARY 1970

Crime	Same Charges Filed	Misdemeanor Filed	No Charges Filed
Burglary	3	1	1
Battery	4	3	0
Grand theft	2	1	0
Forgery	1	1	0
Illegal possession of a weapon	2	0	0
Indecent liberties with a minor	3	1	0
Criminal trespass to a vehicle	1	0	1
Robbery	4	0	1
Total 29	20	7	3

In contrast to the slight modification rate of property crimes (five percent), prosecutors modify crimes against the person and order maintenance offenses much more frequently. Order maintenance crimes, as well as crimes against the person, do not fit the normal pattern of law enforcement. The police officer, and also the courts, are called upon to act more as peacekeepers than to enforce the law. Fully thirty percent of these crimes are downgraded to less serious violations or dismissed altogether. Out of the total fifty-eight arrests in January for these offenses, nine cases were reduced to the least serious criminal offense, disorderly conduct.[16] In addition, eight arrests resulted in no charges at all. A partial explanation as to why order maintenance offenses are altered by the prosecutor but property arrests are not is that there are problems of proof involved. Order maintenance arrests present greater problems of proving an illegal act because there is an absence of tangible evidence. In addition, the conduct of the "victim" may be less than exemplary. Nevertheless, the differences in legal proof do not account for all the alterations in order maintenance offenses. A crucial ingredient is the prosecutor's perceptions of these crimes.

There is no official office policy on how order maintenance and crimes against the people should be handled, but there is an informal set of office norms. Minor batteries, disorderly conduct, and so forth, are viewed as minor, if not "petty crap" to quote one assistant, which divert attention and resources from the more important and interesting work in the office, which has to do with felonies. The office norms view many of these order maintenance cases as private quarrels that should be settled without recourse to criminal law. For example, husband-wife fights are viewed as essentially civil disputes. Prosecutors do not like working with these cases. Often they stem from a long-smoldering feud. The victim and perpetrator normally engage in character assassination and name-calling. Not surprisingly, the two parties have different versions of what happened. These factors, the lack of seriousness, the private nature of the dispute, and the unclear nature of the event and the victim's conduct combine to make the office unenthusiastic about filing charges. As a result, in Prairie City the informal norm on order maintenance situations is "the less involvement the better." This is manifest in the relatively high dismissal rates when arrests do occur.

Domestic Disturbances

The type of order maintenance offense that the prosecutors dislike the most are husband-wife fights. Let us examine this area in greater depth to give some of the flavor of how the prosecutor's perceptions of order maintenance offenses produce dismissals and reductions of charges when the police do arrest.

Domestic disturbance is the euphemism that is currently applied to a husband-wife fight. Probably few areas of the law provide as many problems for the law enforcers as the husband-wife

---

[16] The concept of order maintenance is borrowed from James Q. Wilson, *Varieties of Police Behavior* (Harvard University Press, 1968), pp. 16–17.

quarrel. For the police, the husband-wife fight provides a steady stream of calls. The police are summoned when the husband or wife has become overly aggressive, or the neighbors have become alarmed and disturbed. For the officer answering the call, there are several difficulties. First, he has little beyond common sense upon which to rely. He is called upon to arbitrate a long-seething disagreement. His ability to arrest also is limited. If the dispute is on private property, he has limited arrest powers. In addition, the complainant (usually the wife) may not want to file charges —just quiet her husband down. When an arrest is made, the wife may become belligerent with the officer. Many police officers are killed or injured in handling husband-wife fights.

The Prairie City police disliked handling such offenses. The unofficial policy was to avoid making an arrest. As the chief commented, "What good does it do to arrest—you'll probably end up taking the food money for the kids to pay the fine." Thus, the police prefer to either quiet the situation down, have the wife spend the night at mother's, or employ some other unofficial procedure. If an arrest was the only way to preserve peace for the night, they made an arrest. The police, however, then referred the wife to the prosecutor's office, advising her, "If you want to file charges, see the prosecutor." As a result, Monday mornings were a busy period in the prosecutor's office. The modest waiting room was often filled with women who wanted to have their husbands arrested. Assistants spent a good part of Monday listening to tales of woes that seemed to date to prehistory. The assistants avoided invoking the law as much as possible, trying for a cooling off period. They urged the women to think about it, asking if they really did want their husbands arrested. In their experience, women who had wanted to press charges immediately after the incident took place often changed their minds within a week or two. If this happened, the charge would have to be dismissed for the lack of a complaining witness.

For these reasons the state's attorney unilaterally altered the procedure. Consistent with our earlier discussion of his role vis-à-vis the police, he did not first discuss the problem with them. Instead the office sent out a memorandum instructing the police to conduct the investigation and not refer the wife to the prosecutor's office. The burden of investigation was shifted to the police. Now they were required to hear the tales of woe and decide whether to arrest or not. As a direct result of this change in procedure, fewer husband-wife fight charges have been filed.

In summary, the office is not oriented to full enforcement in order maintenance situations. The unofficial norm is one of lais-sez-faire. The criminal law is seen as having an ambivalent role to play in such situations. Lack of enthusiasm, sometimes border-ing on antipathy, coupled with pragmatic considerations best de-scribe the Prairie City state's attorney's view of order mainte-nance crimes. This attitude has produced two distinct policy out-puts. First, order maintenance arrests tend to be downgraded. The suspect is charged with disorderly conduct, the most minor crimi-nal violation. Second, the office has altered its procedures to greatly restrict the flow of cases, thus removing the need for the prosecutors to make decisions in individual cases.

Effects of the Charging Decision on Later Stages of the Criminal Process

Pre-charge screening of cases should affect later stages in the criminal justice process. We would hardly expect such a major decision-making apparatus not to alter patterns of settlement else-where in the system. Such a displacement effect can be seen in the workings of the preliminary hearing and grand jury in Prairie City. Because cases are reviewed prior to the filing of charged, the intended functions of both the preliminary hearing and the grand jury have been eclipsed.

Preliminary Hearing

The preliminary hearing, or preliminary examination as it is called in some states, represents the first review of a case by a neutral party. At the preliminary hearing a judge reviews the work of the police and prosecutor to determine if there is enough evidence to hold the suspect for the grand jury. The applicable standards, however, are minimal. The state has only to show that there is probable cause to believe a crime was committed and that probable cause exists that the accused committed the alleged act.[17] If these points are proven to the satisfaction of the judge, the defendant is bound over to the grand jury (the technical term is a finding of probable cause). If probable cause does not exist, then the defendant is released although the State's attorney can still present the case to the grand jury.

Preliminary hearings in Prairie City are not used to screen cases. They are very routine. A typical hearing involves a detec-tive testifying about police reports that he may or may not have

---

[17] For a good discussion of the legal status of the preliminary hearing in Illinois see John O'Shea, "The Preliminary Hearing in Illinois—Nature and Practice," *Illinois Bar Journal*, 1969, 57: 556–560.

written (hearsay evidence is admissable in preliminary hearings as well as before grand juries). In a typical case, the testimony shows that a burglary was reported by Mr. Jones. Police investigated and found a break-in had occurred at Jones' store. Later, a Mr. X was arrested, who was in possession of the stolen items. Notice that the bridge from the crime to the suspect is nonexistant. How the police settled on the given suspect is left out unless the victim has identified the suspect. Defendants are allowed to cross-examine witnesses at the preliminary hearing, a right not accorded to suspects in University Towns. The only deviation from the routine pattern is in rape cases. Informants mentioned that in rape cases the arraigning magistrate has indicated that hearsay evidence might not be acceptable. Because there is a good possibility a rape "victim" is not telling the whole truth, the magistrate would require that the victim testify if the story seems suspect.

The preliminary hearing in Prairie City has minimal impact on the processing of cases. With the exception of rare instances mentioned above, the preliminary hearing is not of major importance. Prosecutors view it as insignificant, useless, or both, and think it could be dispensed with except when the preliminary hearing prevents railroading of suspects by putting the case in the public eye and, thus, preventing abuse. The preliminary hearing can function as a safety valve, although the prosecutors see their screening as carrying out the task that the preliminary hearing is designed to do: proceeding against a suspect only if the state has a case. Defense counsel expressed similar views. They believe that in its present form the preliminary hearing does not accomplish what it was intended to do. Either it should be made a critical stage in the proceedings or it should be done away with. They liked the preliminary hearing under the old system when the hearings were almost a minitrial. They liked that system because they knew what the case was all about when the hearing was over.

The routine conduct of the preliminary hearing carries over to the results. Table 9 shows that only four cases were dismissed for lack of probable cause in 1968, which amounts to two percent of the total number of cases. Observation of the preliminary hearing during the study period produced a similar conclusion. During the period of this study only one case was dismissed at a preliminary hearing and this case was far from typical. Indeed, the prosecutor commented afterwards that the case probably should never have been filed in the first place.

TABLE 9

USAGE OF THE PRELIMINARY HEARING
IN PRAIRIE CITY DURING 1968

Outcome	Number of Cases	Percentage
Finding of probable cause	129	52%
Finding of lack of probable cause	4	2%
Defendant waives preliminary hearing, or it is not held*	115	46%
Total	248	100%

* In thirty-five cases the court records do not indicate whether the preliminary hearing was held or waived. These cases have been coded as the equivalent of a waiver of the preliminary hearing.

Although the preliminary hearing in Prairie City is not functioning as intended, it has taken on some other purposes. A well-known latent function of the preliminary hearing is its use as a discovery technique. In some jurisdictions prosecutors use the preliminary hearing to test their evidence and to gauge the witnesses' likely impact on a jury. In Prairie City, however, prosecutors rarely, if ever, use the preliminary hearing in such a fashion. Increasingly, however, the private law firm has been using it in such a fashion. On occasion they have hired a legal stenographer to record the hearings for possible use at trial or in a pretrial motion. But for every action there is an equal and opposite reaction. In response to the private law firms attempt to use the preliminary hearing for discovery, the prosecutors are presenting less evidence. For example, if a legal stenographer is present the state's attorney will not call the arresting officer to testify because this testimony could potentially be used later. Instead another officer, who has just read the police report, will be called. His testimony is hearsay evidence and has no use in the later stages of a case.

Grand Jury

The grand jury and the preliminary hearing are very much alike: both are designed to check abuse through an independent check of official action. In practice this function is seldom performed. Whereas the judge performs the review function at the preliminary hearing, the public through twenty-three men and women performs the task as the grand jury. The grand jury is the first time that a case is reviewed by someone who does not work in law enforcement. Further, the grand jury possesses great legal powers. They can refuse to indict, thus barring prosecution of a felony; investigate criminal activity independently of the judge or prosecutor; and hold other miscellaneous powers. These powers are largely unused, however. Some states have even abolished the grand jury and proceed on informations alone. While Illinois retains the grand jury, and the legal theory of the independent review of cases persists, in actuality the grand jury is the creature of the state's attorney.

The grand jury is controlled by the prosecutor. He decides which cases, if any, it will hear; which witnesses will testify; and the tone of the proceedings. Since only the state's evidence is presented, defense and prosecution alike see it as the prosecutor's rubber stamp. The grand jury indicts the person the prosecutor wants indicted. This aspect of the prosecutional dominance of Prairie City's grand jury is reflected in the lack of no true bills. During 1968 only four no true bills were returned. Even no true bills, however, are a reflection of the prosecutor's dominance of the grand jury. If the prosecutor does not believe a case is strong, he can and sometimes does convey this subtly to the jury. To quote one assistant, the grand jurors "get the feeling when we're not pressing a case real hard." One does not have to be overt to communicate to the grand jurors what you think of a case.

Interviews on the use of the grand jury revealed only one example of a no true bill stemming from independent action of the grand jury. The case was a complex one—a white victim who was drunk contended he was rolled by a black assailant. The grand jurors found it difficult to decide which principle was at fault and returned a no true bill. The extreme nature of the case points out that the grand jurors in Prairie City work the will of the prosecutor, except on rare occasions.[18]

Conclusion

After an arrest, what next? This chapter has answered this question, a question that at first glance suggests its own answer

---

[18] On rare occasions the grand jury can serve as a safety valve for the prosecutor. If a case has received widespread publicity, the prosecutor may hesitate to dismiss the case publicly, even if he believes he cannot obtain a conviction. In such a situation the prosecutor may persuade the grand jury to return a no true bill. A former prosecutor recalled one instance where this had occurred, but felt it happened rarely and that the procedure was never used dishonestly.

—the arrestee will be formally charged with a crime. Indeed, the inattention to postarrest proceedings has reinforced the implicit assumption that criminal charges follow an arrest but being booked in a station house is not the same as being charged in court. Despite the swelling interest in the activities of the police —and their use of the arrest power—there has been relatively little interest or concern with the immediate legal ramifications of an arrest. Much attention has been directed at later stages in the criminal justice process, particularly plea bargaining and jury trial, without realizing that these stages are shaped by earlier decisions.

In Prairie City the charging decision is a crucial stage, second in importance only to plea bargaining, because during the charging phase the prosecutor not only decides which cases merit prosecution, but also which charges will be pressed. We can organize our observations of the effects of the charging decision into four empirical findings. First, some felony arrests are reduced to misdemeanor charges. This is particularly the case with aggravated battery arrests. Second, the prosecutor refuses to file charges for a high proportion of arrests made by the sheriff's department. We noted two interacting explanations: sheriff's deputies concentrate on teen-age activity, but produce little evidence of crimes; and the sheriff's department does not review arrests before forwarding the reports to the state's attorney. Third, the prosecutor alters certain types of crimes more than others. Arrests for order maintenance and crimes against persons are more likely to be downgraded to less serious criminal charges, or dismissed altogether. Finally, the pre-charge screening of cases affects later stages of adjudication. Only rarely do judges find a lack of probable cause or grand juries return no true bills.

Without additional research, we cannot say whether similar effects are observable in other communities. In future investigations the effects of alternative structuring of the charging decision should be of particular interest. In Prarie City the charging decision and the screening function coincide. In other areas, however, the two are separate; the police file charges and then the prosecutor screens cases. Whether such a structure produces similar or different results needs to be researched. This question is important because reformers propose that the prosecutor dominate the charging decision. For example, the President's Commission on Law Enforcement and Administration of Justice suggests that the prosecutor should control the filing of charges because the prosecutor is in the best position to evaluate the evidence.[19] The premise of this reform proposal is efficiency; the system will discard weak cases more quickly. Since Prairie City already operates under such a system we can use our knowledge to inquire into possible unintended consequences. Obviously a study based on a single community cannot be the definitive work on the subject. Nevertheless it is sufficient to suggest that the reformers' drive for greater efficiency has overlooked an important consideration—police reactions.

The charging decision involves an inherent tension between the police's perspective and the prosecutor's perspective on the law. As Neal Milner writes, "There is often conflict between the 'police perspective's' emphasis on prosecuting all those arrested and the 'legal perspective's' emphasis on the necessity for building a good case. . . ." [20] It is difficult for a patrolman to understand, or for a lawyer to explain, why there was probable cause for an arrest but not enough evidence to prosecute. If the policeman thinks he has made a "good pinch," he wants the courts to agree with his assessment. But when the prosecutor screens cases, he may refuse to prosecute some cases, a refusal that the police may interpret as the prosecutor's failure to back them up.

Consider the prosecutor's charging dilemma. Although this is a hypothetical example, real life instances are not hard to find. The police have arrested a suspect for illegal possession of narcotics. In reviewing the arrest reports the prosecutor makes the judgment that the search was illegal and that the judge will probably suppress the evidence. Without the evidence, there is no case. Will the prosecutor file charges nevertheless? Some argue, on the basis of efficiency, that charges should not be filed. The police are not likely to agree with such a decision. Given the prosecutor's working realities—the necessity of maintaining good relations with the police—perhaps it is more expedient to file charges. If the evidence is later suppressed, the judge and not the prosecutor will be the object of police ire. Thus any analysis of the charging decision, and proposed reforms of its operation, must take into account the likely reactions of the police. By contrast a recent study of this subject writes, "Reasons are obvious why a prosecutor would find intolerable a situation in which war-

---

[19] The President's Commission on Law Enforcement and Administration of Justice, *Task Force Report: The Courts* (Government Printing Office, 1967) p. 5.

[20] Milner, *The Courts and Local Law Enforcement*, p. 88.

rants were issued charging a substantial number of persons who later proved unconvictable."[21] But reasons are obvious only if we evaluate the prosecutor in terms of efficiency. If we also consider the prosecutor's working relationship with the police, it is also obvious why some prosecutor might consider court dismissals a small price to pay for the backing of the police.

In short, proposed court reforms must be considered not only for possible increases in efficiency, but also in terms of potential impact upon the working relationships of the major actors. As we noted in chapter 3, tension between police and prosecutor is quite high in Prairie City. Although one cannot attribute all of this tension to the prosecutor's dominance of the charging decision, some of the police displeasure with the prosecutor is tied to it. In Prairie City then two factors occur together: the prosecutor dominates the charging decision and there is tension between the police and prosecutor. On the basis of these common occurrences we can offer two hypotheses. Hypothesis number one: the greater the prosecutorial dominance of the charging decision, the greater police antipathy to the prosecutor. Hypothesis number two reverses the first: prosecutors will dominate the charging decision, that is, not grant the police a role, if they do not place a high value on working closely with the police. Thus we would expect that prosecutors who follow the President's Commission's recommendation of controlling the filing of charges will be the one's who do not define their job as acting as police officers' spokesmen in court.

---

[21] Frank Miller & Lawrence Tiffany, "Prosecutor Dominance of the Warrant Decision: A Study of Current Practices," *Washington University Law Quarterly*, 1964: 12.

CHAPTER 7

The Economics of Justice

The symbols with which people surround their government and major institutions tell a great deal about the values of those people. No more graphic symbol of the law exists in American life than the blindfolded lady holding the scales of justice. The blindfold symbolizes that all who come to her are to receive an equal hearing free of considerations of social status, race, or religion. Such symbols, while they be a good guide to abstract values, are not necessarily a guide to the application of those values. Whether lady justice is indeed blindfolded or whether the consideration of race, poverty, length of hair, or ignorance permeate the blindfold has become a major consideration in American political life.

A growing body of literature shows that the rich and the poor are not treated equally in American courts. In both civil and criminal courts, the rich and the poor are subject to different treatment and experience contrasting outcomes. If, for example, a person of some means is arrested for a felony he can readily post bail and hire his own attorney. By contrast the poor defendant will probably have to await trial in jail. A court-appointed attorney will be made available to him, but until 1962 the poor did not have such a right. Thus they could be charged, convicted and sentenced without a lawyer to argue the case. As the Kerner Commission made clear, a major grievance among blacks is the discriminatory administration of justice.[1]

But why this differential treatment? In some cases the formal law is biased against certain types of defendants. Carlin has termed this *de jure* bias; that is, the law creates one remedy for the rich and another for the poor. Most of the bias in the law is

---

[1] *Report of the National Advisory Commission on Civil Disorders* (Government Printing Office, 1968), p. 111. See also Edwin Schur, *Our Criminal Society* (Prentice-Hall, 1969), pp. 135–139; Patricia Wald, "Poverty and Criminal Justice," *Task Force Report: The Courts* (Government Printing Office, 1967), pp. 139–151.

not a product of such formal differentiation but of *de facto* bias. On paper the rich and poor are treated alike but in fact different practices and results emerge. Such disparities arise by default or inaction, rather than through positive or overt intentions.[2]

In this chapter we will examine some aspects of *de facto* bias in Prairie City. Toward this end, it is helpful to conceptualize the courts as a series of screens. Simply put, the criminal justice system is a sorting process with winnowing and sifting occurring at various levels. It seems reasonable to assume that the defendant's background has a bearing on this sorting process. By background we have in mind such standard indicators as age, race, sex, economic status, intelligence and education, and prior court record. These background factors enable some defendants to function within the court system better than others. One assumes also that such background factors provide important cues to the legal actors in evaluating defendants. Broadly stated, the court process is a series of screens and we expect these screens to affect defendants differently depending on their backgrounds.

Unfortunately data limitations prevent an investigation of all the possible characteristics of the defendants. Court records and the prosecutor's files only yield accurate and representative data for all defendants on age, economic status (through a surrogate measure), prior record, and type of crime. Most notably absent from the records is race, for which no adequate data exists because race is recorded only when a defendant is sentenced to prison. Relying on this measure would obviously not tell us anything about the entire sample. While data on race would be desirable it would not markedly alter the analysis. At the risk of being overbold, and commenting on a touchy issue with admittedly limited data, it is desirable to record impressions. The first is that in Prairie City there are more white defendants than blacks, although there is a larger proportion of black defendants as compared to black population. Second, court observations, conversations with all the participants, and scrutiny of available data indicate that race is not an important factor in how a defendant is treated.[3] As other analyses of similarly situated communities have

---

[2] Jerome Carlin, Jan Howard, & Sheldon Messinger, "Civil Justice and the Poor: Issues for Sociological Research," *Law and Society Review*, November 1966, 1: 9–89.

[3] For an excellent analysis of the studies on race and sentencing, see: Michael Hindelang, "Equality Under the Law," in Charles Reasons & Jack Kuykendall, ed., *Race, Crime and Justice* (Goodyear Publishing, 1971), pp. 312–323.

shown, it is economic status rather than race that provides the cutting edge.[4] Thus racial data would be desirable but its unavailability should not alter the analysis because in the northern court system race and poverty are but two sides of the same coin.

Economics undoubtedly has a major impact on the administration of justice but we should also note that the relationship is not totally deterministic. The influence of poverty is a question of degree. In some communities the penalty for being poor is higher than it is in others. In Prairie City several policies instituted by the arraigning magistrate have served to mute the impact of economics.

Three areas were chosen for scrutiny of *de facto* bias because they represent areas that have received considerable attention in recent years. Each has been the subject of extensive debate and discussion. Two have become major areas of attention as a result of the Warren court's revolution in criminal justice. These areas are confessions, bail, and the appointment of counsel for indigents. In each of these areas, critics of the court system have contended that the rich man receives one type of justice while the poor receives another. The extent to which this is the case is the subject of this chapter.

Confessions

Interrogations are a major police investigation technique. Indeed many police spokesmen believe that without the ability to interrogate suspects and obtain confessions they would not be able to solve many crimes. Critics of police interrogation, however, contend that the process is an unequal one. For example, the reputed member of organized crime seldom tells the police more than his name and the phone number of his attorney. By contrast, the poor and the ignorant, who do not know their rights, are more likely to confess to the police. The Supreme Court has termed

---

[4] The argument is that when investigating racial discrimination one must first control for differences in economic status because blacks are disproportionately poor. See: Kay Calavan, "A Statistical Survey of Champaign County Criminal Courts," Legal Services Agency of Champaign County, unpublished manuscript, autumn, 1968, p. 38. Samuel Funderburk, "A Study of Sentencing Tendencies of a Florida Misdemeanor Court: 1962 and 1966," unpublished Master's Thesis, Department of Political Science, University of Florida, 1967. Maureen Mileski, "Courtroom Encounters: An Observation Study of a Lower Criminal Court," *Law and Society Review*, 1971, 5: 505–507.

interrogations "inherently coercive" [5] and has moved to regulate the interrogation process by requiring that suspects be warned of their right to silence and their right to an attorney before interrogation begins. In Chapter 8 we will look more deeply at the effects of these decisions on the criminal justice system of Prairie City. At this point we will examine why some defendants confess and others do not.

One hundred and fourteen felony defendants made a statement to the police in 1968. Most of these were written confessions but a handful were oral admissions. We would expect that some suspects possessed greater personal strength in resisting police pressures to confess than others.[6] The docket data allow us to examine four factors that appear important in shaping the citizen's response: 1] the nature of the crime, 2] prior criminal conviction, 3] age, and 4] economic status.

Type of Crime

Past studies of confessions have analyzed felony cases and, by implication, have assumed that the legal concept of felony needs no differentiation. Criminologists, though, have found that legal definitions may mask important features of social reality. To see if confessions are related to the type of crime involved, table 10 categorizes crimes into property offenses (burglary, forgery, theft, and criminal damage to property) ; and other, essentially nonproperty crimes (murder, assault, robbery).[7] The results indicate that defendants in property offenses are more likely to confess. Whereas defendants charged with a property crime confess fifty-six percent of the time, defendants in nonproperty crimes make admissions to the police in only thirty-two percent of the cases.

What might explain this pattern? One important factor is the evidence available to the police during questioning. In burglary,

---

[5] Miranda v Arizona, 384 U.S. 436 (1966), 533.

[6] Edwin Driver, "Confessions and the Social Psychology of Coercion," in Marvin Summers & Thomas Barth, eds., *Law and Order in a Democratic Society* (Merrill, 1970), p. 89.

[7] Crimes against property include theft of over $150, burglary, forgery, criminal damage to property over $150, and narcotics. Crimes against persons include battery, robbery, and homicide. Robbery involves elements of both property and the person but was categorized as a crime against the person on the assumption that the victim was more an important consideration than economic motive.

TABLE 10

CONFESSIONS RATES AND BACKGROUND FACTORS
OF THE DEFENDANT

	Total Defendants	Confessions— all cases	Confessions— property crimes	Confessions— non-property crimes
Prior felony conviction	47	17 (36%)	14 (52%)	3 (15%)
No prior felony	127	75 (59%)	57 (66%)	18 (45%)
Young (20 or under)	102	51 (50%)	38 (54%)	13 (40%)
Old	135	60 (44%)	41 (59%)	19 (29%)
Public defender	132	69 (52%)	55 (65%)	14 (29%)
Private attorneys	102	41 (40%)	24 (45%)	17 (35%)
Property crimes	147		82 (56%)	
Nonproperty crimes	101			32 (32%)

Note: The full sample of cases has an N of 248. Due to missing data, however, not every category has all 248 cases.

theft, or forgery cases the police are likely to have physical evidence linking the suspect and the crime, evidence such as stolen goods, fingerprints, or a signature on a check. In nonproperty crimes, however, such evidence is generally lacking for the crime involves fewer tangible pieces of evidence, or the nature of the offense is subject to greater interpretation. The importance of physical evidence during interrogations is suggested by *Criminal Interrogation and Confessions*, a police manual on questioning suspects. The book urges the interrogator to first communicate that he believes the suspect is guilty and then to provide evidence supporting this view.[8] This technique was employed in New Haven where "the detective showed the suspect the evidence to prove they knew his story was false." [9] A similar use of evidence was apparent in the interrogations witnessed in Prairie City. In one case the police listed for the suspect all their evidence: eyewitnesses, a screwdriver in the suspect's possession, arrest near the scene of the crime, and summed it up by saying, "You have to realize you're not going to get out of this by lying." The police showed another suspect the stolen goods they had found in his possession and hinted that his fingerprints had been found at the

[8] Fred Inbau & John Reid, *Criminal Interrogation and Confessions* (Williams & Wilkins, 1962). Driver, "Confessions," p. 79.

[9] Michael Wald, "Interrogations in New Haven: The Impact of *Miranda*," *Yale Law Journal*, 1967, 76: 1544.

scene. Given such evidence it is not surprising that more suspects in property offenses confess than suspects in other types of cases where physical evidence is less likely to be available.

Prior Criminal Record

Several studies have suggested that the suspect's ability to respond to the pressures of police interrogation is shaped by his prior experience with criminal justice. This line of reasoning was used by the Supreme Court in justifying the imposition of procedural restrictions upon police interrogations. Some judges contended that the Court was not creating new rights, only providing a forum for telling the inexperienced person what the experienced one already knew. Given the strange and hostile environment of the police interrogation room, we would hypothesize that suspects with prior experience would be less likely to confess. Table 10 examines this hypothesis, using a prior felony conviction to measure past experience with the criminal justice system. The data supports the hypothesis. While six out of ten suspects without a prior record confess to the police, less than four out of ten (thirty-six percent) with a prior felony conviction provide the police with a confession.

Having found that the ex-con is less likely to confess than the suspect new to the system,[10] we should reverse the question and ask why so many ex-cons do confess? After all almost forty percent of these suspects have confessed. Why? A partial answer is found by reading across table 10, and comparing the type of crime allegedly committed, a factor that we previously found important. Controlling for the nature of the crime shows that even ex-cons respond to police interrogations on the basis of the crime. In property offenses the experienced suspect confesses well over one-half the time, but in nonproperty crimes he confesses only fifteen percent of the time. This specification pattern reinforces our earlier reasoning about the importance of physical evidence. Even the group possessing the skills most likely to enable them to resist police interrogation—the suspects with prior felony records—confesses in fifty-two percent of the property offenses. If the physical evidence is absent the ex-con seldom talks to the detectives.

---

[10] We must temper these conclusions, however, with a note about missing data. Information on prior record is available only when the suspect has been convicted and a pre-sentence investigation has been conducted. Thus, prior record is not available for all suspects.

Age

Experienced suspects are less likely to provide the police with a confession. We would expect also that the inexperienced suspect would be less able to resist the "inherently compelling pressures" of police interrogations. One measure of experience is age. Age is an indirect measure of a person's maturity, and we would hypothesize that older, more experienced defendants would be better able to cope with the unfamiliar environment of the police station and, as a result, confess less often. The Supreme Court has found age to be an important factor in ruling on confessions alleged to have been psychologically coerced. For example, in *Gallegos* v. *Colorado,* the Court held that a "14-year-old boy, no matter how sophisticated, is unlikely to have any conception of what will confront him when he is made accessible only to the police." [11] A study in Denver confirmed this proposition, concluding that older suspects confessed less.[12]

Returning again to table 10, we find that age is not an important criterion in Prairie City. Those suspects who are twenty or younger confess at about the same rate as older suspects. In this situation controlling for the type of the crime does not alter the conclusion. Although the young do confess more often in non-property crimes, the opposite pattern holds in property offenses. Overall then the hypothesis is rejected: younger defendants do not confess more often than older ones.

Poverty

A major criticism of the administration of both civil and criminal justice is that it is biased against the poor. Such biases against the poor may be direct—the absence of money to hire a lawyer or post bail.[13] Or the biases may be indirect—the absence of skills needed for coping with the legal system.[14] The interrogation process has been criticized on the latter grounds. Several studies have argued that because the poor have less education and less self-confidence, they are less able to cope with the pressures

---

[10] Gallegos v. Colorado, 370 U.S. 54 (1962).

[12] Lew Leiken, "Police Interrogations in Colorado," *Denver Law Journal,* 1970, 47: 21.

[13] Charles Ares, Anne Rankin, & Herbert Sturz, "The Manhattan Bail Project: An Interim Report on the Use of Pre-Trial Parole," *New York University Law Review,* 1963, 38: 69.

[14] See generally Carlin, Howard, & Messinger, "Civil Justice," pp. 9–89.

of interrogation and therefore will confess more readily to the crime.[15] One way to test this hypothesis is to use legal representation as a surrogate measure of poverty. Defendants with some money hire a private attorney, while indigents are represented by a court-appointed lawyer—the public defender in Prairie City.[16] We would predict, therefore, that clients of private attorneys would be less likely to confess than those represented by the public defender. Table 10 presents the data need for testing this prediction. While the gross data indicates that the poor do confess more (fifty-two percent) than the rich (forty percent) the relationship is not statistically significant. Further, controlling for the type of crime shows contradictory results. In property offenses the poor, as predicted, do confess more. But in nonproperty offenses, contrary to prediction, the rich confess more. The best conclusion then is that the poor do not confess at different rates than the rich. As a further check on this finding, bail was used as another surrogate measure for poverty. Defendants who posted cash bail (the rich) were predicted to confess less than defendants who could not raise the money (the poor).[17] Again, however, the data fail to confirm the hypothesis. Those who posted cash bail confessed fifty-one percent of the time—slightly higher than confession rates for the poor (forty-five percent).

Thus, in Prairie City, the poor do not confess at any greater rate than the not so poor. This finding is consistent with several other studies. For example, two studies have investigated education (a social status variable that is analogous to economic status) and found that better educated suspects did not confess less. In Denver, defendants with ten years of education or more were just as likely to talk to the police as suspects with less education.[18] An illuminating study was done on Yale graduate students, who were questioned by the FBI in conjunction with a draft protest.

---

[15] Driver, "Confessions," p. 89. Stephen Wasby, *The Impact of the United States Supreme Court: Some Perspectives* (Dorsey Press, 1970), p. 161.

[16] David Neubauer, "Counsel for the Indigent: An Empirical Examination," paper delivered at the Annual Meeting of the American Political Science Association, Washington, D.C., September 2–7, 1968, p. 12.

[17] The data strongly suggests that Released on their Own Recognizance (ROR) suspects have been interrogated less often by the police. Since ROR suspects are usually younger and are accused of minor felonies—theft over $150 or criminal damage to property—it seems likely that the police do not perceive a need to interrogate these types of suspects as often as suspects in more serious felonies.

[18] Leiken, "Police Interrogations," p. 20.

Even these highly educated persons did not understand their rights, did not comprehend what was involved in waiving their right to silence, and answered the FBI's questions. Even after counseling from law professors, these students answered some of the police questions.[19] Differential social status—whether measured by economic levels or educational attainment—is not related to confessions.

Bail

Bail is one of the most dramatic illustration of the economics of justice. Defendants with money are usually released and defendants without money generally await trial in jail. The number of people involved in such pretrial detention is large. The National Jail Census reports that 78,000 defendants were in jail awaiting trial in March 1970.[20] Because of the perceived inequities in the workings of bail, a major thrust of criminal justice reform is bail reform. Concern with bail is premised not only on the hardships imposed by awaiting trial in jail, but also on the negative effect such detention has on later stages of the process. Defendants in jail are likely to lose their job and thus are less likely to qualify for probation. In addition, they are unable to aid in the investigation of their case.[21]

A suspect charged with a felony in Illinois can secure his pretrial release in one of two ways. Illinois law allows for release on own recognizance, which is usually abbreviated ROR. Under ROR the judge releases the suspect on his promise to return to court on the appointed day. No posting of cash is required The second method of pretrial release is posting of cash bail. The cash bail feature of Illinois law is unique and is one of the procedures advocated by bail reformers. In all states, except Illinois, posting cash bail usually involves hiring a bail bondsman. The bondsman requires ten percent of the bail amount as his fee for posting collateral for gaining release. The bail bondsman has been associated with a great deal of abuse in criminal justice and Illinois law reformers moved to abolish the bondsman indirectly. In Illinois clerks of the court can accept the ten percent bail deposit. No bondsman is required. There is a crucial difference, however,

---

[19] John Griffiths & Richard Ayres, "A Postscript to the *Miranda* Project: Interrogation of Draft Protestors." *Yale Law Journal*, 1967, 76: 318.

[20] Law Enforcement Assistance Administration, *National Jail Census 1970* (Government Printing Office, 1971), p. 2.

[21] Ares, Rankin, & Sturz, "The Manhattan Bail Project," pp. 68–70.

between the operations of the bondsmen and the Illinois process. In Illinois when the defendant shows up in court at the appointed time ninety percent of his deposit is returned. Thus, if bail is set at $1,000 (the normal bail required in burglary cases in Prairie City), the defendant can deposit $100 with the court and secure his release. When his case is finished the court will return $90, the remainder being retained to cover costs of administering the program. As a result of the cash bail feature of Illinois law, the bail bondsman has virtually disappeared.

As we have stressed throughout this study, the formal law is not necessarily a guide to action. While it creates the conditions for the exercise of decisions by establishing the permissible categories, legal actors interpret their responsibilities in different ways. In bail there are two major areas of discretion: 1] setting the amount of bail and 2] using ROR. Each of these discretionary decisions involves important consequences. In the first instance, the greater the amount of the bail, the less likely a person can raise the necessary cash to secure his release. In the second instance the law does not require ROR. This is at the option of the judge and the law does not establish any criteria for determining who will be granted ROR and who will be denied it.

In investigating bail practices then it is crucial that we ask who exercises this discretion and what philosophy guides the decisions. In Prairie City the arraigning magistrate is primarily responsible for bail. However, this is not the case in all communities. In some areas the prosecutor sets bail by making a recommendation to the judge and the judge accepts this recommendation.[22] Under such a prosecutor-dominated bail system, bails are often set high for pragmatic political reasons.[23] In Seattle, for example, "The bail system is used to protect the prosecutor from criticism. Thus it is the policy to set bail at a high level with the expectation that the court will reduce the amount." [24]

There is some indication that prosecutors set bail higher than judges. A more critical factor is the officials' view on the purposes of bail. Bail practices in America have been under public scrutiny

---

[22] Lee Silverstein, "Bail in the State Courts—A Field Study and Report," *Minnesota Law Review*, 1966, 50: 623.

[23] Frederic Suffet, "Bail Setting: A Study of Courtroom Interaction," in Richard Quinney, ed., *Crime and Justice in Society* (Little, Brown, 1969), pp. 298–299.

[24] George Cole, "The Decision to Prosecute," *Law and Society Review*, 1970, 4: 341.

not only by reformers, who are concerned with inequities in the system, but also by those concerned with crime. Some picture a direct link between bail and crime. They point, for example, to the suspect arrested by the police who was out on bail awaiting adjudication of another charge. The contrasting philosophies of bail are highlighted by the current debate over preventive detention. Under preventive detention the judge has the power to hold a suspect without bail if a dangerous or violent crime is involved and such detention is deemed necessary for the community's safety.[25] Some judges have been known to apply this principle by setting high bail as a punishment. Civil libertarians argue that such pretrial detention, and the setting of high bail as punishment before a suspect has been found guilty, violate the purposes of bail. In their view bail was instituted to insure that a defendant did appear in court when he was supposed to, and any attempts to use pretrial detention as punishment violate the basic rights of Americans.

Thus the setting of bail involves a basic political dimension. What purposes does the actor assign to the bail process: crime prevention or is it simply a way of insuring that a suspect will return to court? Unfortunately most of the judicial reformers ignore this political dimension. The judicial administration viewpoint was expressed by Lee Silverstein who wrote that the case for bail reform was compelling because "Everyone is disadvantaged in a high bail county—the defendant, his family, the bondsman and the public." [26] If the case is so overwhelming, why does not everyone adopt it? The answer, of course, is that for some the administrative inconvenience of high bail may be the price willingly paid to "fight crime."

Where then does the arraigning magistrate fit on this continuum? His philosophy on bail is that if we mean it when we say a man is innocent until proven guilty, then the only purpose of bail is to insure that the defendant is in court when he should be. Bail is not a punishment and preventive detention is abhorrent. He further believes that misdemeanor bails should be severed from economics as much as possible.

Informants point out, however, that not all judges in Prairie City share the arraigning magistrate's philosophy on bail. Observ-

---

[25] This summary is based on the preventive detention law for the District of Columbia. See Congressional Quarterly, *Crime and the Law* (Congressional Quarterly, 1971), p. 65.

[26] Silverstein, "Bail in the State Courts," pp. 628–629.

ers of the judicial chambers say it is a fight to keep bails low. One judge in particular likes high bails. An incident points up this difference in philosophy. A racial disturbance elicited widespread public attention. The arraigning magistrate, however, set bail in the normal manner and even released some suspects on ROR. Another judge was said to have been furious. Informants say he wanted higher bails to keep the troublemakers in jail. The public reaction was also heated. The arraigning magistrate received hate mail of all kinds from all over the United States. What the people wanted was clear: to keep all the suspects in jail.

The difference in philosophy between the two judges emerged in interviews. When asked about problems of defendants skipping bail, the arraigning magistrate believed Prairie City had had good results and bail-skipping was at a minimum. The other judge, however, stated that bond-jumping was a problem. It seems safe to assume that both judges were commenting on roughly the same number of defendants who had skipped. The differences in their interpretations depended more on their value orientation than on objective reality.

The arraigning magistrate believes that bail should be used only to insure that a defendant returns to court. The practical implication of this position is that he sets low bail amounts. In his opinion, bail and economics should be separated as much as possible. We can gauge the impact of these views by examining table 11, which summarizes the amount of bail by the nature of the offense. In Prairie City, as in most communities, the amount of bail is based primarily, but not necessarily exclusively, on the seriousness of the charge. Thus bail for armed robbery is higher than bail for less serious charges such as burglary or forgery. Based on studies in other cities, the amount of bail required in Prairie City ranks fairly low.[27]

The arraigning magistrate's interest in bail extends beyond the setting of bail. He is also concerned with the fairness of the entire bail process and as a result has taken positive steps to reform the system. Under his guidance and prodding the judges collectively drew up a recommended bail schedule. In the past judges had set bail on an individual basis, which produced disparities. The bail schedule was an attempt to think about the bail question independently of the emotions surrounding a particular

---

[27] Alfred Kamin, "Bail Administration in Illinois," *Illinois Bar Journal,* 1965, 53: 679. *Cf.* Suffet, "Bail Setting," and Silverstein, "Bail in the State Courts."

TABLE 11
AMOUNT OF BAIL AND PRETRIAL RELEASE FOR SELECTED CRIMES—1968

Amount of Bail	Battery	Burglary	Forgery	Narcotics	Robbery	Total All Crimes
$1,000 or under	10 (44%)	27 (43%)	13 (48%)	5 (63%)	0	81 (35%)
$1,001 to $2,000	10 (44%)	27 (43%)	11 (41%)	2 (25%)	6 (20%)	83 (36%)
$3,000 to $4,000	3 (13%)	5 (8%)	2 (7%)	1 (13%)	6 (20%)	30 (13%)
$5,000 to $8,000	0	3 (5%)	0	0	15 (53%)	22 (9%)
$10,000+	0	1 (2%)	1 (4%)	0	2 (7%)	11 (5%)
No bail set	0	0	0	0	0	6 (3%)
Total	23 (101%)	63 (101%)	27 (100%)	8 (101%)	30 (100%)	233 (101%)
Pretrial release						
Not released	7 (29%)	23 (35%)	15 (55%)	1 (12%)	20 (67%)	90 (37%)
Cash bail	10 (42%)	22 (34%)	9 (33%)	3 (37%)	3 (10%)	85 (35%)
ROR	7 (29%)	20 (31%)	3 (11%)	4 (50%)	7 (23%)	66 (27%)
Total	24 (100%)	65	27	8	30	241 (99%)

crime or a particular defendant. But by far the most significant and far-reaching reform instituted by the arraigning magistrate has been the ROR program.

The Vera Foundation has been at the forefront of instituting release without cash. The system operates on the basis of interviews conducted by court personnel. The theory is that a suspect with ties to the community is not likely to skip. Defendants are scored on the basis of ties to the community: length of residency; having a family; holding a job; and having no prior record of skipping bail. Bail reform programs modeled on the Vera plan are now operating in a number of communities. The Prairie City magistrate has instituted this same program but without the creation of a separate agency to administer it and without outside funding to support it. When a suspect is arraigned the magistrate orally administers the Vera checklist The results are shown in table 11. In 1968 twenty-seven percent of the felony suspects were released on ROR. When this figure was shown to the judge he suggested that if more recent data were available, they would show an even higher percentage.

Differential Distribution of Pretrial Release

Bail has often been compared to ransom; release is gained by posting cash, and those without money are at an obvious disadvantage. Prairie City, however, has adopted policies that mute the relationship between pretrial release and economic status. The arraigning magistrate's setting of low bail, coupled with use of ROR, result in release before trial of two-thirds of the felony suspects. But the operation of these factors still leaves certain defendants untouched. For example when bail was set at $1,000, sixteen percent of the defendants could not raise the $100 necessary to secure their release. In addition forty-one percent could not meet a $2,000 bail. (See table 12). No matter how low the bail is set, some defendants cannot raise the necessary cash and they

TABLE 12
AMOUNT OF BAIL RELATED TO PRETRIAL RELEASE

	$1,000	$2,000	$3,000	$4,000	$5,000
No release	13 (16%)	34 (41%)	11 (41%)	1 (33%)	21 (64%)
ROR	35 (44%)	14 (17%)	8 (30%)	1 (33%)	5 (15%)
Cash bail	22 (40%)	35 (42%)	8 (30%)	1 (33%)	7 (21%)
	80 (100%)	83 (100%)	27 (101%)	3 (99%)	33 (100%)

do not qualify for ROR. Why then are some defendants able to secure their release while others are not? It is perhaps best to reverse the question and ask who benefits most from the bail policies in Prairie City? The data suggest that age, type of crime, and prior conviction are related to differential rates of pretrial release.

Age

In Prairie City teen-agers fare better than their elders in terms of pretrial release. Table 13 shows that twenty-nine percent of the teenagers are not released compared to forty-one percent of those twenty years of age and over. This high proportion of release, however, does not stem from posting cash bail. Teen-agers generally are an impecunious lot who do not post cash bail although the amount of their bail is low. Teenagers' lack of economic resources undoubtedly means that they either do not have a job, or if they do have one that it is low paying. Although the young do not have financial resources for bail they do qualify (disporportionately) for ROR. Forty-two percent of the teenagers are released on their own recognizance compared to only seventeen percent of those over the age of twenty. Predicting what would happen to teen-agers if there was no ROR is difficult because it is obvious that some could post cash bail who now are released on their own recognizance. But this factor may have little weight. Teen-agers commit a high percentage of economic crimes, which is probably indicative of a lack of money. Thus one speculates that ROR works to the major advantage of teen-agers. Without it many more would await trial in jail.

Prior Felony Record

Having a prior criminal record works to the detriment of being released prior to trial. There is a disproportionate tendency not to release defendants with a prior record. Such defendants have difficulty posting cash bail, probably because their economic status resulted in their committing a crime. Having a prior felony conviction also reduces the likelihood of qualifying for ROR. According to table 13 defendants with a prior record seldom receive ROR. Although a prior conviction greatly reduces the probability of being released, there is no evidence that prior felons have higher bails to meet. The relationship between a prior record and high bail is slight, which almost exactly parallels the relationship of a prior felon having committed a serious offense. Lack of a prior record interacts with age. One reason teen-agers fare as well

TABLE 13

PRETRIAL RELEASE RELATED TO AGE, PRIOR RECORD AND TYPE OF CRIME

	Total number of defendants	No release	ROR	Cash bail	ROR—percent of those not posting cash bail
Age					
16-19	97	28 (29%)	41 (42%)	28 (29%)	59%
20-29	87	39 (45%)	15 (17%)	33 (38%)	28%
30+	47	21 (45%)	7 (15%)	19 (40%)	25%
Prior criminal record					
No prior record	51	12 (24%)	19 (37%)	20 (39%)	61%
Juvenile or misdemeanor arrest	73	23 (32%)	24 (33%)	26 (36%)	51%
Felony record	47	31 (66%)	5 (10%)	11 (23%)	14%
Type of crime					
Property offense	169	68 (40%)	43 (25%)	58 (34%)	43%
Non-property offense	62	22 (35%)	13 (21%)	27 (44%)	33%

Note: See discussion in table 10 concerning missing data.

as they do in the bail system is their lack of a prior felony conviction. Only sixteen percent of the teen-agers have a prior felony record compared to thirty-five percent of their elders.

Type of Crime

Pretrial release is also related to the type of crime involved, but the relationship is not what one would normally expect. One would expect that the more serious the crime, the less likely the person would be released. At the extremes this is true for few people charged with murder or manslaughter are released. However, if we exclude the most serious offenses, we find that the bail procedures work to the advantage of those charged with crimes of violence. Consider the last columns of table 13. Defendants charged with a crime against a person post cash bail forty-four percent of the time, a higher percentage than those who are charged with crimes against property. This finding is doubly important when we consider that in crimes against the person, bail is set higher (table 11). One expects the explanation for this relationship relates to the different types of people involved. Crimes against property are the product of poverty and thus we do not expect this group to have much money for posting bail. In contrast, crimes against the person involve a wider strata of society. In this sense then cash bail produces an anomaly. Those charged with burglary are more likely to stay in jail awaiting trial than those charged with assault.

Appointment of the Public Defender

The Supreme Court has firmly established the right of any suspect, rich or poor, to have a lawyer in a felony case.[28] The quality of the legal representation available to the poor, however, has been questioned, a criticism that we discussed in chapter 4.[29] In this section we want to examine two interrelated additional aspects of the right to counsel for indigent defendants. First, we will discuss the appointment process in Prairie City to see if it meets the spirit, as well as the letter, of the law. Second, we will compare background characteristics of defendants with private attorneys and defendants with court-appointed attorneys to determine what, if any, differences result.

The public defender in Prairie City is a private law firm that

---

[28] Gideon v. Wainwright, 372 U.S. 335 (1963).

[29] For a summary, see Lee Silverstein, *Defense of the Poor* (American Bar Foundation, 1965), pp. 20–32, 45–47.

represents the criminal indigents in the county as part of its legal practice. The public defender is normally appointed at the preliminary hearing. Since the preliminary hearing in Prairie City is held within a day or two of charges being filed, the public defender enters the case at a relatively early stage. In sixty-four percent of his cases, the public defender has been appointed within a week of charges being filed. By the second week, he has been appointed in seventy-nine percent, or four out of five cases. Compared to national figures Prairie City appoints the public defender as quickly as any locality in the nation.[30] In the handful of cases where he is not appointed until later, some special circumstance is usually involved. Typical is the defendant who initially states that he will hire his own attorney, but later finds that legal aid is more expensive, or his resources more limited than he has assumed. In such a situation the public defender will not be appointed until after the grand jury indictment. Excepting these rare circumstances, however, the Prairie City public defender is appointed quickly.

The quick appointment of the public defender is a reflection of the way Prairie City approaches the appointment of counsel for indigents. The major participants believe that the vast majority of defendants who request appointment are indigent. Those with some money will be questioned closely, but the dominant attitude is that these defendants will not be able to hire their own attorney so the public defender should be appointed as quickly as possible. This attitude is in contrast to the dominant idea in University Towns. There several officials, including judges, expressed the view that some people are trying to waste taxpayers' money by requesting the public defender when they could hire their own attorney. Thus defendants on the borderline of indigency are instructed to try and hire their own attorney and if they cannot, one will be appointed later. This delays the appointment of the public defender. Although precise figures are hard to come by, scrutiny of the court studies in University Towns indicates that a fair proportion of defendants do not have the public defender appointed until several weeks after charges are filed.[31]

When the lawyer is appointed relates directly to eligibility standards for court-appointed attorneys. The American Bar Foundation survey on bail revealed twenty-one counties where

---

[30] Neubauer, "Counsel for Indigents. . . . ," p. 7.

[31] Kay Calavan, "Statistical Survey of Champaign County Criminal Court Dockets," p. 38.

release on bail precluded the possibility of receiving a court-appointed attorney. This is labeled a bail test. Under a bail test, if you have enough money to secure your release you are presumed to have money enough to hire a lawyer. The study further showed that in an additional forty counties pretrial release was the primary though not the sole test for determining eligibility.[32] The bail test does not operate in Prairie City. Table 14 shows that a quarter of the public defender clients were able to post cash bail, while still qualifying for a court-appointed attorney.

Eligibility for appointment of the public defender is not limited to felony cases. Prior to the Supreme Court's 1972 decision in *Argersinger* v. *Hamlin*[33] there was no requirement that indigent misdemeanor defendants be provided with a court-appointed attorney. In Prairie City, however, the dominant view was that indigent misdemeanor defendants should have a lawyer and one was appointed if requested. Most defendants did not request one, probably on the basis of the minor nature of their crime. Where the misdemeanor was a serious one, however, or where the defendant was likely to receive a long jail term, a lawyer was usually present for the indigent.

The legal actors who are responsible for appointment of counsel in Prairie City are in accord with the principle that indigents are entitled to a lawyer at state expense. The public defender is appointed quickly, posting of cash bail is not a prime factor in determining who is eligible, and the class of eligibles extends to misdemeanors. By contrast, the dominant view in University Towns is that some defendants are trying to waste tax money and as a result the public defender is not appointed as quickly, and it seems more likely that a bail test is employed. Although exact figures are lacking it appears that misdemeanor defendants are less likely to receive a court-appointed lawyer if they are indigent.

While the appointment of counsel for indigents has been researched, relatively little attention has been paid to the type of defendant the court-appointed attorney represents. As a result, some past studies have compared court-appointed attorneys with private attorneys without considering how the clients differ. From a statistical viewpoint the selection of defendants is not likely to be a random process and therefore any comparison of the two types of attorneys must likewise consider differences in the backgrounds of defendants. The most basic difference, of course, stems

---

[32] Silverstein, "Bail in the State Courts," p. 622.

[33] 92 S. Ct. 2006 (1972).

from economics—public defender clients are too poor to hire their own attorney. It is reasonable to assume that such differences in relative affluence may affect the outcome of the process. As Skolnick comments, "It is instructive . . . to compare some of the factors distinguishing the clientele of the private defense attorney from that of the Public Defender, to understand how distinctions in the character of the clientele might generate such criticisms of the Public Defender as suggested by . . . Sudnow." [34]

We can replicate Skolnick's analysis of wealth of the defendants by concentrating on bail. The most direct and immediate indication of economic status is the ability or inability to post cash bail. As table 14 shows twice as many private attorney clients as

TABLE 14
CONTRASTING BACKGROUNDS OF DEFENDANTS
WITH PRIVATE AND COURT-APPOINTED ATTORNEYS

	Private Attorney	Court-Appointed Attorney
Pretrial release		
Not released	18 (18%)	70 (53%)
ROR	35 (35%)	30 (23%)
Cash bail	48 (48%)	32 (24%)
	101 (101%)	132 (100%)
Prior records		
No prior record	25 (36%)	27 (26%)
Misdemeanor or juvenile record	30 (43%)	43 (42%)
Felony record	14 (20%)	33 (32%)
	69 (99%)	103 (100%)
Type of crime		
Property	67 (66%)	113 (82%)
Nonproperty	35 (34%)	24 (18%)
	102 (100%)	137 (100%)

Percentages do not always add up to 100% due to rounding. See note in table 10 on missing data.

public defender clients can afford cash bail in Prairie City. It is possible that the relationship is spurious. Public defender clients may have to post a higher amount of bail. The data, however, in-

---

[34] Jerome Skolnick, "Social Control in the Adversary System," *The Journal of Conflict Resolution*, 1967, 11: 64. See also David Sudnow, "Normal Crimes: Sociological Features of the Penal Code in a Public Defender Office," *Social Problems*, 1965, 12: 255.

dicate the opposite. Although the relationship is small the data show that private attorney clients are required to post higher bail than public defender clients. Thus simple measures of economic means, cash to hire an attorney and cash to post bail, indicate that the public defender represents an economically poorer group of clients.

Skolnick's data allowed him to consider only bail and economic factors in comparing the two types of attorneys. The docket study employed in Prairie City provides additional information on the defendants background that provides a specification of the gulf between the types of clients. One such factor is ROR. By excluding the defendants who post cash bail, we can concentrate on defendants who might qualify for ROR. Perhaps the public defender client can compensate for his lack of money by qualifying to a higher degree for ROR. The data indicate the opposite however. Not only do clients of the public defender have less money for bail, they also qualify less often for ROR. While two-thirds of the defendants who can hire a lawyer can qualify for ROR, only thirty percent of the defendants with court-appointed lawyers can qualify. Thus the inability to post cash bail is not overcome by a greater ability to secure a noneconomic form of pretrial release. By combining cash bail and ROR figures we can see that only eighteen percent of the defendants who hired their own lawyer await trial in jail as compared to over one-half of the clients that the public defender must interview in jail.

The reason public defender clients do not qualify for ROR to a greater extent relates to their prior felony record. One-third of these defendants have a prior felony conviction compared to only one-fifth of the clients with private attorneys. The significance of the prior conviction record will become obvious in later chapters on sentencing. To look ahead, defendants with a prior record have little likelihood of receiving probation.

The contrast in the background of defendants is also revealed in the type of crime committed. According to table 14 those too poor to hire their own lawyer commit predominately economic crimes. While the majority of defendants with private attorneys (sixty-six percent) have been charged with property crimes (forgery, burglary, theft, robbery) almost ninety percent of the public defender clients have been charged with these offenses. Thus there is a moderate relationship between representation by a court-appointed lawyer and being charged with a crime whose motive is primarily economic.

Skolnick's conclusion that Westville's public defender represents a particularly disadvantaged class of defendants applies equally to Prairie City. Although the social and economic status of those charged with felonies is not presumed to be high, there nevertheless are gradations in the degree of deprivation. By definition, the indigent cannot afford to retain a lawyer and the lack of money is reflected in the relative inability of Prairie City defendants to post low cash bails. Underlying this economic division of defendants are even greater cleavages that reinforce the lack of money. In comparing the clients of the public defender to the clients of private attorneys, we noted that the former qualify less often for ROR. The former group of defendants are also more likely to have a prior felony record, as well as having committed property crimes. The public defender's client scores lower on all available indicators of the status of defendants: lack of money; release on ROR; having a prior conviction; and the nature of the crime. Besides the differences between the two types of clients, we presume that these differences work to the disadvantage of the public defender's client. It also seems reasonable to assume that the attorney has little control over these factors. These are the givens that the client comes with and the attorney is only able to marginally alter the situation. The only possible way the attorney can aid is to attempt to secure his client's release from jail.

Conclusion

It is useful to think of the criminal court process as a series of screens. Stages and procedures in the administration of justice act as filters, sorting defendants into different categories. In the last chapter we saw how one of these stages—the charging decision—screened cases on the basis of the legal strength of the case and on the basis of the type of crime. This chapter has examined the type of sorting that takes place between arrest and trial to categorize defendants into varying groups. Since it is presumptive that police interrogations, the setting of bail, and the appointment of the public defender will produce differential results, we have examined the background characteristics of defendants. Let us place our findings in perspective by examining classes of defendants to see how they fare in Prairie City.

Teen-agers in Prairie City receive some major benefits from the system or, at least, are not discriminated against by it. Teen-agers do not confess in disproportionate numbers, but they are released more often than adults.[35] By contrast the defendants with

---

[35] Cf. Stuart Nagel, "Disparities in Criminal Procedure. *UCLA Law Review*, 1967, 14: 1272–1305.

a prior conviction exhibits the opposite pattern. They confess less and are released less often. The nature of the crime also provides a significant cutting edge in the differential treatment of defendants. Defendants in property crimes are more likely to have confessed and are slightly less likely to be released on bail. This pattern is an important one for it suggests that in less serious offenses like burglary, theft, and forgery, the criminal process operates differently than in the more severe offenses, particularly assault. One would expect that in crimes of violence the defendant would receive fewer of the advantages, but in actuality the opposite is the case.

These findings point to an interesting conclusion. The advantages and disadvantages resulting from the system are not necessarily cumulative: a defendant who is disadvantaged by the results of one stage of the proceedings is not necessarily disadvantaged at another. For example, the poor in general receive fewer of the advantages of the system (primarily pretrial release and hiring a private attorney) but at the same time they confess in the same proportion as the not so poor. This conclusion parallels one reached by Robert Dahl in his study of New Haven politics. "In the political system of today, inequalities in political resources remain, but they tend to be noncumulative. The political system of New Haven, then, is one of *dispersed inequalities*." [36] Much the same can be said about disparities in the outputs of criminal justice in Prairie City—disparities are not uniform. This is not to say that the poor do not overall receive fewer of the advantages than the rich, but it does suggest that one must differentiate among types of disparities.

One area where disparities are largely cumulative, however, is that of the clientele of the public defender. The public defender, unlike the private attorney, has no control over the people he will defend. He must represent those who cannot accumulate enough money to pay a private attorney. The clients of the public defender consequently are markedly different than the clients of private lawyers. The client of the public defender is more likely to have been charged with a property crime; more likely to have confessed; to be poorer; not to have been released on bail; and to be somewhat younger and less experienced. While not all of these disadvantages are necessarily cumulative—younger defendants accused of a property crime are likely to get probation—on the whole the disadvantages of the public defender client are multi-

---

[36] Robert Dahl, *Who Governs?* (Yale University Press, 1961), p. 85.

plied throughout the rest of the system. This lack of resources make it less likely that the public defender can secure an acquittal for his client or qualify him for probation.

In a larger setting we have suggested that Prairie City has adopted policies that mute the effects of economics on the administration of justice. Returning to an earlier theme, bail and appointment of counsel for indigents are not simply questions of judicial administration, as some reformers assume. Rather, they involve questions of the allocation of justice—a political dimension. We can most readily see this point by examining variations in pretrial release. Where one lives has a direct bearing on the likelihood of obtaining pretrial release. In a survey of medium-sized counties (population ranging from 100,000 to 400,000), release rates varied from a low of twenty-nine percent to a high of ninety-two percent. We can best compare Prairie City to the larger universe by considering the median. In the above study the median release rate was forty-nine percent. By contrast Prairie City releases sixty-three percent. Prairie City, therefore, releases a higher proportion of defendants than most communities. Of the twenty-one cities in the study just cited only five released a higher percentage of defendants before trial than did Prairie City.[37] In addition the public defender is appointed as quickly as in any community in the nation.

In this sense then Prairie City is a model of reform. Many of the reform proposals advocated in the United States are in operation in Prairie City. This suggests a broader question—what are the political conditions associated with the adoption of reform? The dominant factor in Prairie City is the philosophy of the arraigning magistrate, who believes that a defendant should not be penalized for poverty. On his own initiative he has moved to have a uniform bail schedule established; sets low bail amounts; and initiated the use of ROR. The arraigning magistrate has been a catalyst for change but we must be careful not to draw the conclusion that reform is a one-man endeavor. The way reform touches the other legal actors and their actions (or inactions as the case may be) are also crucial. Some of the bail reform mea-

---

[37] The same conclusion is reached when we compare Prairie City to other Illinois counties. As part of the larger Silverstein study, reports were prepared individually for each state. The Illinois report shows the following release percentages by county: Cook (Chicago), 25%; Du Page, 48%; Madison, 73%; Peoria, 53%; Piatt, 60%; Sangamon, 20%; and Will, 39%. Weighted percentage, 32. See Donald Dowling & John Yantis, "Defense of the Poor in Criminal Cases in Illinois," *Chicago Bar Record*, 1966, 47: 222.

sures, for example, depend upon the acquiescence of other legal actors. The prosecutor could take a more active role in bail-setting and urge higher bail amounts, but he does not. The state's attorney's office finds the bail policy reasonable. It has even urged the police to adopt a more liberal ROR procedure in misdemeanor. The police also play a role in bail in misdemeanor arrests. Illinois law provides that in a misdemeanor the police do not have to require cash bail but can instead issue a "notice to appear." The notice to appear functions much like a traffic citation; by signing the form the suspect agrees to show up in court. The Prairie City police have begun using the notice to appear.

The importance of the police and prosecutor in bail, and the political dimensions involved, is highlighted by a brief comparison to University Towns. There the judges have been urging a more liberal pre-release policy but with little success. The police flatly refused to use the notice to appear, the prosecutor did not back an ROR program, and the arraigning magistrate set much higher bails than his brethren in Prairie City. The typical felony bail in University Towns is about $3,000, which is much higher than in the study city. All this suggests that positive action by one official will only be successful if other actors either acquiesce or offer their support. In Prairie City these conditions have been met.

The Impact of the Supreme Court

"You have the right to remain silent. You have the right to a lawyer. If you cannot afford a lawyer, one will be provided. Anything you say can be used against you." This police ritual can be witnessed almost every night, courtesy of prime-time TV. Invariably the warnings are delivered in a perfunctory manner, the detective reading from the *"Miranda* card" in an atonal voice. For once TV detective shows have not dramatized the real world of the police. The *Miranda* warnings are the most visible, best known, and probably the most controversial part of the Supreme Court's revolution in criminal justice. Responding to criticisms that police procedures were unfair and that the police were not adhering to the procedural requirements of the law, the Supreme Court imposed additional restrictions on police investigative techniques such as searches, interrogations, and line-ups. In turn the Court's decisions produced extensive political controversy. As with the rulings on school desegregation, school prayer, reapportionment, and obscenity, the Court's decisions on criminal justice drew public attention, much of it negative.

Spurred by the political dialogue, a number of political scientists have investigated the impact of these decisions. Polemics aside, they have probed what effects, responses, and evasions have actually occurred.[1] For example, after *Miranda* many wondered whether the police would give the warnings. A study in New Haven found that originally the police did not give the required warnings. As they became familiar with the decision, however, the warnings were given.[2] Another common query concerning

---

[1] Stephen Wasby, *The Impact of the United States Supreme Court: Some Perspectives* (Dorsey Press, 1970), provides an excellent overview not only of the controversies surrounding Supreme Court decisions, but also studies the impact of *Mapp* and *Miranda*.

[2] Michael Wald, et al., "Interrogations in New Haven: The Impact of *Miranda," Yale Law Journal,* 1967, 76: 1521–1648.

Miranda centered on the number of confessions that would be obtained. People wondered whether the rate of confessions would decline. Overall it appears that even after the warnings, defendants are talking to the police, although there is some scattered evidence that confession rates have decreased slightly.[3]

Since there is such a broad range of responses to the criminal justice system, one must limit the analysis. Therefore this chapter focuses on the impact of the Court's decisions limiting police investigation powers (primarily *Mapp* and *Miranda*) on the Prairie City criminal courts. Thus the emphasis is on the impact on the courts—an emphasis omitted in past research. As the police were the ultimate target of the Court's restrictions, research has concentrated on police responses, accommodations, and evasions to the Court's decisions. One should not omit, however, the lower courts, since they are the primary link between the Supreme Court and the police. The activities of the lower courts play a critical role in shaping the impact of the Court's decisions. The judiciary is like any large organization; the policy directives issued at the top are not necessarily the same as the policies implemented at the lower level. The social network of the lower courts, coupled with the role orientations of the law appliers, filter the decisions of the upper court. But bef re we examine how the police, prosecutors, defense attorneys and judges of Prairie City have shaped the application of *Mapp* and *Miranda,* let us briefly examine what these decisions held and their significance.

The Warren Court's Decisions on Criminal Justice

Mapp and *Miranda* are the major cases in the Supreme Court's revolution in criminal justice. Although the decisions deal with different areas, *Mapp* with searches and *Miranda* with confessions, they are similar in that they both impose additional restrictions on police investigations. In addition, both deal with areas central to the law enforcement area. Although criminal justice has been on the Court's agenda since the thirties, until 1962 the decisions of the Supreme Court dealt largely with the trial process—right to counsel, for example. In *Mapp* and *Miranda* the court moved these procedural safeguards further back in the process, to the police station.[4]

In *Miranda,* the Court supplemented (not supplanted) earlier

---

[3] Wasby, *The Impact of the United States Supreme Court,* p. 155.

[4] Neal Milner, *The Court and Local Law Enforcement: The Impact of Miranda* (Sage Publications, 1971), pp. 29–32.

decisions on confessions. The traditional rule was that confessions would be admitted at trial if they were "free and voluntary." [5] Confessions obtained by physical coercion (beatings, torture) were not allowed into evidence because they were not trustworthy—a man in fear of a beating is not likely to give truthful statements. He will say what his antagonists want to hear. In the thirties the Court rejected confessions based on physical coercion and, subsequently, such practices ceased. The Court then was confronted with the slightly different issue of confessions obtained as a result of lengthy interrogations, psychological ploys, and the like. The Court reasoned that confessions based on psychological coercion should be rejected just as if they were based on physical coercion because such statements were not likely to be free and voluntary. But it is not easy to define what constituted psychological coercion and in over twenty cases the Court sought to spell out what factors the trial court should use in making this determination.[6]

The Court standards, however, were far from precise. In an attempt to provide more precision, the Court in *Miranda* wrote some new requirements. These requirements did not relate to psychological coercion but dealt instead with the procedures the police were to follow before and during questioning. The police were required to tell the suspect of his right to remain silent; to have a lawyer present; to provide a court-appointed attorney for the indigent, and to end questioning when requested. In addition, *Miranda* shifted the burden of proof. In psychological coercion cases, the defense had to prove that the confessions were not "free and voluntary." Under *Miranda* the police and prosecutor must prove that they had adhered to the requirements.[7]

The Court has enforced analogous restrictions on police searches. Until *Mapp* v. *Ohio*[8] in 1962, the United States had operated largely under the common law rule, "If the constable blunders, the crook should not go free." This meant that if the police made an illegal search ("search without probable cause" is the legal term), the evidence obtained still could be used in

[5] Brown v. Mississippi, 297 U.S. 278 (1936). For an excellent overview of the major decisions of the Supreme Court see: Lucius Barker & Twiley Barker, *Civil Liberties and the Constitution* (Prentice-Hall, 1970), pp. 236–257.

[6] Gallegos v. Colorado, 370 U.S. 54 (1962).

[7] Miranda v. Arizona, 384 U.S. 436 (1966).

[8] Mapp v. Ohio, 367 U.S. 643 (1962).

court. The issue of improper police search was a separate issue. Evidence was admitted in court on the basis of its truthfulness, not on the basis of how it was obtained. Under this common law rule there were no effective controls on police conduct during a search. The policeman faced no sanctions if he searched illegally. In an effort to combat such police abuse, the Supreme Court imposed the exclusionary rule. Under the exclusionary rule evidence may not be admitted at trial if it has been improperly obtained. The Court reasoned that if the police were denied the benefits of using an illegal search, they would search legally. The exclusionary rule, however, has brought to light additional problems, mainly that the criteria for searches are somewhat ambiguous and, furthermore, often require the police officer to make on-the-spot decisions. As a result police spokesman, as well as some judges (notably Chief Justice Burger) argue that the exclusionary rule hampers the police and should be modified.[9]

Pretrial Motions: A Question of Facts

The remedy, if a defense attorney believes his client's rights have been violated by an illegal search or an improperly obtained confession, is to file a pretrial motion to suppress the evidence.[10] In Illinois such pretrial motions are held before the trial. The judge hears the evidence and makes a ruling as to whether the fruits of the search or the confession may be admitted at trial. If he finds that the defendant's rights have been violated, the evidence will not be allowed into court.

A basic question then in assessing the impact of *Mapp* and *Miranda* is how many pretrial motions are filed and how many are sustained? The answer is relatively few—at least in Prairie City. During 1968 only seven confessions were challenged via a pretrial motion. Only two searches were alleged to be improper. The same conclusions apply to the number of motions sustained. During 1968 only one confession and one search were found to

---

[9] Bivens v. Six Unknown Named Agents, 403 U.S. 388 (1971). Chief Justice Burger dissenting.

[10] A study of Chicago and Washington, D.C. found more pretrial motions than in Prairie City. For example in 12 court days in Chicago 649 pretrial motions to suppress physical evidence were filed. These motions, however, were concentrated in three crime areas: narcotics, weapons, and gambling. Dallin Oaks, "Studying the Exclusionary Rule in Search and Seizure." *University of Chicago Law Review*, 1970, 37: 682. Thus one reason for the relatively few pretrial motions in Prairie City is the absence of vice crimes, as explained in Chapter 2.

be improper. This pattern carried over to the period of observation (late 1969 and early 1970). During the study only five pretrial motions were filed, with one being sustained. It is conceivable
that the absence of challenges to confessions and searches is a
reflection of the lack of confessions and searches, but that does
not prove to be the case. Of the 248 defendants in the 1968 docket
study, 46 percent made either a written or oral admission to the
police. Figures on police searches are less precise, but at least
twenty of these cases did involve a search.

These objective indicators strongly indicate that the impact of
Mapp and *Miranda* has been minimal in Prairie City. Whether
one is counting the court docket, observing in the courtroom, or
talking to the participants, one finds little activity. This lack of
activity is not wholly unexpected. In a study of the impact of the
Court's school prayer decisions, Dolbeare and Hammond concluded that events that are controversial at the national level,
may produce only a ripple at the local level.[11] Why, though, are
so few pretrial motions filed in Prairie City? This is the basic
question we wish to answer in this chapter. We shall begin by
analyzing the pretrial motion.

A pretrial motion to suppress evidence, like other court hearings, reduces to two basic elements: facts and law. After the facts
are determined, the law is applied to the situation as reconstructed
in court, and a decision is reached. The distinction between facts
and law is associated with Jerome Frank, a legal realist. Frank
argued that lawyers and judges in trying to arrive at clear and
precise laws had overlooked the facts. As he writes: "The 'facts,'
it must never be overlooked, are not objective. They are what the
judge thinks they are." [12] Pretrial motions to suppress evidence
are graphic illustrations of the fact-law distinction in operation.
At a pretrial hearing the basic dispute is over the facts—what
happened. To be sure, the law is not exactly clear and straightforward—lawyers and judges may disagree on precisely what an
appellate court decision means—but the dynamics of the situation
hinge on the facts.

"The real question in Supreme Court cases is what's going on
at the police station," is how one defense attorney phrased it.

---

[11] Kenneth Dolbeare & Phillip Hammond, "Local Elites, the Impact of Judi-
cial Decisions and the Process of Change." Paper delivered at the Annual
Meeting of the American Political Science Association, Washington, D.C.,
September 6–9, 1969, p. 11.

[12] Jerome Frank, *Courts on Trial* (Athenum, 1969), p. 55.

There is seldom unbiased evidence on what happened because the only witnesses are the participants—police and defendant—who, not surprisingly, sometimes have different versions of what happened. Thus pretrial motions have been called "swearing matches." Although the Supreme Court imposed new rules, it has not altered the dynamics of this encounter. Prior to *Miranda,* the dispute centered on the "voluntariness of the confession," now it centers on how the *Miranda* warnings were given.[13] James Vorenberg, who was executive director of the President's Commission on Law Enforcement and Administration of Justice, said that *Miranda* "just moves the battleground from the voluntariness of the confession back to the voluntariness of the waiver. . . . the police have done pretty well with these swearing contests over the years." [14] The nature of this swearing match is typified in the following pretrial motion. While such motions are rare, the dynamics of this encounter will illustrate why so few motions are filed or sustained.

A Faked Robbery?

Call him Danny. He was 17, white, and a high school dropout. To support himself and his pregnant wife, Danny worked at a gas station. According to his original report to the police, a man walked into the station, pointed a gun in his face, and took the large denomination bills from the cash register. The police investigated but could find no corroboration for his story. Other people who had been in the area did not remember seeing a big black man leaving the gas station. Other discrepancies in Danny's story led the police to believe that he had reported a false armed robbery to cover up his theft. They interviewed him, and after signing the custodial interview form, Danny signed a confession, admitting he had stolen the money. The defense attorney challenged the confession, contending that the *Miranda* warnings were not properly given, and that the confession had been psychologically coerced. At the hearing the testimony of the detectives and the defendant agreed on only two points: the custodial interview form had been signed and a confession given. Beyond these basics, however, the testimony clashed sharply on five key points.

Two detectives testified separately, but they told the same

---

[13] Robert Cipes, "Crime, Confessions and the Court," *The Atlantic Monthly,* September, 1966, p. 55.

[14] As quoted in Cipes, p. 55.

story. They went to Danny's house and asked him to come to the police station—a request with which he willingly complied. Once at the police station, the custodial interview form was signed and the detectives then told Danny their theory: the armed robbery report was a cover up for his theft of the money. At this point Danny confessed, saying he had needed the money to pay his bills. After making a written statement the defendant asked if he could go home, saying he had never spent the night away from his wife and felt that he should be with her since she was pregnant. The detectives indicated that in the normal felony arrest the suspect must first post bail, but since Danny had been cooperative they would ask their supervisor if he could be released on his own recognizance. The sergeant reluctantly agreed. At the end of the interrogation, Danny asked about his chances for probation. The detectives replied that the court normally gave first offenders in theft cases probation, especially if they had been cooperative.

Danny told a different story. He had not wanted to go to the police station, but the detectives had insisted. Once at the station he was questioned for a long time and not until midway through the interrogation was he asked to sign the custodial interview form. The defendant claimed that he had repeatedly denied his guilt and asked to go home, at which point the detective replied that the defendant could not go home until he confessed. Further, if he did confess he could go home right away. In addition, Danny said the police told him that if he confessed he would get probation so there was nothing to worry about. Because he just wanted to go home and be with his wife, Danny said he signed the confession, although he did not commit the theft.

It is obvious that Danny's and the detectives' testimony clash on a number of major points. This is significant because the contrasting versions lead to different decisions. For instance, the defense attorney, in his summation at the end of the hearing, argued that the evidence showed a psychologically coerced confession. The defendant almost had been forced to go to the station house; the interrogation had lasted a long time; promises of pretrial release and mention of probation were illicit inducements. These factors taken together meant the confession was not "free and voluntary." He further argued that the *Miranda* warnings had not been properly given since the defendant's testimony indicated that the custodial interview form was not signed until midway in the questioning.

By contrast the state's attorney pictured the facts as showing a routine police interrogation. The defendant had gone willingly to the police station, the interrogation had been a short one, and probation had not been used as an inducement since the defendant had first raised the issue. Releasing the suspect on ROR was portrayed as a product of the detectives' humanity. As for the *Miranda* warnings, the prosecution concluded that the detectives' testimony showed that the custodial interview form had been presented before questioning and that the time on the form supported the police version.

This pretrial motion graphically illustrates that the dominant issue in Supreme Court cases is the facts. The nature of the issue —the dispute over the facts—structures and apportions the roles that the police, defense attorney, judge, and prosecutor play. The police are in a favorable position because they control the generation of the facts the court will hear. The defense attorney is forced into a catalytic role since he must search out the issues. The judge, by virtue of his power of fact-finder at the hearing, becomes the supreme umpire that legal theory indicates he should play. The prosecutor, at least in Prairie City, is forced into a quiescent role.

As for Danny—he lost the battle but won the war. The judge accepted the detectives' testimony and ruled that the confession could be introduced as evidence during the trial. During the trial, however, the defense attorney hit hard at the circumstances surrounding the confession. Evidently the jury was more sympathetic to Danny than the judge because he was acquitted. The police had a cynical reaction to the verdict. They thought the jurors were influenced by the visibility of Danny's pregnant wife during the trial.

The Police and Pretrial Motions

Although the police are presumed to be at a disadvantage during a pretrial motion since under *Miranda* the police must prove that the law's requirements have been met; the police in reality are at no such disadvantage for they control the flow of information. The position of the police is analogous to the insurance adjustor. Both are judged by their superiors, but both control the flow of information on which these judgments are based. The insurance adjustor fills out the required forms to minimize his supervisor's possibility for challenging him.[15] Similarly, the police by initially obtaining the suspect's signature on the custodial interview form, are able to forestall potential challenges to confessions.

---

[15] H. Laurence Ross, *Settled Out of Court: The Social Process of Insurance Claims Adjustment* (Aldine, 1970), p. 56.

In response to *Miranda,* the police and prosecutor in Prairie City prepared a one-page form entitled Custodial Interview Form. Standard police procedure—which was confirmed by observations at the police station—is to begin by asking the suspect if he understands his rights. If so, he is asked to sign the custodial interview form. Although the police treat this as a formality— "Do you understand your rights?"—legally it has a greater significance because the suspect's signature is normally sufficient proof in court that the police have complied with *Miranda.* The police are fairly successful in obtaining the suspect's signature. Of the 248 felony defendants in 1968, 171 (69 percent of the total) signed the form. We have no way of telling how many of the defendants did not sign because they were not interrogated. Detectives do not necessarily question all felony suspects. The prosecutor's records indicate that only eleven (four percent) of the suspects refused to sign. The police use a similar form—entitled "Consent to Search"—when they make a search with or without a search warrant.

The custodial interview form forestalls most legal challenges to police interrogations. The presence of the suspect's signature restricts any wholesale challenge to police procedures. In short, the major response to *Mapp* and *Miranda* on the part of the Prairie City police department has been the generation of reams of paper showing compliance.

The police ability to generate paper proofs resonates with another feature of the social network of Prairie City. The court officials perceive that the police act properly most of the time. Such perceptions are of critical importance because these court officials have little direct knowledge of police practices. Without such direct knowledge their mental images of what the police do become important guides to their actions.

A good starting point in assessing police practices is to inquire what the natural critics of the police—the defense attorneys— think.[16] If they fail to perceive major problems then we are on fairly solid ground in concluding that the police basically are in compliance with the law. The majority of defense attorneys perceived no problems in the area of searches or confessions. The following answer was typical: "If the police have searched I ask my client about it. Invariably the client replies that he gave the police permission to search." Another defense attorney stated that he believed the *Miranda* warnings were being given.

---

[16] Jerome Skolnick, *Justice Without Trial* (John Wiley, 1966), p. 28.

Prosecutors agree with this assessment. As we noted in chapter 3, the state's attorney's office is critical of certain police activities. But when asked about problems with confessions and search and seizure, the prosecutors replied that there were no problems in this area. "The police do a pretty good job on search and seizure," is how one of them phrased it. Another commented that, "Every once in a while, the police will blow a case, but this is not a large enough county for that to be a big problem." This statement sums up the dominant views of the judges, prosecutors, and defense attorneys. They perceive that occasionally the police do not conform to the requirements of the law but this is viewed as aberrant. Most of the court officials appear willing to accord the police the aura of procedural regularity. They perceive that in the normal processing of cases the police are in compliance with the law. While they do see the possibility of error, such errors are treated as the occasional blunders that will occur in any organization.[17]

We should place these assessments in perspective by noting that there are several dissenters from this majority view. Three defense attorneys saw more of a problem. As one stated, "The police give only the rhetoric of warnings. They use inducements and coercion [left undefined] to gain confessions." Another commented, "Obviously the warnings are not given the way the police say." One attorney discussed how the police improperly influence the outcome of cases. He stated that there is "lying on the part of the police. They see nothing wrong with lying." This statement, in context, is not as bombastic as it first appears. He went on to say that the police would neither testify falsely about the guilt of the suspect, nor would they even consider planting evidence or fabricating it. Instead, the police officer is concerned with factual guilt. Further, they view the court's requirements as technicalities that let some guilty suspects off the hook.[18] Therefore, on questions involving police adherence to procedural requirements, they can shape their testimony. Such shaping can be very subtle, a word here, a deleted sentence there, or simply not remembering certain things.

He elaborated on this point by saying that a major impact of *Mapp* and *Miranda* has been that the police have learned what to

---

[17] On procedural regularity see: Herbert Packer, *The Limits of the Criminal Sanction* (Stanford University Press, 1968), p. 159. The concept used here differs somewhat from the value approach of Packer.

[18] Skolnick, *Justice Without Trial*, Chap. 9.

say in court and what not to say. He cited a recent case in which a young detective made some damaging admissions, and evidence was suppressed. He felt the next time this detective testified he would know what to say. Thus these three defense attorneys see more problems with search and seizure and interrogations than the majority. Even these dissenters, however, do not perceive any wholesale abuses. As one summarized it, "There are no flagrant police abuses, where they simply knock the door down."

The Catalytic Role of the Defense Attorney

Signatures on the custodial interview form, coupled with the court officials' perceptions that the police adhere to the procedural requirements of the law, dictate that wholesale challenges to confessions, or searches, will not be productive. But some cases potentially involve a police violation. Here the defense attorney plays the dynamic role because unless he takes action, no challenges to the police activity will be raised. The task of the lawyer then is to separate the potentially atypical situation from the more numerous ones where the police have not violated the Supreme Court's decisions. Lawyers in civil practice face the same task. Most clients who come to a lawyer for a will or a contract present no great legal problems. Most are easily solved by filling in a blank will or a standard contract. The mark of the good lawyer is knowing when a case should be handled differently than the rest.

This is no easy task in the case of potential violations of the Supreme Court's criminal justice decisions. As one lawyer commented:

> Illegal searches are hard to get at. . . . The defendant doesn't know if the police had probable cause. Sometimes the police get an anonymous phone call that a burglary is in progress . . . Or the police get a tip that guns are in a car. Well, the prosecutor doesn't tell you that. You have to root around to find out if probable cause existed. You have to ask, "How did the police get to it in the first place?" A search without probable cause is hard to find out about.

Possible violations of *Mapp* or *Miranda* do not come into the lawyer's office prepackaged just awaiting a court hearing. On the contrary the lawyer must frame the issue and determine if enough facts exist to support his contention. Often the attorney is unaided by his client. As the lawyer just quoted went on to say, "For the defendant the case starts when he's arrested. Search and seizure and probable cause, however, start before that." A prosecutor familiar with the problems of the defense attorney expanded on this point, saying that clients are often so inarticulate that they cannot tell their lawyer what happened.

The defense attorney then faces major barriers in finding out if probable cause existed for the search or if the confession met the requirements of the law. In addition, violations by the police are relatively rare. Even if they occur more often than appears to be the case, they are hard to document. These factors mean that even the most knowledgable and diligent attorney is not likely to be successful in suppressing evidence in a large number of cases in Prairie City. Notice that pretrial motions on evidence reverse the burden of proof. In a criminal case the state must prove the suspect guilty. Similarly in *Miranda,* the state must prove that the warnings were given. But in a pretrial motion challenging a search or a confession, the defense lawyer must assume the burden of proof. He must search out and document the alleged infraction.

These factors dictate that enforcement of the Supreme Court's criminal justice decisions is a direct function of specialized attorneys. As with most areas in a complex society, only a specialist possesses the necessary knowledge and skill to effectively handle a given problem. The impact of the Supreme Court decisions is tied to the existence of lawyers who keep up on the changes in the law in this area. Prairie City has such a specialist. Most of the pretrial motions come from his office. In addition it appears that few lawyers, even those in criminal practice, qualify as specialists. Neal Milner's study of four Wisconsin cities found that lawyers varied in their knowledge and use of *Miranda*. In some cities, such as Green Bay, lawyers had only limited knowledge of the Court's decision. In several communities, however, there was at least one lawyer who was particularly knowledgable about the decision and it was only in those towns that challenges were raised in court.[19]

The Judge as Fact Finder

Normally the defense attorney plays a reactive role, responding to the state's case. In pretrial motions to suppress evidence, however, he must play a catalytic role, searching out and developing the facts. The fact dispute inherent in these cases produces another reversal of roles within the social system of the Prairie City courts. Although, in theory, the judge possesses the greatest

---

[19] Milner, *The Court and Local Law Enforcement,* pp. 111–113.

power, it should be recalled that in Chapter Five we noted how this power has been eclipsed in Prairie City. During plea bargaining the defense and prosecution largely determine guilt and sentencing—tasks normally associated with the judge. When a confession or a search is challenged, however, the judge is the most important member of the Prairie City criminal justice community. The judge alone is the finder of fact. Through his fact-finding, the judge gives the issues of the case the shape they shall retain through all subsequent litigation.

Returning to the example of the pretrial motion concerning the armed robbery that may have been faked, recall that the judge accepted the police version of the facts, thus upholding the confession. Such findings are seldom reviewed by appellate courts. On appeal, upper courts examine whether the law was correctly applied by the trial judge. They will rarely scrutinize the facts to which the law was applied. Such deference toward the trial judge is based on his proximity to the event. Only the trial judge has the opportunity to observe directly *how* a witness testifies, his responsiveness to questions, his attempts at concealment. Such nuances are not reflected in the trial court transcript. A prosecutor pointed to an additional reason why appellate courts do not scrutinize the trial judge's finding of fact.

> If a defense attorney appeals on an unsuccessful pretrial motion, the appellate court would have to find that the trial judge abused his discretion. When an appeals court reverses in one of these cases they are saying that another judge abused his discretion. They are understandably reluctant to do so. Normally appellate courts accept the trial judge finding of fact because he is closer to the action.

Thus the trial court judge possesses virtually unfettered discretion in making findings of fact. This discretionary power can be used to buttress the judge's opinion on how a matter should be decided.[20] As one attorney put it, "A judge who knows what he is doing can keep making findings of fact so that no appellate court can ever rule he didn't apply the law properly." Thus a judge out of sympathy with Supreme Court decisions, by making findings of facts, can distinguish the given case from the decision that in theory should govern. Let us therefore investigate judges'

---

[20] Lucius Barker & Twiley Barker, *Freedoms, Court Politics: Studies in Civil Liberties* (Prentice-Hall, rev. ed., 1972), pp. 44–51. Barker and Barker analyze a famous Supreme Court decision (Finer v. N.Y.) and show how the Supreme Court's decision was based on the trial judge's finding of fact.

attitudes about *Mapp* and *Miranda* to see if these views may affect their decisions.

The chief justice showed no reticence in expressing his displeasure with the Supreme Court decisions. The following comment is typical: "The motion to suppress is a very popular approach and most [sic] not the slightest grounds for objecting. The defense attorney is just hoping to get lucky. They're filed to cause trouble." Later in the interview he elaborated further. "Things have gotten carried away, gone to ridiculous lengths. Need to be changes made [sic]. . . . the police have been dealt with unfairly, their hands have been tied." Defense attorneys interpret the judge's opinions—which are well known among the law appliers—to mean that it is virtually impossible to get evidence suppressed by the chief judge. As a result, pretrial motions are filed before the other judges.[21]

The other judges expressed greater support for the Supreme Court's decisions on criminal justice, but none could be called ardent supporters. One of these judges was interviewed a few days after he had suppressed a confession. He prefaced his remarks by saying that he "doesn't complain about the police." He then indicated that suppression of evidence did improve police procedures for it acquainted them with the problem. When asked if more search warrants should be used, he replied that they should be, but, "I sometimes wonder if the police know what they are searching for." These statements indicate a more receptive attitude toward the procedural requirements imposed on the police by the Supreme Court than the chief judge's. Still another judge who hears criminal cases also was less critical of the Court than the chief judge.

Even without a judge's displeasure with *Mapp* and *Miranda*, defense attorneys believe it is hard to win a pretrial motion. In their view, structural considerations explain why so few motions to suppress a confession or a piece of evidence are sustained. One

---

[21] These comments are based on an interview with the judge, observations in his courtroom, and interviews. As such they are based on the *perceptions* of the actors. We should note that subsequent events have somewhat modified the conclusions stated. The judge later indicated informally that no one knew how he would rule, since pretrial motions were never filed with him since attorneys preferred other judges. When motions were filed, the judge did sustain several of them. This is another illustration of the complexity of the chief judge. As we discussed in Chapter 5 the judge not only has strong beliefs but also strives to follow the law. Thus his actions indicate a willingness to set aside his personal views and follow the upper court decisions.

reason is that the dispute over the facts invariably involves a conflict between the suspect and the police. In such a situation it is hard not to defer to the police. As one attorney explained it, "These cases often involve a conflict between the police officer's version and the defendant's version. Judges never believe the defendant. . . ." The consensus among the lawyers was that pretrial motions would be successful only if the officer's testimony showed an error. For example, in the two cases where evidence was suppressed during the time of the study the defense attorney believed the suppression was the product of the police testimony. Unless they can gain damaging admissions from the police, defense attorneys do not think they can get evidence suppressed.

According to the defense attorneys, judges are reluctant to suppress evidence for a second reason—unfavorable publicity. If a piece of physical evidence is not allowed before a jury, or if a confession is not admitted into evidence, the press reports that the judge suppressed the damaging material because of a legal technicality. Negative public reaction usually accompanies such suppressions, either in the form of letters to the editors or comments on the local radio talk show. One attorney summarized this factor as follows: "Even though the judges deny that they pay any attention to public reaction, they have to be affected by negative publicity when they suppress evidence."

The Other Side of the Social System

The impact of the Supreme Court's criminal justice decisions are shaped and modified by the lower courts, the courts that must directly apply the Court's rulings. The social system operates as a filter through which the decisions must pass. And because the dominant issue in one of these cases centers on the facts—not the law—some actors are in a more favorable position than others. The police are in a favorable position because they are able to generate facts showing their compliance. The defense attorney is in an unfavorable position because he must search out the issue. Finally, the judge is the dominant legal actor because he is the fact finder. In combination these factors produce few challenges to police procedures. Further, the few challenges that are raised are seldom sustained by the courts.

The social system of the courts thus constricts the impact of *Mapp* and *Miranda*. But if the social system constricts formal challenges, it also provides for informal avenues of redress. The impact of *Mapp* and *Miranda* involves not only formal court suppression of evidence, but also informal pressures. The operation of these informal channels is illustrated in the following case. Although this is a single case, its effect extends much beyond the immediate defendants.

Four suspects were charged with armed robbery. From an evidentiary standpoint the prosecutor had a strong case; eyewitness identification and physical evidence (the stolen money and a gun) found in a suspect's possession. After the arrest the police questioned the suspects and obtained a signed confession. The defense attorney believed, however, that the confessions were the product of illicit promises made by the detectives. As he viewed the case, filing a pretrial motion to suppress the confession would be futile because even without the confession the state had sufficient evidence for a conviction. He, therefore, recommended that his clients plead guilty—a decision that he described as the most difficult one he had made as a lawyer. Rather than challenge the confession through the formal means of a pretrial motion, the attorney chose a different route. This is how he explained his decision:

> Very few officers use improper means to get a statement. I know because I hear about it when it does occur. But one particular officer I have heard complaints about from all types of defendants —all races, creeds, crimes, situations, etc. In all of these cases invalid promises are being made to defendants. Invalid promises to get him probation, to keep the case out of the paper, or that no charges will be filed. Of course the officer later denies making any promises. By way of contrast, I have never heard a complaint about some officers.
>
> I have recently informed the court and the state's attorney about this particular officer. If he is not stopped, then I will make a vendetta out of this. I will take case after case until there is enough evidence that they will have to believe that this officer is not telling the truth.
>
> We had the same situation with the sheriff's department. I went to the boss and laid it on the line and it has stopped.
>
> This may sound horrible, but it is the most effective means to stop this sort of thing. Motions to suppress in court don't get anywhere so it is better to try and get to the source.

The essential outlines of this statement are supported by the comments of others. During an interview with one of the judges, he mentioned when asked about communications with the police, "We may have a little problem, i.e. today came to our attention the overeagerness to get a confession. This will be looked into."

A similar comment was made by the prosecutor during an interview: "There is *more* than an indication that the police mention probation during interrogation." Although the author was not privy to the conversations that ensued from the defense attorney's statement to the judge and the prosecutor, the effects were visible. A few days later the police brass met with the state's attorney— an unusual occurrence. There was every indication that police interrogations were discussed. The defense attorney reported a similar reaction. He concluded the statement quoted above by saying: "I know it has reached the officer because of the way he has acted toward me."

Thus the impact of *Mapp* and *Miranda* must be measured not only in the light of formal court proceedings but also in terms of actions taken outside of the courtroom. The small size of the criminal justice community in Prairie City provides alternative avenues for achieving results, avenues that some defense attorneys believe are ultimately more successful than formal challenges. We need to make two points about such informal challenges. First, only those with close working ties with the other law appliers can raise such challenges. Such access is one of the benefits for working within the system, as we discussed in Chapter 4. At the same time, it is important to notice that these informal challenges serve to protect the system. No public statements are made, statements that might lead others to question the integrity of the system. Second, these informal challenges operate only with major violations or, at least, what appear to be major violations to the defense attorney. If the issue was a fine one, if the search had been on the borderline of being illegal, informal challenges would not be an effective means to raise such technical points.

The Limited Role of the Prosecutor

We have mentioned the prosecutor seldom in this chapter, which must seem to be an oversight. We would expect that the most important member of the criminal justice community—the prosecutor—would play a critically important role in shaping and applying the Supreme Court's criminal justice decisions. A state's attorney has great potential for shaping the impact of the Court's decisions by monitoring police compliance with the law and/or communicating the decisions to the police. In Prairie City, however, the prosecutor plays only a limited role. The part he plays, its impact, and why it is limited is the subject of this section.

Monitoring Cases

Prosecutors can play a critical role in the impact of the Court's criminal justice decisions by monitoring police adherence to the procedural requirements of the law. Typically, such monitoring involves the refusal to file charges when police practices are questionable. Thus tainted evidence could be suppressed effectively without a formal pretrial motion because no charges would be filed. Legal reformers urge prosecutors to act in this fashion.[22] The Prairie City prosecutor, however, does not refuse to file charges because of possible police irregularities. One assistant explained it this way: "A search is not illegal until a judge rules that it is. The issue is a question of fact and unless the state's attorney is to act as a judge, then he should present the case in court." All the assistants supported this position, although one added the following qualification: "If the violation is really aggravated, then we won't press charges because the police would be embarrassed." Otherwise the prosecutor does not monitor cases for possible violations of the Supreme Court's requirements.

In one area—the drafting of search warrants—the prosecutor does monitor police activities. A search warrant is issued by a judge upon a written complaint. The complaint must show sufficient facts to establish probable cause for the search, describe the place or person to be searched, and specify the objects to be seized. If these criteria are not met, the judge can refuse to issue the warrant. The police, as well as the general public, assume that if the judge does sign the search warrant that any evidence seized will be admitted into court. This assumption is false. Evidence seized under a defective warrant will be suppressed. Thus even with a search warrant, police actions may later be held invalid.

Because they are complex legal documents, the prosecutor drafts all the search warrants. The police are not perceived to have the necessary legal expertise. The prosecutor's control of search warrants is a form of preventive medicine: in drafting the complaint the prosecutors attempt to minimize potentials for challenges by the defense. The state's attorney's office, however, issues search warrants only reluctantly. Although a search warrant in theory provides greater legal protection for the police search, the prosecutors believe that in reality a warrant makes the police actions more vulnerable. For them, search warrants are like the proverbial clay pigeon; they invite defense objections. An examination of the complexities of a search warrant will explain this.

---

22 Wayne LaFave, *Arrest* (Little, Brown, 1968), p. 515.

From the prosecutor's perspective, the very specific statement of facts required by a search warrant is a major drawback. When the police request a search warrant, not all the necessary facts may be available. This obviously hampers the drafting of the warrant. Further, these documents require anticipation of what is likely to happen when the police search. As pretrial motions show, reconstructing past events is difficult. But the foresight required in writing a search warrant is even more difficult. The failure to anticipate events may make the warrant defective. But the major liability is that the search warrant commits the police and prosecutor to a specific statement of facts, which cannot be altered later. When the police search without a warrant, the ambiguities of the situation generally work to the prosecutor's advantage—it will be the defendant's word against the police, and the police normally win such swearing matches. The precision of the search warrant, however, works to the advantage of the defense, for the state has locked a set of facts into the record. The typical problems the defense attorney faces in reconstructing events has been solved by the prosecution.

From the prosecutor's perspective a second deficiency of search warrants is the lack of clarity in search and seizure law. Recently both state and federal courts have imposed more stringent requirements on the issuance of search warrants. For example, in search warrants based on the statement of an informant (a not uncommon occurrence), the prosecutor must show that the informant not only has personal knowledge of the event, but also has given reliable evidence in the past. These requirements make it difficult to obtain a search warrant when an informant is necessary. The effect of the tightening of requirements for the use of search warrants by the courts also means that the law is in a state of flux.[23] The law at the time the warrant was issued may have changed by the time the warrant is litigated.

A third, but less central, liability of the search warrant involves police execution of the warrant. According to the Prairie City prosecutors, the police do not understand the limits of a search warrant. "All the police want is a piece of paper," is the way one assistant phrased it. The dominant view is that once the police have a warrant, they think that their search is proper. They pointed to cases where the police were overzealous and seized

---

[23] Arthur Burnett, "Search Warrants: Impact and Application of *Chimel and Spinelli and Related Problems*," *Federal Bar Journal*, 1970, 29: 170. Wayne LaFave, "Search and Seizure: 'The Course of True Law . . . Has Not . . . Run Smooth'," *University of Illinois Law Forum*, 1966: 255–265.

evidence that was not listed on the warrant. While this evidence may be helpful it is legally inadmissable. Although such extra evidence is not a major handicap to the prosecutors, they believe that the police officers' attitude that the warrant is all they need can cause problems that are best avoided.

In spite of the fact that the courts have been encouraging (and, some would say, requiring) greater use of search warrants, Prairie City prosecutors see few advantages in them and many liabilities. The prosecutors are reluctant to issue a warrant because of the possible pitfalls of a specific statement of the facts, the stringent new requirements that have produced even more uncertainty in the law, and the police failure to respect the limits of a search warrant. Therefore, when the police request a warrant, the state's attorneys encourage the police to search in some other way, such as visual inspection. If they see something remiss they may be able to search under the "plain view doctrine" that does not require a search warrant. Requesting the suspect's permission to search is another common alternative. The police use a permission-to-search form, which is analogous to the custodial interview form. The suspect's signature largely preempts later challenges to the legality of the search. Even when the police are armed with a warrant, they request permission to search. If the suspect agrees, the warrant is not executed. Prosecutors report that suspects normally consent to searches, thus forestalling later legal challenges.

The prosecutors may elect a third alternative—not issuing a search warrant but allowing the police to search. Unless they believe the warrant has a good chance of standing up in court, the prosecutors may decide the odds are better if they later try to reconstruct an ambiguous situation rather than prematurely commit themselves to the specifics required by a search warrant. The prosecutor's reluctance to authorize search warrant results in few warrants being issued. The court records for 1966 through 1969 show an average of only seven a year.

The prosecutor's discouragement of search warrants shows how the goals of the upper courts may be deflected by the actions and perceptions of the officials who make the day to day decisions. Justice Harlan pointed in this direction in his concurring opinion in *Chimel.*

We simply do not know the extent to which cities and towns are prepared to administer the greatly expanded warrant system

which will be required by today's decision: nor can we say with
assurance that in each and every local situation, the warrant requirement plays an essential role in the protection of those fundamental liberties protected against state infringement. . . .[24]

This writing is perceptive for it points out the inherent clash
between the law in action and legal theory.

While the courts have been placing a greater stress on search
warrants, the practitioners discourage its use. The lack of certainty is the basic reason for this discouragement. While the
courts, police, and laymen believe that a warrant ensures a legal
search, such is not the case. Rather, the rules are in a state of flux.
As Skolnick succinctly puts it, "Whenever rules of constraint are
ambiguous, they strengthen the very conduct they are intended to
restrain." [25] This applies to search warrants. The uncertainty of
the law coupled with the ambiguity of the facts means the Prairie
City prosecutor authorizes a search warrant only as a last resort.
Without a warrant the state has the advantage of hindsight. With
one the state has all the liabilities of a smoky crystal ball.

The Prosecutor as Communicator

Communication plays a vital role in the impact of Supreme
Court decisions. Obviously a decision will have no affect if those
to be affected have not read it or heard about it. Just as importantly, communications may distort the message. In some areas
court decisions are rapidly and accurately transmitted. For example, business executives subscribe to services of commerical
clearing houses that specialize in reporting tax and antitrust
decisions. With literally millions of dollars involved, no business-
man can afford to decide tax questions or approve a merger based
on last year's law. He needs to know what the court ruled yesterday. But not all decisions are conveyed this rapidly or this accurately. Studies of the impact of the Court's decisions banning
school prayer from the classroom, found that those most affected
(school board members and principals) often knew little about

---

[24] Chimel v. California, 89 S. Ct. Reports, 2034, (1969), J. Harlan concurring.

[25] Skolnick, *Justice Without Trial*, p. 12.

the Court's rulings. Further their knowledge sometimes was inaccurate.[26]

Where does criminal justice fall on this continuum? Are the communication channels like business cases or are they similar to the ones that operated in the school prayer decisions? The imperfect communications network causes criminal justice people to be more like school officials than businessmen. Copies of court decisions are rarely available at the police station. The police do subscribe to publications that summarize the leading cases, but communications involves more than dissemination—it also includes interpretation. The meaning of a decision for specific police practices needs to be spelled out, but the police are not equipped to translate the legalistic verbiage of the appellate courts into policy guidelines.

In a time of rapid, almost revolutionary, change in the criminal law, how do the police learn about these changes, and who helps them to interpret the law? The answer usually is that no one does. Only some of the largest police departments employ staff attorneys. Prosecutors normally do not perform these functions. The President's Commission found:

> Very few prosecutors' offices endeavor systematically to provide legal counsel to the police. Excepting those few departments which employ legal advisors, most police forces receive only sporadic counsel from the prosecutor's office or from individual prosecutors who have developed a special relationship with certain squads or officers.[27]

This conclusion applies to Prairie City.

On rare occasions, the state's attorney sends the police a memo on a recent court decision. The prosecutor does not inform the police of every major decision. Thus the state's attorney's office does not, on a regular basis, attempt to keep the police abreast of recent changes in the law. Further, the memos are not geared to the police audience but are legalistic in tone. They convey the major holdings of a case but they do not explain its implications for police procedures. Interpreting the decisions is left to the police.

Formal memos are one way that prosecutors can communicate

---

[26] For an extensive discussion of the communication of Supreme Court decisions see, Wasby, *The Impact of the United States Supreme Court*, pp. 83–98.

[27] The President's Commission on Law Enforcement and Administration of Justice, *Task Force Report: The Police* (Government Printing Office, 1967), p. 50.

with the police. Informal police-prosecutor contacts are another. In Prairie City, however, such informal interactions are minimal for the police and prosecutor maintain no regular working liaison as we noted in Chapter 3. As a result police-prosecutor contacts are confined to specific cases or controversies: requests for search warrants; pretrial motions; or trials. Such interactions can be vehicles for educating the police, but in Prairie City they rarely are. These contacts have only a limited educational role. Several factors lessen their potential educational value.

Typically, the police come to the state's attorney's office, state their problem, and ask how to search (or perform similar tasks) in conformity with the law. They want answers. But the prosecutors are unable to provide the certainty that the police desire. Where the police see simple problems, the prosecutors see complex issues and respond, "It's six of this and half a dozen of the other." In short, the prosecutors cannot provide the simple answers the police think they should. The time element also limits the educational role of such police-prosecutor contacts. On several occasions the police were observed waiting several hours before an assistant could draft a search warrant—the attorneys were busy with scheduled court appearances. Such delays, which the police understandably dislike, reduce the likelihood that the police will request advice in the future. One other factor needs to be considered: the nature of the interaction. In most cases, but particularly with pretrial motions, the occasion for the interaction is an alleged police violation. Such confrontations place the police in a defensive posture that leads to abrasive interactions, not to educational dialogue. During the field work, several somewhat heated interchanges between police and prosecutor were overheard.

The Prairie City prosecutor plays only a limited role in communicating changes in the law to the police. Although, as we have mentioned, memos are occasionally issued, they only partially bridge the gap between the police and the courts. Less formal police-prosecutor contacts also fail to educate the police. This lack of communication stands in sharp contrast to another finding from this study; the police lack of knowledge about the law represents potential problems for the prosecutor. As we just noted, prosecutors think the police do not understand the limits of a search warrant. Here is another example. During the drafting of a search warrant, one of the detectives commented, "I thought *Chimel* gave us the power to search [the trunk of a car]." But *Chimel* did the opposite—limiting police searches to within arm's reach of the suspect, a clarification the state's attorney quickly noted.

Given the prosecutor's unease with police knowledge about the law, why does the office not attempt to educate the police more effectively? The President's Commission suggests such a role for the prosecutor. "The prosecutor is in the most favorable position to bring about needed coordination among the various law enforcement and correctional agencies in the community." [28] The Prairie City state's attorney failure to perform such coordination and communication roles is tied directly to the office's conception of itself as a law firm. This law firm orientation does not stress working with the client, in this case the police. The focus is on the internal workings of the office, with little attempt at outreach. In only one area—the drafting of search warrants—does the Prairie City state's attorney play a major part in the shaping of the Supreme Court decisions. Why the prosecutor dominantes search warrants is also explained by the law firm orientation. Search warrants are legal documents that require a lawyer's attention. Further, the drafting of search warrants does not require the prosecutor to go to the police. The police must come to the courts through the state's attorney's office. In short, the law reformer's suggested role for the prosecutor as a strong communicator of changes in the law and a coordinator of the parts of the criminal justice system requires a prosecutor with a wider frame of reference than that of a law firm.

Conclusion

The polished marble of the Supreme Court in Washington, D.C., and the antiseptic green of the police station in Prairie City are separated by more than miles. Several layers of appellate courts, the local court, prosecutors, and even newspapers, mediate between the Court's decisions and their ultimate impact. This chapter has examined the impact of the Court's criminal justice decisions (*Mapp, Miranda,* and the follow-up cases) from the perspective of the local court system. The attitudes of these officials, as well as the everyday pressures of their jobs, play a major role in shaping the impact of the Court's decisions.

The relative powers of the judges, defense attorneys, and prosecutors are apportioned according to the nature of the dis-

---

[28] The President's Commission on Law Enforcement and Administration of Justice, *Task Force Report: The Courts* (Government Printing Office, 1967), p. 72.

pute. Although we are accustomed to thinking of these cases in terms of the formal law, a more basic issue is what is happening at the police station. The question over the facts provides the basic dynamics of the process. Contrary to popular belief, the police have not been overwhelmed by the Court's decisions because they largely control the facts. The defendant's signature on the custodial interview or the permission-to-search form heads off most potential challenges to police activities. The opposite is true for the defense attorney. The defense attorney is the activator, the catalyst, because he must dig to find if the facts may support a pretrial motion. We have suggested that a necessary condition for the adjudication of *Mapp* and *Miranda* cases is the existence of specialized defense attorneys. Short of blatant police disregard for the law (which all admit is rare) only a specialist can effectively search out and frame these issues.

The judge, by virtue of his almost unrestrained power as fact finder, has the pivotal position in pretrial motions to suppress evidence. For the judge alone decides which version is more believable, and normally sides with the police. Finally, the prosecutor plays a more limited role than one would expect. Although he is the dominant figure in Prairie City, he plays only a minor role in the implementation of the *Mapp* and *Miranda* decisions. He makes little effort to communicate changes in the law to the police. The only area where he does play a major part is the drafting of search warrants. This area is the most graphic illustration of how the attitudes of the officials at the working level can deflect the thrust of decisions reached in the higher courts. Although the courts have been encouraging greater reliance on search warrants, the Prairie City prosecutors see numerous liabilities and few benefits from using them. As a result the prosecutor discourages the use of search warrants while the upper courts encourage their use.

In combination, the roles played by the legal actors in the implementation of Supreme Court decisions is strikingly different from the roles played in the processing of the normal case. The Prairie City judges, for example, play a restricted part in the disposition of felony or misdemeanor cases. In a pretrial motion, however, the judge is the pivotal person. Similarly, the prosecutor plays a dominant role in most areas of the local criminal justice process, but has only a bit part in a pretrial motion. Such reversals have a major bearing on the conclusions one can reach from studies of the impact of Supreme Court decisions. Impact studies have adopted a top down view. But these issues involve a different ordering of local actors than is true of the typical case. As a result, one can make only limited generalizations about the workings of the criminal justice system from studies on the impact of the Supreme Court.

Part Three · TRIAL

INTRODUCTION

Courtroom 2-A was a little more crowded than usual because this was plea day. The defendants, Terry Boldt included, sat on the court's pew-like benches waiting to go before the judge. The drawn lines on the defendants' faces were matched by the nervous restlessness of their families. It was the nervous restlessness of those trying to keep quiet but not knowing what to do. Several lawyers also were waiting in the courtroom, but they sat near the judge's bench, behind the barrier separating the laity from the law people. This physical separation between the lawyers on the one side and their clients on the other was reflected in a difference in demeanor. The tension of the defendants and their families was not apparent among the lawyers who bantered or talked quietly to each other.

"All rise, all rise, the court of Prairie County is now in session, the Honorable Judge . . . presiding," called the clerk of the court. The formalities over, the clerk intoned in his deep baritone, "*The People* vs. *Boldt*." Terry Boldt and his lawyer approached the bench by separate paths. The lawyer spoke first:

"Your honor, my client wishes at this time to withdraw his previous plea of not guilty and wishes at this time to enter a plea of guilty to the offense of burglary."

The judge responded, "Mr. Boldt, before this

court can accept your plea of guilty, we want
to make sure that this is your decision,
that you fully understand what it happening.

"First, do you know that for the crime
of burglary you can go to prison for one to ten
years?"

The defendant spoke for the first time
replying with a barely audible, "Yes, your
honor."

The judge went on, "Second do you understand
that you have the right to a jury trial. At that
time the state would have to prove its case
to twelve men and women, or you would go free.
Knowing this, do you still want to waive
your right to a jury trial?"

"Yes, your honor."

"We want to make sure that this guilty plea is
your decision. Did anyone mistreat you, beat
you up, deny you food or water? Did anyone do
anything to pressure you into pleading guilty?"

"No."

"Did your lawyer pressure you into entering
this plea? Did he say he wouldn't defend you
at trial if you didn't go along with him?"

"No, your honor."

"Finally the court wants to make sure that the
only reason you are pleading guilty is because
you actually committed the crime in question. Did
you do it?"

The suspect hesitated, caught perhaps by
the directness of the question. He glanced at his
family and then at his lawyer before replying,
"Yes."

"The court then finds you guilty of the crime
of burglary. The probation officer will prepare
a presentence investigation. You are to return
to court in two weeks for sentencing." [1]

"*The People* vs. *Porter*," the clerk intoned.
Thus ended Terry Boldt's day in the

---

[1] The dialogue between the judge and the defendant is made
a part of the official record of the case. The purpose of the
detailed questions is to prevent the suspect from later contending that his plea was not free and voluntary.

Prairie City court. His appearance lasted about fifteen minutes. In other jurisdictions, particularly large urban ones, the time may be considerably shorter. Such brief courtroom appearances are the dominant reality of criminal justice.[2] Although trials are equated with criminal justice, very few suspects ever receive a trial. Rather, like Terry Boldt, they plead guilty. It is hard to say how many plead guilty because statistics on the court system are notoriously unreliable. The best estimates indicate that over eighty percent of the felony cases (and probably over ninety-five percent of misdemeanor cases) end with a plea. There is a sharp contrast between the ideals of the system (a jury trial) and the reality (guilty pleas). Further, the finding of guilt is usually viewed as a public process involv'ng two adversaries locked in combat in open court, but more typically the assessment of guilt is the product of negotiations conducted in private.

The significance of the guilty plea is not the formal court appearance but what happens behind the scenes. The dynamics of plea bargaining occur behind closed doors because most pleas are the product of negotiations between defense and prosecution. But such negotiations are not always included in the formal court record.[3] Although the defendant normally states in open court that no promises have been made, that is not the case. Promises, or at least understandings, have been reached.

Part Three examines the "deals" that result from negotiations, as well as the other final stages

---

[2] For a discussion of arraignment and pleas in large urban courts see Martin Mayer, *The Lawyers* (Dell, 1967), chap. 5.

[3] Since this research was completed, the Illinois Supreme Court has imposed new rules regarding guilty pleas in court. Now the court must be advised of negotiations that have taken place. If later the apparent arrangement is not forthcoming, the defendant has the right to withdraw his plea.

of the criminal process. These are some of the
questions we want to answer: What types of deals
are arranged? What standards are employed
during negotiations? Why do cases not go to
trial? Why do participants view bargaining as
necessary? Finally, and most important,
who gets what from such a structure? Toward
this end, it is helpful to divide the final stages of
a case into two analytical questions: what
did the suspect do? And, what should be done
with the guilty suspects? We can call the
first question guilt adjudication. To the layman
guilt adjudication is a question of what did
the suspect do? Did he steal the money? Did he
beat up Tom Porter? To the lawyer, however,
guilt adjudication is more complicated because he
must approach guilt adjudication in terms of
legal proof. The question for the lawyer is less one
of what did the defendant do, than what can
be proven about his conduct. This difference in
phrasing is a basic one, for everyone may "know"
that Terry Boldt burglarized the house, but
proof of the burglary may be lacking. Thus the
final stages of the court process must decide
what can be proven about the suspect's conduct.

The second question hinges on the
disposition of the guilty. In theory, society
can impose a variety of punishments, or
treatments. In reality, however, the court's options
are more limited. In a felony case, the court
process must decide whether to send the
person to prison or place him on probation.
Technically, the suspect could also be fined but
a fine is not a live option in most felony cases.
In Illinois, if the decision is made to send
the suspect to prison, an additional determination
must be made as to how long the prison sentence
should be.

Chapter 9 examines the plea-bargaining
process, paying particular attention to the
types of pleas that are common in Prairie City
and the negotiations between lawyers.
Chapter 10 explores the jury trial. Most, but

not all, suspects plead guilty. In the chapter
on jury trials we first want to see how the
possibility of the jury trial affects plea bargaining
and, second, consider why some cases go to
trial while others do not.

Chapter 11 deals with sentencing. The
defendant in a criminal case is primarily
interested in what is going to happen to him. Is
he going to go to prison or will he be placed on
probation? Chapter 11 examines how
these decisions are made. As we shall see,
sentencing considerations play an important part
in the plea-bargaining process.

While our discussion is divided into three
parts, we must keep in mind that the
process is more unified than our tripartate division
may indicate. For example, during negotiations
between the defendant and the prosecutor (the
subject of chapter 9), the lawyers
not only discuss the likely result of a jury
trial (the subject of chapter 10) but also the
likely penalty (chapter 11). But, because it
is impossible to treat everything all at once,
it is best to look at the major phases of
the process individually. This separation should
cause no problem if we keep in mind the
interrelations of the phases.

CHAPTER 9 **Plea Bargaining and the Adjudication of Guilt**

Trials fascinate the American public. Every year numerous books, countless short stories, and endless numbers of television dramas use courtroom encounters to entertain. Trials of well-known persons, such as the Chicago Seven, Angela Davis, the Berrigans and Charles Manson, receive extensive national publicity. Even a local murder trial is the subject of many newspaper accounts, as well as conversation. Most of us think of the trial as the prime ingredient of the criminal courts. But it is not. For Terry Boldt, and countless defendants like him, will never have a trial because they plead guilty.

Why is it that the very premise of the system (a jury trial) has become a rarity? Few trials are held because they are costly both in terms of money and time. An average felony trial lasts two or three days. During this time a judge, a defense attorney, a prosecutor, and twelve citizens sitting as a jury are needed to dispose of a single case. Given the large number of cases on the court docket it is obvious that if there were more trials, fewer cases would be disposed of, unless the resources of the criminal courts were greatly expanded. Because trials are so costly to the system, an alternative pattern of settlement has developed. It is plea bargaining. Before trial, the prosecutor, defense attorney and, in some areas, the judge discuss the case and negotiate a possible settlement. As in any negotiations, each side has something it wants, and it can achieve this goal only by offering a concession on something else. The prosecutor wants to secure a conviction, but has more cases to try than time in which to try them. But he can gain a conviction without a trial by offering the suspect inducements. Such a plea is also more certain than a jury verdict. In return for his plea, the prosecutor can offer to let the suspect plead to a less serious charge, dismiss multiple charges, or offer a light prison sentence. If the defendant pleads guilty, the court also benefits because its crowded docket is relieved. Thus all sides normally receive something they desire in return for concessions on other points.[1]

This process goes by a variety of labels and euphemisms—plea bargaining, negotiating a settlement, copping a plea. But whatever one calls it (we prefer plea bargaining), it is the most critical stage in the criminal justice process. It is during plea bargaining that the guilt or innocence of the million or so felony suspects is decided each year. In addition, plea bargaining either decides the sentence or shapes what the sentence is likely to be. Clearly, plea bargaining is the most critical stage in the criminal justice process. It is the most important determinant of who gets what from the criminal justice system. In this chapter we want to explore how the lawyers conduct plea bargaining and the results of these negotiations. But before considering how the process operates, it is helpful to consider past normative and empirical analyses of the process.

A number of normative criticisms have been raised about plea bargaining. Although plea bargaining is the dominant reality of the lower courts, it is not universally accepted. This is to be expected because the ideals of the system point to a trial, yet reality undercuts this ideal. Second, plea bargaining is often a secret process and many are suspicious of secret deals. We do not plan to enter this debate. As the preface indicated, this book holds to the fact-value distinction. But it is appropriate to discuss what normative critiques have been made of the plea bargaining process. This outline will allow the reader to draw his own conclusions.

Some criticize plea bargaining because an innocent suspect may be pressured into pleading guilty to a crime that he did not commit. The critics of plea bargaining point to the pressures upon the suspect to plead guilty, and particuarly the universal assumption that most defendants are guilty.[2] While some believe that plea bargaining may put the innocent at a disadvantage, others are critical of plea bargaining because it works to the advantage of the guilty. For example, the police criticize plea bargaining because they believe the suspect gets a lighter penalty than he should.[3] Blumberg contends that the current system of

---

[1] This discussion is based largely on Donald Newman, *Conviction* (Little, Brown, 1966).

[2] See David Sudnow, "Normal Crimes: Sociological Features of the Penal Code in a Public Defender Office," *Social Problems*, 1965, 12: 255.

[3] Albert Reiss, Jr. & David Bordua, "Environment and Organization: A Perspective on the Police," in David Bordua, ed., *The Police* (John Wiley, 1967), pp. 36–37.

negotiations "probably tends to serve better the interests and requirements of the guilty." [4]

Thus while plea bargaining is the dominant reality of the lower courts, it is viewed with a great deal of skepticism by some people. This skepticism is most graphically revealed in official government reports. The President's Commission on Law Enforcement and Administration of Justice wrote: "Plea bargaining *may be* a useful procedure . . . (emphasis provided)." [5] Such normative ambivalence over the proper role of plea bargaining in the administration of justice is typical of most commentaries and analyses. Recently, however, the call has been sounded to abolish plea bargaining altogether. The Nixon administration convened a new commission to update the earlier one. Called the National Advisory Commission on Criminal Justice Standards, their report urged the abolition of plea bargaining within five years. [6]

One additional point is worth bearing in mind—plea bargaining operates largely outside of judicial scrutiny. Appellate courts largely have been silent on plea bargaining. While they regularly rule on issues of pretrial and trial procedures, they usually totally ignore the most critical stage in the criminal justice process— plea bargaining. Only a few courts have ever even mentioned plea bargaining and then only in the most general way. [7] As one analyst concluded: "Indeed, one gets the impression that our law does not feel quite ready to face up to the theoretical and practical problems involved. . . . Likely this judicial shyness expresses a recognition that we really do not know very much about the practice of plea bargaining." [8] Judicial reticence in discussing plea bargaining has, however, begun to change. Several Supreme Court decisions, while upholding the validity of plea bargaining, have

---

[4] Abraham Blumberg, *Criminal Justice* (Quadrangle Books, 1967), p. 30.

[5] President's Commission on Law Enforcement and Administration of Justice," *The Challenge of Crime in a Free Society* (Government Printing Office, 1967), p. 11.

[6] "Commission Proposes Hundreds of Methods to Reduce Crime, Improve Criminal Justice," *LEAA Newsletter* (Law Enforcement Assistance Administration, U.S. Dept. of Justice), 1973, 3: 12.

[7] For a discussion of appellate court decisions on plea bargaining see Lawrence Friedman & Stewart Macaulay, *Law and the Behavioral Sciences* (Bobbs-Merrill, 1969), p. 141.

[8] Arnold Enker, "Perspectives on Plea Bargaining," in President's Commission on Law Enforcement and Administration of Justice, *Task Force Report: The Courts* (Government Printing Office, 1967), p. 108.

sought to place greater procedural protections around it. For example in *Santobello v. New York* the defendant entered a guilty plea based in part on the prosecutor's recommendation of a light sentence. When he received the maximum the defendant sought to withdraw his plea of guilty but the lower court refused.[9] Chief Justice Burger ordered the guilty plea vacated. Similarly, a number of state and lower appellate courts have sought to place greater procedural protections on plea bargaining, as well as formalizing the process.

Considering the dominance and importance of plea bargaining, we would expect that this process would have been extensively examined. Such is not the case. Indeed, most of the research has been done by one man—Donald Newman. Newman studied plea bargaining in Wisconsin during the fifties and later wrote the American Bar Foundation volume, *Conviction*.[10] As in other volumes of this series, however the research perspective is judicial administration. Legal categories are stressed more than social realities. The mechanics of plea bargaining are analyzed but seldom the dynamics.[11]

In this chapter we want to examine the dynamics of plea bargaining to discover what types of pleas are made and why. We want to examine the standards used by defense and prosecution in arriving at a settlement. In short we want to step inside the plea bargaining process and see how and why it works. Our discussion will be divided into four parts: [1] the setting of plea bargaining [2] the types of pleas entered in court [3] actual negotiations and [4] the effects of the social system on plea bargaining.

---

[9] Santobello v. New York 404 U.S. 257 (1971); North Carolina v. Alford 400 U.S. 25 (1971).

[10] Newman, *Conviction*; Donald Newman, "Pleading Guilty for Considerations: A Study of Bargain Justice," *Journal of Criminal Law, Criminology and Police Science* (March–April, 1956), 46: 780–790. Other important works include: Albert Alschuler, "The Prosecutor's Role in Plea Bargaining," *University of Chicago Law Review*, 1968, 36: 50–112, and Dominick Vetri. "Guilty Plea Bargaining: Compromises by Prosecutors to Secure Guilty Pleas," *University of Pennsylvania Law Review*, 1964, 112: 865–895. For a useful article that reviews the major studies and argues, from a sociological perspective, for a structure like plea bargaining, see Arthur Rosett, "The Negotiated Guilty Plea," *The Annals of the American Academy of Political and Social Science*, 1967, 374: 71–81.

[11] These critiques of plea bargaining research may be found in Blumberg, *Criminal Justice*, p. 193; James Klonoski & Robert Mendelsohn, eds., *The Politics of Local Justice* (Little, Brown, 1970), pp. 5–6

The Setting of Plea Bargaining

The defense attorney initiates plea bargaining. Such initiation is of interest, for in a number of competitive situations (chess, for example) the opening move is critical. It sets the stage for subsequent maneuvering. Such is the case in plea bargaining. The Prairie City prosecutors believe it would be a sign of weakness if they initiated plea bargaining and they prefer for the defense to make the first overture. In turn, defense initiation is surrounded with expectations. In fact, it would be considered a violation of the norms of the Prairie City criminal justice community if a defense attorney did not try to negotiate for his client. As noted earlier, the practice of criminal law involves some elements of civil law. In this instance lawyers expect to negotiate with the opposition to see what the other side is willing to offer, what his case looks like, and if an equitable agreement can be reached.

Plea negotiations occur a week or two before the trial is scheduled. To review briefly the sequence of a criminal case, the defendant is first arraigned on a charge. If the case is a felony, then a preliminary hearing is held, at which time the suspect is usually bound over to the grand jury. The grand jury returns an indictment and the suspect is then arraigned a second time on the grand jury charge. At the arraignment, trial is set for six weeks later. As the trial date approaches, the attorneys begin to negotiate. By this stage each side has a fairly well-developed idea of what the case involves. The prosecutor already has presented the case to the grand jury, thus indicating that he views the case as serious and wishes to prosecute. By this stage the defense has had an opportunity to discuss the events with his client. Further the defense has filed pretrial motions requesting the state to produce a copy of any statement made by the defendant as well as a list of witnesses the prosecution intends to call.

Negotiations between defense and prosecution (notice that the judge is not a party for reasons explained in Chapter Five) are best viewed as a trading of ideas between two professionals over what can or cannot be proven in court. For example, in a misdemeanor case, the preliminary dialogue went like this

Defense counsel: "Tell me what you can prove."
State's attorney: "No, you tell me why I can't prove my case and, if you can, I'll dismiss it"

The standards of these negotiations are the standards of the trial.

The two professionals trained in the law conduct a minitrial in the prosecutor's office.

The prosecutor generally has the upper hand in the negotiations over the facts. This is attested to not only by the statements of prosecutors but also by comments of defense attorneys. For example, one defense lawyer estimated that the state has a strong case at least seventy-five percent of the time. A consideration of the evidence available to the prosecution bears this out. If the case involves stolen property (burglary, for example), the stolen goods were likely to have been found in the suspect's possession. In a forgery case, the suspect's signature on the check can be verified by a handwriting expert. In a battery case, the victim is normally available to testify. In addition, the state has a confession from the suspect almost half of the time. In short, by the time a case progresses to a grand jury indictment, the state's attorney's office has a fairly solid case against the suspect. To be sure, the state does not possess strong evidence in every case, but the facts are on their side in most cases.

The facts of the case then put the prosecutor in a strong bargaining position. He uses the facts at his disposal to demonstrate to the defense attorney that he has enough evidence to convict his client. Here we should note an important difference between civil and criminal law. In a civil case both sides are required to disclose their case. Through such disclosure the law tries to encourage a settlement of a case before trial. Such disclosures were not required in criminal cases at the time of this research.[12] The state is required by law to make known only a small part of their case (prosecution witnesses, and the presence of a confession). Otherwise they can wait until trial to disclose the rest. In Prairie City, however, the prosecutor's office follows an open file policy. That is, assistants are free to reveal the evidence to the defense. Prosecutors believe that such disclosures will convince the defense attorney, and his client, that the State will win at trial.[13] Thus disclosure of evidence is used to induce a plea.

---

[12] Again recent changes in Illinois law alter the legal basis of the process, but do not undermine the dynamics of the process. The Illinois Supreme Court now requires the prosecution to give the defense a copy of the police reports. Thus criminal law is moving in the direction of full disclosure as in civil cases.

[13] While the office has an open file policy, there is no requirement that assistants divulge all of the case. One assistant discloses just enough to induce

A good example of how such disclosures produce guilty pleas is shown in the following case. According to the prosecutors, defendants often tell their lawyer's only part of what happened. Therefore, by telling the defense attorney what evidence the prosecutor possesses, the defense attorney can "bring his client around" to seeing that contesting the matter is hopeless. The case involved a liquor store burglary. The client told his attorney that the police had stopped him several blocks from the alleged break in, and he had nothing to do with it. The prosecutor relayed a different version. According to the police reports, the squad car was on routine patrol checking stores. When the car pulled into the parking lot the car lights illuminated someone inside the store. The officers went to the back of the store, and observed a suspect leaving the store and entering a car. They chased the car, stopped it several blocks away, discovered the car "loaded with goodies," and arrested the defendant. After such disclosures the prosecutors contend that the lawyer goes back to his client and says, "You lied to me, you bastard. Tell me the truth or I'll pull out of the case."

Thus plea bargaining in Prairie City involves a discussion between the two opposing lawyers about the facts of the case. One prosecutor termed it a "trading of ideas." Another encapsuled the process in the following sentence: "The pervasiveness of the facts should indicate to any competent attorney that the elements of prosecution are present and a successful prosecution is forthcoming." The two lawyers analyze the evidence of each side. Given the body of evidence available to the state the rhetorical question is, what would a trial decide? In most cases the professionals, using common standards of proof (based on what juries will do), can agree on the likely outcome of the trial.

It is important to place our findings from Prairie City in perspective. As we have just explained, plea bargaining centers first of all on guilt adjudication. That is, the lawyers analyze what can be legally proven about what the suspect did. Such discussions of guilt adjudication in plea bargaining have been largely absent from past studies. Plea bargaining in the Newman study is portrayed as an auction over the sentence. In reading these studies one gains the impression that the lawyers seldom discuss the legal guilt or innocence of a suspect.[14] That is not the case in Prairie

---

a guilty plea. Defense attorneys know of this policy and understandably object.

[14] In particular, see Newman, *Conviction*, and Enker, "Perspectives on Plea Bargaining."

City. According to one defense attorney, about half the time in plea bargaining is spent discussing guilt adjudication, the other half on sentencing. In Prairie City, at least, plea bargaining is best viewed as a minitrial where the two professionals analyze what the likely jury verdict would be.

The Pleas Arrived At

Thus a central aspect of plea bargaining in Prairie City is the discussion of the facts of the case. These discussions are much like the discussions in civil cases where the opposing lawyers try to resolve the conflict before trial. We must stress, however, that these negotiations are in no way automatic. Some negotiations are relatively short, while others are long. In some cases the two sides barter back and forth for a week or longer. In this section we want to examine the pleas that are arrived at. We have already explored the setting for these negotiations, now let us turn to the output of these negotiations.

Table 15 presents the basic data on the type of "pleas" that are arrived at. There are five basic types of outputs of the plea-

TABLE 15
OUTCOME OF FELONY CASES
ACCORDING TO THE CHARGE

Charge	Total	Dismissal	Plea to a Misde-meanor	Plea—Less serious felony	Plea to felony	Jury Trial
Criminal damage to property	12	0	9 (75%)	0	3 (25%)	0
Theft	34	5 (15%)	10 (29%)	0	17 (50%)	2 (6%)
Forgery	23	0	1 (4%)	0	22 (96%)	0
Burglary	60	2 (3%)	4 (7%)	2 (3%)	48 (80%)	4 (7%)
Narcotics	7	0	1 (14%)	0	5 (71%)	1 (14%)
Battery	23	1 (4%)	10 (43%)	0	6 (26%)	6 (26%)
Robbery	12	2 (17%)	2 (17%)	0	6 (50%)	2 (17%)
Armed robbery	24	3 (13%)	0	3 (13%)	12 (50%)	6 (25%)
Sex offenses*	10	0	7 (70%)	1 (10%)	0	2 (20%)
Homicide**	16	1 (6%)	1 (6%)	6 (38%)	3 (19%)	5 (31%)
Totals	221	14 (6%)	45 (20%)	12 (5%)	122 (55%)	28 (13%)

* includes rape and indecent liberties with a child
** includes murder, voluntary manslaughter and involuntary manslaughter
Note: The data is based on active prosecutions of defendants accused of felonies during 1968.

bargaining process. First, the case may be dismissed; second, the suspect may plead to a misdemeanor; third, a reduced charge might be arranged; fourth, and most common, the suspect pleads to one or more of the original charges; and, finally, no agreement may be reached and the lawyers end up going to trial. A brief scanning of table 15 reveals two important findings. First, some types of settlement predominate. Most cases end with a plea to one of the original charges. Relatively few cases are dismissed or reduced to a less serious felony. Furthermore, pleas vary by the type of crime. For example, most burglaries end with a plea to burglary, whereas most battery cases end with a plea to a misdemeanor or a dismissal. We will postpone a discussion of the jury-trial category until the next chapter. At this point, let us examine the four plea categories to see why these pleas occur and why they vary by the type of crime.

Dismissals

A defendant (and his attorney) naturally hope to secure a dismissal, for a dismissal terminates the case without the expense, as well as the uncertainty, of a trial. But the likelihood of this occurring in Prairie City is small; the prosecutor dismisses few cases once charges are filed. At first glance, though, the figures in table 16 seem to belie this proposition for altogether seventy-

TABLE 16
DISMISSALS OF CASES IN THE TOTAL
SAMPLE OF 1968 FELONIES

Convicted companion case	40	
Probation or parole violation	10	
Juvenile or mental hearings	2	
Convicted another jurisdiction	2	
Dismissed on merits	18	
	—	
Total	72	(23% of all cases)

Note: This table is based on all *cases* filed during 1968. By contrast table 15 was based on all active prosecutions of *defendants* during 1968.

two cases (twenty-three percent the total) were dismissed during 1968. A closer examination of these figures, however, shows that few of these dismissals were outright dismissals; instead, most dismissals actually involve a finding of guilt or some penalty.

Of the seventy-two dismissals in 1968, over half of the defendants were convicted in a companion case. It is standard practice for the prosecutor to dismiss all additional charges when the suspect pleads to one offense. For example, if the defendant has been accused of three burglaries, two of these charges will be dismissed if the suspect pleads to one. From the defendant's perspective, however, the practical implications of such dismissals are minimal. Although the defendant could be sentenced to consecutive sentences if he was found guilty on all charges, in practice sentences run concurrently, so the prosecutor actually gives up very little when he dismisses additional charges. Nevertheless, a major outcome of the plea bargaining process, at least in Prairie City, is that the defense attorney is able to secure dismissals of multiple charges against his client.

Cases are dismissed for other reasons. For example, if a suspect is on probation or parole and is charged with a crime, the usual practice is to violate him, that is, revoke his probation or parole and send him to prison. The charges then are dismissed. By violating the suspect on his parole or probation, the state has a lighter burden of proof than if they conducted a full trial. Charges also are dismissed when a suspect is convicted in another jurisdiction, or is subject to juvenile or mental proceedings. In all of the above situations the suspect is subject to some sort of penalty or legal proceeding.

When we separate the dismissals stemming from muiltiple charges, violations on probation or parole, convictions in another jurisdiction, and mental or juvenile proceedings, we are left with only eighteen cases (six percent of the total) that actually are dismissed on the merits. These figures back up the statements of the prosecutors that they will rarely dismiss a felony case outright. They will dismiss only if they have a "lousy" or "unprovable" case. For example, occasionally the prosecutors will file a charge based on the statement of a complainant only to discover later that the complainant was not telling the truth. The police provided the following illustration. A janitor was charged with rape. The police on further investigation prior to trial discovered that the "victim" had made a similar rape complaint in another city, a complaint that had been found to be untrue. This case was dismissed. But such situations are rare. Instead, if the prosecutor believes he has a weak case then he will offer a plea to a misdemeanor rather then dismiss outright.

Pleas of Misdemeanors

The defense attorneys' first preference is to negotiate a dismissal of the case but, as we have seen, such outright dismissals are relatively rare. Therefore, defense attorneys believe a more realistic objective is to try to secure a plea to a misdemeanor. In particular they want to avoid a felony conviction on their client's record. Table 15 shows that in roughly one-fifth of the cases the defense attorney is able to secure such a reduction. Such reductions, however, are not uniform. Rather, certain types of crimes are more likely to be reduced to a misdemeanor than others. Petty property crimes and certain crimes against the person disproportionately end with a plea to a misdemeanor.

Table 15 points out that forty-one percent of larceny and criminal damage to property cases (both are felonies if more than $150 is involved) are reduced to misdemeanors. Crimes of violence without an economic motive also have a disproportionate number of reductions. About half of all sex and battery charges (seventeen out of thirty-three) are reduced to misdemeanors. Since it is presumptive that such reductions in charges are beneficial to defendants, we should ask what accounts for this important allocation of justice? Who benefits and why?

To answer this question, we must begin where the prosecutor begins, the state of the evidence. Sex and battery cases taken as a group are the most difficult cases for the state to prove and it is presumptive that these proof problems explain why so many cases are reduced to misdemeanors. Prosecutors pointed to ambiguities over culpability. For example, determining who was the aggressor in a battery case may be difficult. Further, victims may be hesitant about cooperating. The cooperation of the victim in sex cases is often the fatal hurdle for the prosecution. Mothers are understandably hesitant about allowing their child to repeat the story in public, fearing the child will only be harmed further. Additionally, the victims in sex and battery cases may be untrustworthy witnesses or may not be viewed as worthy victims by juries. All of these proof problems make sex and battery charges the hardest cases to prove. This view is given further credence when we examine the proportion of cases going to trial. According to table 15 a high proportion of sex and battery cases (twenty-four percent) go to trial. This indicates that, in cases not reduced, professionals cannot agree on the state of the evidence.

But what explains the disproportionate number of reductions

in petty property crimes? We do not expect that the prosecutor would have any great proof problems in larceny or cases involving criminal damage to property. The proof problems of these cases would certainly not be greater than proof problems in burglaries, where few cases end with a plea to a misdemeanor. The reason that so many minor property felony cases end with a plea to a misdemeanor is that the prosecutor views these as the least serious of all felonies, and since they are relatively minor not all should be treated as felonies. Thus, we hypothesize that evidence is probably sufficient for a conviction but prosecutors exercise discretion by reducing the charge. If discretion is involved, as distinct from judgment on evidence, then we would expect certain groups of defendants to be more favored than others. We would predict that teen-agers and those with money would be more likely to have their case reduced to a misdemeanor or dismissed outright. Alternatively, we would expect that in sex and battery cases where judgment on the evidence is the crucial dimension, that the favored groups would show no such benefits. Table 17 provides a limited test of these hypotheses and generally confirms them. In petty property crimes, teens, those with their own lawyer, and those released on bail have their cases disproportionately reduced to a misdemeanor or dismissed. All three of these relationships support the hypothesis. In sex and battery cases, two out of the three relationships support the hypothesis that the cases are disposed of on the basis of the evidence and not on the basis of the background of the defendant. The only exceptions are teen-agers in sex and battery cases. In general, the data support our hypothesis that petty property crimes involve discretion while sex and battery cases involve judgment of the nature of the evidence.

Pleas to a Less Serious Felony

A common type of plea arrangement in many communities is a plea to a less serious felony. For example, the suspect will be charged with armed robbery, but the defense attorney will work out a plea to robbery.[15] We would expect that Prairie City similarly would have a large number of pleas to a less serious felony. Such does not prove to be the case. Instead pleas to a less serious felony are rare (only twelve defendants or five percent of the cases ended with such a plea).

Although the actual number of reductions is small, these reductions are important because they occur in the most serious

---

[15] Enker, pp. 108–110.

TABLE 17
AGE, TYPE OF ATTORNEY, AND BAIL AS FACTORS
IN DISMISSAL AND REDUCTIONS.

	AGE			
	Petty Property		Sex and Battery	
	Teen-ager	Adult	Teen-ager	Adult
Dismissal or misdemeanor plea	12 (60%)	12 (48%)	7 (78%)	12 (52%)
All others	8	13	2	11
Total	20	25	9	23

	TYPE OF LAWYER			
	Petty Property		Sex and Battery	
	Public Defender	Private	Public Defender	Private
Dismissal or misdemeanor plea	6 (37%)	16 (57%)	6 (55%)	11 (52%)
All others	10	12	5	10
Total	16	28	11	21

	BAIL			
	Petty Property		Sex and Battery	
	No Release	Release	No Release	Release
Dismissal or misdemeanor plea	3 (38%)	21 (55%)	7 (70%)	13 (52%)
All others	5	17	3	12
Total	8	38	10	25

Note: The data is based on active prosecutions of defendants accused of felonies during 1968.

cases. During 1968, five murders, one manslaughter, one rape, and three armed robberies (plus two burglaries) were reduced to less serious felony charges. Omitting the two apparently atypical burglary cases, all of these charge reductions represent a significant advantage to the defendant. Conviction for murder and rape automatically excludes a suspect from probation. Thus a lawyer wants to secure a plea to a lesser felony to keep open the possibility of probation, although this is not likely. More importantly, the defense attorney tries to secure a charge reduction to reduce the possible prison term. If, for example, the suspect pleads to voluntary manslaughter then prison term is one to twenty, which is significantly less than the minimum of fourteen (maximum of life) on a conviction for murder. Thus defense attorneys attempt to have the most serious felonies reduced to less serious ones to minimize possible prison time. Defense attorneys mentioned an additional motive for seeking a charge reduction. As we discussed in chapter 5 the chief judge believes in long prison terms. He normally goes along with the prosecutor's sentence recommendations but at some future time he might not. Therefore by obtaining a plea to a less serious felony, the defense attorney has hedged his bets. Even if the judge imposes a higher prison penalty he can not go that much higher.

In Prairie City, therefore, relatively few charges are reduced to less serious felonies, although these reductions are important because they involve the most serious offenses. In this way Prairie City deviates from past studies. Why it deviates can best be explained by examining the final plea category—pleas to the original charge.

Pleas to One of the Original Charges

The majority of guilty pleas in Prairie City are pleas to the original charge. While most studies of plea bargaining have emphasized the charge reductions that occur, this does not prove to be the case in our study city. Of the 134 pleas to a felony during 1968, 122 (91 percent) were pleas to the original charge. Although we lack reliable comparative data, it does appear that Prairie City has a high proportion of on-line pleas. Two factors seem to explain why most of these pleas are on line: Illinois law, which provides the legal categories, and the prosecutor's initial screening of cases.

Charge reductions are often ways to avoid legislative mandates. The statutory law in many states is inflexible and charge reductions are used to provide flexibility in the system. In Michigan, for example, state law does not allow probation for defendants convicted of armed robbery. Since judges sometimes wish to grant probation in armed robbery cases, they will not accept a guilty plea to armed robbery. Instead, suspects plead to robbery.[16] In other instances the criminal code's categorization of crimes does not agree with the views of the working officials. Some states maintain a distinction between daytime and nighttime burglaries, with nighttime burglaries having stiffer penalties. To avoid such harshness in the law, suspects regularly plead to daytime bur-

---

[16] Donald McIntyre, ed., *Law Enforcement in the Metropolis* (American Bar Foundation, 1967), pp. 132–135.

glary, although they were originally charged with burglary at night.[17]

Such charge reductions then provide flexibility to the system where the law has erected immutable principles. But such charge reductions to gain flexibility are not needed in Illinois because the criminal code sets forth a few coherent crime categories. There are no classes of burglary, no degrees of assault and battery, and probation is denied only to murderers, rapists, and sellers of narcotics.[18]

A second factor that appears to explain why so many of the guilty pleas in Prairie City are on line is the screening performed by the prosecutor. As we noted in chapter 6, the prosecutor reviews each case before filing charges. He eliminates the weak cases, as well as squaring the charge to the facts (recall that the police often overcharge). One hypothesizes that in jurisdictions where the prosecutor does not perform such a screening function that plea bargaining would produce different outputs. We would expect a higher proportion of dismissals and a higher proportion of charge reductions because the state has fewer strong cases. Only future research can confirm these hypotheses, but on first examination it does seem to explain why so many cases in Prairie City end with a plea to the original charge.

We need to comment on one additional factor surrounding on-line pleas. In some jurisdictions, on-line pleas are obtained through the filing of multiple charges. The defendant will be charged with two or three offenses on the same information or indictment. The prosecutor can use such multiple charges to gain the defendant's plea to the most serious offense in return for dismissing the other counts. Such a practice is rare in Prairie City, for a defendant is normally charged with only the most serious charge involved in the alleged criminal act. The only time a suspect will be charged with multiple counts is where the offenses occurred at different times, that is, a burglary defendant accused of several separate burglaries. In this case, the prosecutor would dismiss the additional counts in return for a plea to one, as discussed earlier.

---

[17] Newman, *Conviction*, p. 53.

[18] Enker reaches a similar conclusion based on his experience in the Federal courts. "Perspectives on Plea Bargaining," p. 110.

Guilt Adjudication in Misdemeanors

So far we have dealt mainly with felony cases and the guilty pleas that dispose of most of these cases. In misdemeanor cases a trial is even more rare than in felony cases. Here too, most suspects plead guilty. But the guilty plea in misdemeanors is different from that of felonies because in misdemeanors there is less negotiation, for most defendants do not have an attorney, and plead guilty on their own.

For most misdemeanor defendants, their case ends on their first or second appearance in court. On the first appearance in court the judge informs the suspect of the charges against him, and the maximum penalty he may receive if convicted. In addition, the magistrate outlines the suspect's rights to hire a lawyer or have a court-appointed lawyer if he is indigent, his right to a jury trial and to bail. He then asks the suspect to plead guilty or not guilty. Many enter a plea of guilty and are sentenced immediately (usually a fine of $25 to $100 depending on the seriousness of the offense). Some enter an initial plea of not guilty but on their next court appearance plead guilty. Thus most misdemeanor and traffic cases are disposed of speedily by a guilty plea involving a direct transaction between the defendant and the judge.

Plea bargaining, however, can and does occur, in misdemeanor and traffic cases. In rare cases, the suspect will come to the prosecutor's office to explain his side of the case. Most plea bargaining in misdemeanor cases occurs after a suspect hires a lawyer. It is hard to provide exact figures on how many misdemeanor and traffic defendants hire a lawyer, but figures from the misdemeanor cases started during January, 1970 show that twenty-seven percent of the suspects did hire a lawyer.

Hiring a lawyer is a major economic decision, because it costs money to retain a lawyer. Lawyers are reluctant to disclose their fees lest the competition discover how much (or how little) they charge. Nevertheless all of the defense lawyers did discuss their fee schedule with the researcher. In the interests of privacy we will not break down these fee schedules by type of attorney. It is sufficient to point out the range of fees. If a suspect in Prairie City wants to hire a lawyer in a misdemeanor or traffic case, he will have to pay between $100 and $400. Why would suspects spend from $100 to $400 for a lawyer? Answering this question will provide important background for our discussion of the actual plea bargaining process in misdemeanor cases.

In discussing misdemeanor cases with defense lawyers, they point to three reasons why a suspect hires a lawyer. First, some are scared by the maximum penalty. For example, if they are accused of battery they can go to jail for a year. They do not know that few, if any, suspects ever receive such a severe penalty. Second, some crimes involve jail penalties. Driving without a license in Illinois, for example, carries an automatic jail term. In addition, people convicted of drunk driving may also be sent to jail, particularly if they have been convicted before. Lawyers can help their clients avoid serving time in jail. It is seldom, if ever, that a suspect represented by counsel is sent to jail. As one defense attorney observed, "The only people who go to jail in traffic cases are people who don't have a lawyer. If a suspect goes in, pleads guilty and begs the mercy of the court, the judge may still send him to jail. Very rarely will a suspect represented by counsel be sent to jail."

A third reason a suspect might hire a lawyer is to keep his driver's license. In Illinois conviction for drunk driving (abbreviated DWI for "Driving While under the Influence of Intoxicating beverages") carries with it an automatic revocation of the driver's license for one year. Understandably, those charged with DWI want to avoid this. Therefore, they hire a lawyer who can negotiate with the prosecutor to let the suspect plead to reckless driving, which does not involve loss of license. As one lawyer pointed out, clients will go to almost any length to keep their driver's license.

The defense attorney is in a favorable position to avoid a DWI conviction because breathalyzer results are not admissible in the Prairie City courts. A breathalyzer mechanically determines the level of alcohol in a person's blood stream. The law assumes that a person with more than .10 parts alcohol is "driving under the influence." The results of the breathalyzer are not admissible in the Prairie City court because the police department has not obtained the required certification that the machine is properly maintained. During plea bargaining the lawyers discuss the results of the breathalyzer but such information is not admissable in court.

In these situations the lawyer is functioning much like the inside dopester we referred to in Chapter Four. The lawyer's main commodity is his knowledge of what goes on at the courthouse. He has access to the prosecutor's office, an access not usually afforded the suspect. The lawyer's fee secures for the client what similarly situated suspects receive. The fee is a toll for access over the bridge between the layman and the professional.

The Dynamics of Plea Bargaining

After a suspect has hired a lawyer, the lawyer usually demands a jury trial. The case is then placed on the jury trial setting. The week before the case is scheduled for trial the attorneys negotiate. To appreciate the dynamics of the plea-bargaining process, as well as to reinforce our earlier discussion about the importance of evidence in such negotiations, we shall report below most of the plea bargaining in misdemeanor cases for one week that involved one prosecutor.

The misdemeanor jury setting is called once a month. During the month on which this report is based there were eighty-seven defendants accused of one hundred and seven separate offenses. The list was divided among three assistant state's attorneys on the basis of the lawyers handling the cases. One assistant took the public defender firm, another the major private firm, the third took the remainder. (The assignments are rotated on a monthly basis to prevent any one defense attorney from developing "ins" with the prosecutor.) According to one assistant, "We want to prevent any defense attorney from being able to say 'I pled a guy guilty last time, so give me a break on this one.'" In the following discussion we will observe the negotiations of the state's attorney who is handling the miscellaneous law firms. As none of the Prairie City lawyers have more than a handful of cases, the prosecutor will be dealing with several lawyers and we will be able to gauge the contrasting styles of negotiations.

Case One. The first attorney came by on Tuesday afternoon. He was representing several clients accused of drunk driving. The first case, he said, looked like a strong one for the state, but it was not. The suspect took several pills and therefore was not drunk. The state's attorney read the police report and commented that the suspect made some damaging admissions such as, "I've been drinking all afternoon." The defense attorney replied, "He didn't tell me that. The guy claims he took pills that affected him, made him look drunk, and he has a doctor's statement." The state's attorney replied, "The breathalizer shows he tested at .25. I want a plea to DWI." The defense attorney retorted, "My client wants a reduction to reckless driving."

Case Two. The attorneys proceeded to the next defendant. He was charged not only with DWI, but also illegal transportation of liquor and illegal possession of firearms. The defendant had admitted hitting three cars but had not taken the breathalyzer test. Counsel contended that the defendant had one and a half beers and then took some pills which, according to witnesses, had had an immediate effect. In addition, the lawyer said he believed the police search for the liquor and weapons was illegal. The state's attorney replied he had to be consistent. Many suspects now contended that it was pills, not liquor, that made them look drunk. He was trying a case that month (postponed from the previous month) where the defendant was presenting medical evidence on the effects of pills. Therefore to be consistent, he could not reduce this charge until he had seen what the jury decided.

Case Three. Having failed to reach agreement on the first two cases, the lawyers went on to the third case. Defense said this case was no problem, for the defendant was willing to plead to DWI (evidently because he had a past conviction for a similar offense). Initially the state had offered a plea to DWI and a $300 fine but the defense attorney negotiated a reduction to $200. Having completed this case, they briefly discussed the others and agreed to continue case one until next month. The state's attorney said he was not sure what he would do in the other case until he talked to his witnesses.

After the defense attorney left, the prosecutor discussed the plea bargaining session. He said that this law firm had four DWI cases on this month's setting. He did not want to appear to be a real "hard nose" by not reducing any, but that was the position he was in. This, and other discussions, indicated that the state's attorney did not want to sell out, but at the same time did not want to appear to be unreasonable.

Case Four. Another defense attorney came by and joked with me that his client *really* was guilty. When the prosecutor returned, the lawyer made the same statement, indicating that he was just interested in collecting his fee. The state's attorney looked at the file (the case involved driving on a suspended license) and recommended three days in jail. The defense attorney said he would recommend that to his client, commenting, "Sounds best to me." Evidently the defendant had a previous record.

Case Five. The defense attorney opened by saying he wanted the charges dismissed because his client did not do it. After reading the police report on the shoplifting case, the state's attorney replied, "From the police reports, it doesn't look like this guy should even have been charged. There was a shoplifting but there is no evidence to connect it with the defendant. The co-defendant has a prior shoplifting record and he was in possession of the stolen goods." The attorneys agree to a dismissal with the defendant paying court costs.

Case Six involved a charge of reckless driving. Again the defense attorney opened, this time offering a plea to running a stop sign, "Since that's what he did." The state's attorney again examined the police report—normally in misdemeanor cases the prosecutor does not examine the file until the attorney enters the office—and agreed, saying all he can show is that somehow, sometime the car got in the ditch. The defense attorney replied that the client admitted he could not stop in time. They agreed to a plea to the stop sign offense and a $10 fine.

Case Seven involved another shoplifting charge. The defendant was accused of stealing a package of meat loaf from a neighborhood grocery store. The two lawyers quickly agreed to a plea and a $50 fine. According to the defense attorney, the defendant was probably drinking and did not know what he was doing. The lawyers also discussed the defendant's past record, which accounted for the higher than normal fine.

Case Eight was settled just as quickly. A woman had been charged with DWI, but no breathalyzer figures were available. A plea to reckless driving was agreed to, but the state did not formally agree until the next case was settled.

Case Nine was the most serious. (Notice that in the negotiations on the first group of cases the most serious offense was reserved for last.) The defendant had been charged with both DWI and fleeing a police officer. Both offenses carry an automatic revocation of the driver's license. To compound the defendant's problems, he had almost hit another car while fleeing the police and also had a prior DWI on his record. This time the prosecutor opened, saying he had good evidence in this case: lay witnesses, and the breathalyzer, which tested at .25 (a high figure). The prosecutor said that jail time would not hurt, but he would recommend the minimum fine on each charge—$50 for fleeing and $100 for DWI—but wanted a plea to both charges. The defense attorney replied that he had to check back on this case because another member of the firm was handling it. The state's attorney replied that he would like a policy of withdrawing all plea recommendations on Friday (jury trials were scheduled to begin on the next Monday). If not accepted by then, all bets are off. He added that if the case went to trial and the defendant was found guilty then he would definitely recommend a jail sentence.

The two attorneys had discussed and largely settled five cases in a little over half an hour. There was now time for conversation. Defense commented that lay witnesses were usually good for the state and put the state in a better bargaining position. The prosecutor disagreed, saying, "To be frank, I don't rely on lay witnesses since they can screw you up. Lay witnesses don't observe well and might say he didn't look drunk. I would rather rely on police officers."

After the lawyer left, the state's attorney had time to give me his side of the negotiations. He discussed the most serious case (nine) first. He believed he was in a pretty strong bargaining position. He wanted a plea to DWI at least and, if the lawyer pushed, he could still dismiss the second count. It seemed unlikely to him that the defendant would risk a jury trial with his record, as well as the strong possibility that a jail sentence would result. As a result, at least one plea to DWI seemed assured. He then referred back to case eight, which involved the woman accused of DWI. He said there was more to that case than met the eye. The arresting officer had called earlier in the day and said the case was a weak one. The woman had been verbally abusive to the police but when she was taken to the police station there was no one there to give the breathalyzer. The state's attorney said he could not have proven much at trial, so he had quickly agreed to reduce the charge, thus making the lawyer think he was not being unreasonable.

At that point, the phone rang to announce that another attorney was in the waiting room. The prosecutor commented that this attorney would not try cases. In contrast the first attorney would try cases but was not that effective. The lawyer entered and the prosecutor allowed him to read the police reports on the DWI charge. *Case Ten.* This was unusual since state's attorneys ordinarily only read the reports aloud, and would not let the lawyer actually see the report. As counsel read, the state's attorney commented that he had read the report and thought that this was the type of case that should be tried. Defense counsel explained that he thought the police were mistaken when they said "reckless driving" because the road was bad. Anyway the defendant was a truck driver. The state's attorney responded, "I won't try to convince you your man was drunk and counsel won't try to convince me he wasn't." The prosecutor said he had not talked to witnesses yet, but that when he did, if he decided that he could not win, he would fold and reduce the DWI charge to reckless driving. For the third time the lawyer mentioned that his client was a truck driver. Thus a conviction would mean not just "re-

voking the license but taking a man's livelihood away from him."
The prosecutor replied, "I don't think the law is just, but that's
not the issue. I have to be consistent and I think that this is a
tryable case. If I have a fifty-fifty chance of winning a jury verdict
then I'll go to trial." The defense lawyer countered, "You have
to make a judgment and you're not doing justice." The state's
attorney responded, "I don't see it that way." No agreement had
been reached in the case but they quickly disposed of case eleven;
the state dismissed a speeding charge for costs stating that in auto
accidents civil cases should take care of the damages.

By Thursday several other negotiations had taken place. The
phone had stopped ringing and no court appearances were scheduled, giving the state's attorney time to reflect on where he stood.
Up to that time, he had only five deals firmed up. He had twelve
cases that could be called a "possible trial." Of these twelve cases,
he thought about six defendants would fold and take the state's
offer. In three or four other cases, the lawyer would not try cases
so those were not likely to have a jury trial. In one or two other
cases the prosecutor, after talking to his witnesses, would fold
rather then go to trial. He was thus in a state of flux, but controlled flux. He was fairly certain that he would not have more
than two trials on this jury setting, but he did not know yet which
cases would go which way. Besides these twelve cases he had
others on the jury setting but these other cases were so minor that
they would not go to trial. Rather than try them, he would make
an offer that the defendant could not refuse.

The defense lawyers were also in a state of flux. They also
faced the possibility of a trial, but the possibility was not a very
large one. Nevertheless, they reflected on their bargaining position in much the same way as the prosecutor. This was apparent
while talking to one defense attorney. He had four cases. We sat
in his office talking about what approach he would take the next
day when he negotiated with the prosecutor we have been following. His comments indicated that lawyers often think in terms
of what is possible, not what they would like to see. Of the four
cases, he thought one would probably end with a plea to DWI
since the state not only had a good case, but the defendant had
a prior DWI reduction. In two others he thought he could get a
reduction of DWI to reckless. The fourth case was the most interesting. On that case the defense wanted a dismissal. His client was
arrested late at night at his home and charged with DWI. The
client had admitted drinking that night but contended that the
car was found on the other side of town. Counsel did not see how

the state could link the drinking client to the car. Thus he wanted a dismissal.

Unfortunately other events intervened and I was not able to observe the negotiations on these cases. The results, however, went as the lawyer predicted, with one exception. I talked to him just after he had left the prosecutor's office, and he began by saying that there was no way that he could take his fourth case to trial. It seemed that his client was so drunk when arrested that he did not know where he was. What he thought was his living room was actually the police station.

Postscript: The prosecutor we spent the week with had only one trial at that jury setting, the rest were pled out. That case involved drunk driving with the defendant contending that the pills he was taking (on doctor's orders) had made him appear drunk although he only had a beer or two. The jury agreed with the defendant. The prosecutor felt his bargaining position was steadily eroding. He now was below fifty-fifty with winning drunk-driving cases with a jury, a fact that defense attorneys pointed up the following month.

Analysis

These examples should illustrate that plea bargaining is a dynamic, give-and-take process that must be assessed not only through the use of statistics on the outputs of the process, but also by viewing the process in action. While the cases discussed were misdemeanors and traffic violations they are, with a few exceptions, illustrative of the plea-bargaining process in felony cases as well. The first exception is that felony cases involve much greater preparation on the part of the attorneys. The prosecutor normally takes a hard look at the evidence in a misdemeanor case when the defense attorney walks in the door. In felony cases, on the other hand, both sides investigate a case more thoroughly. For example, attorneys in a felony case will interview witnesses and if the case looks like a potential trial will spend even more time interviewing, investigating, and so on. Such preparation is largely absent from misdemeanor cases.

Plea bargaining in misdemeanor and traffic cases differs from plea bargaining in felony cases in a second way—the minor cases are treated with greater flexibility. One state's attorney made the following comment: "There is a lot more movement and flexibility in misdemeanors than in felonies." As we noted earlier, prosecutors do not view misdemeanor and traffic cases as very serious, and try to dispose of them as best they can. To quote another assistant, "We're interested in getting a plea on every case because that way you can't lose. Sometimes, though we have to caution ourselves not to make too good of a deal." In felony cases there is relatively little movement from the original charge, but in misdemeanor and traffic cases there is quite a bit of movement. Prosecutors generally want a plea, and are less interested in the exact charge to which the defendant pleads.

Negotiations in misdemeanor cases follow roughly the same pattern as negotiations in felonies, with the two exceptions we have just noted. With this in mind, let us further analyze the process. Reporting the transcripts of negotiations can leave the impression that the process is random, but this is not the case. While there is a give-and-take in negotiations, they proceed within some well-defined patterns. Let us examine these patterns or parameters of the system, starting with the most general and moving to more specific ones.

Plea bargaining is shaped by the social network of the legal actors. The legal community is a relatively small one and in such small communities reputation is a vital, if not overriding, consideration. A major factor in Prairie City is that the two sides basically trust one another. This is an extension of the civil practice model that we developed in Chapters Three and Four. Both the prosecutors and defense attorneys have roots in civil practice. It is accepted in civil cases that the two sides negotiate. Similarly, it is expected that the lawyers will negotiate in criminal cases. A primary norm in such negotiations is reasonableness. Recall the state's attorney's discussion after the first bargaining session. He had refused to reduce any DWI's to reckless and felt that he might appear to be unreasonable to that attorney. But at the same time that a lawyer is expected to be reasonable during negotiations, he is also judged by his peers on whether he is too easy to deal with. Thus lawyers for both sides, but particularly the prosecutors, must tread the line between reasonableness in negotiations and being too easy to bargain with. One prosecutor nicely described this intangible element by saying, "If at the end of a jury setting I would have looked back and found that I had reduced every DWI to reckless, I wouldn't have felt right." Thus lawyers strive for a mental balance between reasonableness and hard bargaining.

These general norms of law practice then provide external restraints on plea bargaining. Within these external restraints bargaining takes into account several factors. Plea bargaining proceeds along definite lines. One factor is the seriousness of the offense. Prosecutors work on a rank order of the seriousness of the offense. For example, a DWI case in which someone was injured or an accident almost occurred, is viewed as more serious than a DWI case where no such dangerous behavior was observed. DWI cases also are viewed as more serious than a simple battery case. The less serious the offense, the less resources the prosecutors will invest in the case. As one assistant stated it, "I'm happy to reduce some charges as long as I get pleas on the stronger ones."

A second factor that is closely related to the first is the suspect's past conduct. If the defendant has never been charged with DWI before, he stands a good chance of getting his case reduced to reckless. However, if he has had a previous DWI reduced, then prosecutors are reluctant to agree to a second reduction. It will be remembered that in case eight the suspect had a prior charge that had been reduced. In such instances the prosecutor begins talking about jail time, indicating that if the suspect does not accept the plea and is found guilty at trial he can expect to spend some time in the county jail. Such threats usually secure the defendant's plea to DWI.

A third factor, which underlies the first two, is the strength of the prosecutor's case. As we discussed earlier in this chapter, evidence is an important consideration in felony plea bargaining. This is also the case in misdemeanor and traffic negotiations. Lawyers, as professionals, are always cognizant of the burden of proof, and this factor is an important consideration in determining which cases are reduced and which ones are not. The importance of evidence is revealed not only during the plea bargaining between two attorneys but also in other instances as well. On more than one occasion I observed prosecutors dismiss or reduce cases because they did not think they could prove the case in court. These dismissals or reductions occurred not just with cases involving lawyers but also with unrepresented defendants.

The seriousness of the offense, the past record of the defendant, and the legal strength of the case then are primary factors shaping the plea-bargaining process. On the basis of these factors, the prosecutors decide which cases are worth fighting and which ones are not. Just as important is the fact that defense attorneys also accept these same factors. Lawyers negotiate on the basis of what they can reasonably expect to get, not on the basis of what they would like to see. Basically they think it is reasonable that a person who has committed a more serious offense and/or has a prior history of this type of misconduct should have a higher penalty than other suspects. In short, the defense attorneys work on the basis of the same rank orderings as the prosecutors and, informally, would probably agree that these rank orderings are reasonable.

Thus plea bargaining in Prairie City operates within the general setting of civil legal practice and three factors shape the actual bargaining—strength of the evidence, seriousness of the offense, and past conduct. These considerations largely determine who gets what. But within this framework the skills of individual attorneys may have marginal effects on the outcomes. There are no great disparities in how the cases of one law firm are handled vis-à-vis the cases of another law firm. The norms of legal practice prevent the prosecutor from running roughshod over one lawyer or law firm. Nevertheless, some lawyers are more skillful and successful than others. Let us examine these factors.

Prosecutors divide defense attorneys into three categories. Although I never heard them express it in this way, it was implicit in their statements that some lawyers are viewed as good trial lawyers; others are lawyers who would go to trial with a varying degree of success; and others who would not try a case. The higher a lawyer is on this trial-willingness, trial-ability scale, the better his relative bargaining position. Recall that prior to case ten the prosecutor said that this particular lawyer would not try cases. Consequently he began bargaining by stressing that he would go to trial on this case. It is doubtful whether he would have used this tactic with other lawyers who are effective in the courtroom.

A second factor, which is harder to evaluate, is the type of appeals the lawyer makes. In case number eight the lawyer on several occasions brought up the employment background of his client—a truck driver—thereby hoping to influence the prosecutor that revocation of the driver's license would be unjust. In another case, a lawyer referred to his client as "a really good-looking kid." These can be termed particularistic appeals. The lawyer is trying to bring out some background factor that might induce the prosecutor to place his client in a category less than normal. How successful these particularistic bargaining ploys are is hard to gauge because prosecutors become immune to them. One defense attorney made this point, "When I was a state's attorney, defense attorneys would come in and whine. They'd say this is a special case, point out what type of guy his client was. So I don't do that. I say what's your best offer and then tell my client. This saves time." Not only did his experience as a prosecutor indicate how jaded state's attorneys can become to such appeals (and hence unaffected) but, given the number of cases these and other dominant attorneys handle, they are in no position to make particularistic appeals in every case. Handling anywhere from five to twenty clients a month, they cannot afford to cry "Wolf" lest they expend their credibility uselessly and have none left for when it can be effective.

These parameters, coupled with the tactics of the defense attorneys, become apparent after observing negotiations and interviewing the participants. A factor, which is less apparent because it operates over a large number of cases, also needs to be examined. These attorneys deal with one another over a long period of time, and therefore they try to bargain from strength. For example, one heard occasional comments that, "I hope you didn't think I gave you too good of a deal on that case." This factor is less tangible than the others and is akin to Parsons' concept of system maintenance.[19]

In Prairie City cases are bargained on an individual basis. There is no mass bargaining of the "If you'll give me this one I'll give you someone else" type.[20] That would be a violation of the norms. But the large number of cases handled results in other pressures. The attorney must consider his overall bargaining position for the long run. Thus, in some cases, he is not only interested in settling that case but also interested in improving his bargaining position overall. One state's attorney commented, "Sometimes you have to let an attorney know that he can't settle all his cases via plea bargaining. You have to let him know he was to try some cases." Several isolated comments by the participants indicated that such overall considerations of plea bargaining position influence some marginal decisions. In one instance a prosecutor made an offhand comment that "One law firm has been winning too many cases recently." At the same time this law firm was handling a drug-sale case defendant (who was an unsophisticated, not a professional, pusher). Normally in such cases the charge would be reduced because the minimum is ten years in jail. Yet this case was not reduced but went to trial. This seems to be indirect proof that some individual cases are handled in such a way to improve the overall bargaining position. Another facet of this was revealed in a statement made after the research was done. A participant pointed to some individual match-ups between

---

[19] Talcott Parsons, *The Social System* (Free Press, 1951).

[20] There are no "package deals" in Prairie City as in other cities. Cf. George Cole, "The Decision to Prosecute," *Law and Society*, 1970, 4: 340.

defense and prosecution. One prosecutor had not won a jury trial against a particular defense attorney for over a year. Another defense attorney had not won a jury trial in over a year. These sub rosa elements obviously have a bearing on how cases are handled above and beyond the individual case.

Conclusion

Plea bargaining is the dominant reality of the lower courts. While popular mythology and the ideals of criminal law stress a jury trial, most defendants are found guilty not after the combat of a trial but after secret negotiations. In this chapter we have looked at the guilt adjudication aspects of plea bargaining in Prairie City, employing interviews, observations, and statistical data to provide a well-rounded picture of the process. In the next chapter we examine the jury trial, and particularly look at how the possibility of a jury trial affects the plea bargaining process. The chapter after that will look at the negotiations over sentence. At this point, however, we should review our major findings and point out how they differ from past studies and, finally, suggest that these findings argue for a reexamination of the plea bargaining process.

Plea bargaining in Prairie City is best viewed as a minitrial conducted in the prosecutor's office. Prime considerations are the facts in the case (is there enough proof for a guilty verdict?) and judgments as to what a jury is likely to do. Professionals employing common standards of trial normally can reach an agreement. This process is best summarized by the state's attorney who stated, "The pervasiveness of the facts should indicate to any competent attorney that the elements of prosecution are present and a successful prosecution is forthcoming." It is important to recall, though, that the defense attorney is operating as an agent for his client. The client has the final say. The lawyer functions to give his client an opinion on what the evidence is and what the likely result would be if the case came to trial.

Given this synopsis of plea bargaining in Prairie City, we should point out that our findings differ greatly from past studies in three ways. First, plea bargaining in Prairie City involves extensive negotiations about evidence. Past studies, however, have only tangentially mentioned this factor. Instead, they have stressed the bargaining over the sentence. Bargaining over sentence does occur in Prairie City but it occurs after bargaining over guilt adjudication.

A second major difference in findings between this study and others is the nature of the final plea. In Prairie City the majority of suspects plead to the original charge. Past studies have stressed the bargaining to secure a reduced charge. In Prairie City the only significant charge reductions are to misdemeanors. Prairie City has fewer reduced charge pleas than other areas for two reasons. First, Illinois law has been codified, a codification that removed numerous degrees of crimes. Second, Prairie City screens its cases before charges are filed, a practice not typical of many areas.

A third major difference is that in Prairie City the type of charge has a great bearing on plea bargaining and the final plea. Past studies have normally analyzed felonies and, by implication, have seen no need to subdivide this category. Our data suggest, however, that there is a big difference by type of crime. For example, few burglary cases end with a plea to a misdemeanor but a large proportion of battery cases do. The major factor accounting for such differentiation is the type of evidence available in each case. While burglary cases are likely to be straightforward, personal-violence crimes involve more complications and therefore more problems of proof. As a result, many more crimes of violence end with reduced pleas than do property offenses.

I think that these findings argue that we need to reassess the role of plea bargaining in the criminal justice system. Although parts of the plea-bargaining process have been analyzed, the larger perspective has gone largely unattended. In seeking to place plea bargaining in a broader perspective a useful starting point is to ask a functional question: what functions does plea bargaining perform? [21] In the simplest terms, negotiations between prosecutor and defense attorney settle disputes. In this sense plea bargaining in criminal cases is hardly unique. On the contrary, such dispute settlement devices predominate in the rest of the legal system. Every day countless disputes between landlord and tenant, husband and wife, debtor and creditor, and one car driver versus another come to the courts for settlement. Each party by right can have a jury trial in most of these disputes, but most do not. Instead, the law settles these cases short of a trial.

---

[21] On the uses and limitations of functional analysis see William Flanagan and Edwin Fogelman, "Functional Analysis," in James Charlesworth, ed., *Contemporary Political Analysis* (Free Press, 1961), pp. 72–85. Arthur Rosett has usefully applied functional analysis to plea bargaining and reached similar conclusions. Rosett, "The Negotiated Guilty Plea," *Annals of the American Academy of Political and Social Science*, 1967, 374: 70–81.

It is useful to view plea bargaining in criminal cases as analogous to dispute settlement in civil cases. The utility of this civil model was suggested by several judges, defense attorneys, and prosecutors.[22] When the interview schedule shifted to a discussion of plea bargaining, the interviewee on numerous occasions spontaneously compared plea bargaining to negotiations in civil cases. To paraphrase one defense attorney "I cooperate with a prosecutor to the same extent I cooperate in a civil case." The law requires negotiations between the opposing lawyers. The participants see negotiations as the way law is practiced.

Viewing plea bargaining from the perspective of civil law has several advantages. First, the civil law model is value-free. Many discussions of plea bargaining are heavily value-oriented, and seem more intent on criticizing the process than explaining why it happens. For these discussions the ideal is a jury trial and deviations from this ideal are suspect. Yet, in a civil case when we learn that the automobile accident involving Smith and Jones was settled without a trial, we do not immediately raise a normative question about the settlement. But when *The People* v. *Smith* is settled without a trial, many do raise a normative question. This seems unfortunate because in the process the nature of the plea bargaining process is lost.

Viewing plea bargaining from the perspective of civil law has a second advantage: it suggests the empirical basis of the process. The study of the legal system must not be content merely with pointing out the deviations between the ideal and the real.[23] It must try instead to explain why these "deviations" occur. An empirically based view of plea bargaining as a dispute-settling device is better able to explain this process than the normative model of criminal law that stresses the ideal of the trial.

---

[22] Reiss and Bordua have suggested the utility of a civil law model for analyzing criminal law. Reiss & Bordua, "Environment and Organization," in David Bordua, ed., *The Police* (John Wiley, 1967), p. 30.

[23] Jerome Skolnick, *Justice Without Trial* (John Wiley, 1967), p. 26.

CHAPTER 10   Juries: Amateurs in Criminal Justice

Jury trials are the opposite side of the coin to plea bargaining. Since there are few bench trials in Prairie City, the real choice on guilt is the decision to go to trial or plead out the case. Unfortunately, this crucial aspect of juries has been little researched. Past studies of juries have concentrated on the internal workings of juries, or juries in controversial cases that had extensive pre-trial publicity. Erlanger argues that we need a "broader perspective" on jury research, particularly the use of juries. He suggests a start by considering "the jury as part of a system of interrelated institutions and practices concerned with adjudication and try to define the role of the jury in the system." [1] A question of particular interest in analyzing juries in Prairie City is:

> What is the role of the jury in a system in which the overwhelming majority of criminal trials are dealt with by negotiated plea? Does a different type of case come to trial? Do outcomes differ? How is the jury perceived by the various participants in the two systems? [2]

Erlanger also identifies a widespread variation in the use of juries.[3] Although he stresses a regional variation, variations in jury trials are also found within states. For example, in one Illinois circuit twenty-three percent of the felony cases were decided by jury trials while in another only four percent were decided in that way.[4] It is presumptive that such variations are related to the role of the jury in the system.

---

[1] Howard Erlanger, "Jury Research in America: Its Past and Future," *Law and Society Review*, 1970, 4: 357.

[2] Ibid., p. 358.

[3] Ibid., p. 357.

[4] Administrative Office of the Illinois Courts, *1967 Annual Report to the Supreme Court of Illinois* (Springfield, Illinois), p. 55.

Our examination of Prairie City cannot answer all the questions suggested by Erlanger, but, hopefully, it can begin the accumulation of data that can answer some of these broader concerns. Our discussion has already indicated that the anticipated reactions of juries plays a major role in plea bargaining. This chapter considers additional features of jury trials: the participants' perceptions of juries; the amateur element that they introduce; and why some cases go to trial but others do not. Let us begin with a brief discussion of jury selection.

Jury Selection

In Prairie City potential jurors are randomly selected from the voter-registration rolls. The potential juror receives instructions to report to the county courthouse on a given day. Certain classes of persons are exempt from jury duty—notably school teachers, clergy, lawyers, and other miscellaneous groups. On the appointed day other potential jurors may indicate that it would be a hardship to serve because of their job, transportation difficulties, illness in the family, and so on. After excusing some from jury service, the chief judge lectures the potential jurors on their duties and responsibilities.

Next, a given number of jurors (usually twenty-four) are sent to the courtrooms where trials are scheduled. Each juror is assigned a number and the court clerk randomly selects twelve names for the jury panel. The voir dire, or the questioning of the jurors, follows. Prosecution and defense question the potential jurors to insure that they have an open mind and are not prejudiced either by prior knowledge of the case or through personal acquaintanceship with any of the persons involved. Each side may challenge a juror, that is, excuse him. Challenges may be for cause (which requires an explanation) or through a peremptory challenge (which do not require an explanation). In a peremptory challenge one side says the state (or the defendant) wishes to excuse Mr. Sampson. Each side is allowed ten peremptory challenges. The defense, in particular, uses its questioning to educate the jurors on the concept of innocent until proven guilty.

Jury selection is an imperfect art rather than an exact science. Lawyers have a mental image of the types of persons most likely to be responsive to their side. Although each side attempts to get jurors that will be favorable, virtually every attorney can point to examples where the opposite result occurred.

From the jurors' perspective, jury duty and the selection

process involve great delay. A week of jury duty may result in the hearing of only one case. The rest of the time the jurors may simply wait. For example, if a juror is challenged, or if he is near the end of the list and not called at all, he is told to return to the main courtroom to await reassignment. Even after being selected to sit on a jury, the juror may hear or see little action. The trial may involve numerous challenges, which are heard by the judge while the jury is removed from the courtroom. Or the jury panel may be selected and sworn only to have the defendant plead guilty, or to have the case fall through for some other reason. Such delays usually are focused on the judge, for the judge will have to face a room full of citizens who have been called to serve the ends of justice, not expecting that such service entails more waiting than deciding.

The Prosecutors' Views of Jury Trials

In discussing jury trials, prosecutors stress the drawbacks of taking a case to trial. Their primary objective is securing a guilty verdict. Viewed from this perspective, jury trials are liabilities because the state must assume a difficult burden of proof. One prosecutor commented, not wholly in jest, "We're interested in everyone pleading guilty. With a plea we can't lose, but we have to caution ourselves not to make too good of a deal." Several major, and some minor, drawbacks of jury trials were mentioned: the time element; technical problems; problems with witnesses and the unpredictability of juries.

From the prosecutors' perspective, one disability of a jury trial is the amount of time consumed. A normal trial lasts two or three days. Preparation time may be as lengthy. In sum, the state's attorney's office does not believe that they could try many more cases than they presently do. The pressure of caseloads must be placed in perspective, however. A number of commentaries have stressed that large caseloads lead to pressures to plead cases out. But in Prairie City the press of cases is considered a minor element relating to why cases are pled out. In their view, plea bargaining is simply the way things are done; it is an acceptable element in the practice of criminal law.

A second perceived disability of jury trials, which also must be labeled relatively minor, relates to technical problems that arise from the conduct of the trial itself. For example, an appellate court may reverse a conviction and order a new trial. Retrials may be particularly time-consuming. When one case was reversed a year and a half after the initial trial, the prosecutors had to locate uncooperative witnesses in Florida, and even Viet Nam, and make arrangements for their return. If the defendant pleads guilty the possibility of a retrial is removed. Another technical problem arises from the possibility of a mistrial. A misphrased question, a witness's overelaboration, or the prosecution approaching the borderline on inadmissible evidence may result in a mistrial. If the judge declares a mistrial, then the process must begin anew the following month, tying up additional time. Two illustrations should clarify the point. One drunk driving case went to trial three times. The judge declared a mistrial the first two times, and the third time the jury was hung (could not reach a verdict). At that point, the prosecutor pled the case out, not wishing to invest any more time in it. Another illustration involved a defense attorney who was particularly skilled at getting a mistrial declared. As one prosecutor put it, "If you can get his cases to the jury, you're alright, it's just hard to get to the jury with him." Such technical problems with a jury trial are avoided, of course, if the defendant pleads guilty.

By far the most critical drawback of jury trials, from the prosecutor's perspective, are problems with witnesses. A major concern to the prosecutor are "poor, inarticulate, biased, or uncooperative witnesses." In some cases the battery victim refuses to testify, or the mother may refuse to let her daughter testify in a rape case. Prosecutors continually talk in terms of what kind of witness a victim will make. For example, pretrial interviews include notations as to whether the complainant will make a good, fair, or bad witness. Prosecutors examine not only lay witnesses but also police officers to see how convincing they will be to a jury. Police officers are the state's most consistent supply of witnesses and, therefore, are closely evaluated. Officers who are too soft-spoken or too belligerent alienate jurors. For this reason, the prosecutor evaluates the effectiveness of an officer's trial appearances. After a rookie testified in a misdemeanor trial, a prosecutor remarked, "He made a darn good witness. Even if this was only a minor case, it's good to know that you can count on him in a big case to be an effective witness."

The persuasiveness of a witness is only one consideration. Another is the changing story, or the surprise on the witness stand. An assistant was discussing his first felony trial involving an aggravated battery case that supposedly had been adequately researched. During the trial, however, a major surprise developed. The victim was asked what she was doing just prior to being shot. She replied, "I was rushing at him with a knife in my hand."

Somehow, this crucial aspect of the "victim's" conduct had not been relayed to the prosecution.

The final drawback of juries are the jurors themselves. Jurors are amateurs in the criminal business and, hence, somewhat unpredictable. The consensus among the prosecutors is that in big cases you do not have to worry, jurors will return guilty verdicts. But in less serious matters, juries are more likely to return not guilty verdicts. An example of such unpredictability came in a narcotics case when two little old ladies announced during jury deliberations that "only God can judge" and refused to vote, thus hanging the jury. Another grandmother type, after a not guilty verdict, put her arm around the defendant and said, "Bob, we were sure happy to find you not guilty, but don't do it again." Such elements of unpredictable behavior by the laity add uncertainty to the process, an uncertainty that is usually removed through plea bargaining.

Trial hazards are part of the prosecutors' folklore in Prairie City. Technical hazards, problems with witnesses, and the vagaries of laity are among the hazards of going to trial. But the uncertainties of jurors and the perils of jury trials must be placed in proper context. Young state's attorneys want trials. As one commented, "I came here to try cases and that is what I want to do." Young prosecutors are eager for trial experience and do take weak cases to trial just for the experience.

Defense Counsels' Views on Jury Trials

When contemplating a jury trial a major concern of the attorney is whether the defendant's story is believable. To sell a jury, a story must be plausible. One lawyer claimed that some clients come up with "half-baked" stories that juries cannot believe, and so the defendant is found guilty. If the defendant's story sounds unreasonable, the jury will probably reject it. The plausibility of a defendant's story presents particularly difficult problems for the public defender. Although both private and appointive counsel have problems managing certain types of clients, the public defender's problems are more acute because he has less leverage with his client.[5] For one thing, he cannot threaten to withdraw or say to the client, "You've paid me for my judgement and expertise, now take it." Added to this is the sensitivity to charges that public defenders sell out or do not conduct a vigorous defense.

---

[5] Jerome Skolnick, "Social Control in the Adversary Process," *Journal of Conflict Resolution*, 1967, 11: 65.

Thus the public defender is less able to talk his client out of an implausible story.

When asked if clients ever force attorneys to trial even though counsel feels the client's story is implausible or dishonest, attorneys said this happens only occasionally. One public defender, however, reported trying an armed robbery case where the defendant's story was that "he was looking at his shoelaces the whole time." The defendant was found guilty. The attorneys' stance in such instances is not a comfortable one. This particular attorney believed that if a defendant wants to make a fool of himself that is his business.

A defense attorney in considering a jury trial must also be highly conscious of the probability of a much more severe penalty if the jury returns a guilty verdict. When asked if there was a penalty for defendants demanding a jury trial, one defense counsel's first reaction was an incredulous look and then the following statement:

> No question there is a harsher penalty if there is no plea. An unwritten rule of practice here is that if you go on trial and lose, there will be a harsher penalty. Maybe in one case in 500 there will be an exception and the defendant will get the same after the trial as he would have with a plea. Otherwise, the penalty is always more.

Statistics bearing this out are not hard to come by. During 1968, fifteen juries returned a guilty verdict and none of these defendants received probation. Furthermore, fourteen out of the fifteen received minimum jail terms of two years or more. By contrast the minimum for defendants who plead guilty is one year. We can illustrate the penalty for demanding a jury trial by examining three cases where we can compare the state's sentence recommendation on a plea and the penalty after jury trial. In one burglary case, the defendant had a prior conviction and the state offered three to twenty years on a plea. After the jury verdict he received fifteen to fifty years. In two robbery cases the state offered two to ten years on a plea. After the verdict one defendant received twelve to twenty years and the other fifteen to thirty years. These three examples put flesh on the statistical skeleton; defendants in Prairie City can expect a harsher penalty if they are found guilty at trial.

Prosecutors express the view that the penalty for a jury trial is not punishment for a defendant exercising his rights but for compounding the crime. They try to convey the idea that if the state has a good, provable case and is forced to trial, or if the defendant lies on the stand, then he has compounded the crime. The state claims that the penalty for a jury trial is not for the exercise of constitutional rights, but rather to discourage the defendant from hoping a rabbit will come out of the hat at the last moment. A University Towns' prosecutor expressed the same thoughts. "There is no higher penalty for exercising the right to trial," he said, "but if a defendant testifies falsely, or gets witnesses to misrepresent [the truth] then the state seeks a higher penalty."

Defense attorneys vary in their evaluations of the jury-trial penalty. One thought that in the long run it works to the advantage of the defendant, believing that it did not force the innocent to plead guilty, but encouraged the guilty to plead. In his view the guilty are better off with a light sentence rather than risking a higher penalty. Most defense counsels, however, disagreed because the trial penalty resulted in exorbitant sentences. They believe there should be one appropriate penalty whether this is a trial or not. One attorney conceded the obvious, however: if there was one set penalty there would be more trials.

In analyzing the penalty for jury trials, one must also consider the role of the judge for the jury-trial penalty is dependent on the judge. In actuality, the penalty for a jury trial stems from a lack of agreement between counsel. Lacking an agreement, each side makes a recommendation. One attorney wryly commented, "This amounts to me arguing for probation and the state asking for five to fifteen years, and the judge choosing." Thus the result is the penalty the judge thinks proper, because he is not bound by any agreement between the lawyers.

In Prairie City, this invariably means a high penalty. The judges have the power to go along with a penalty for jury trial or not. In Prairie City they do because they agree with it. One judge said, "If the defendant does it the hard way [an interesting term for a jury trial], then he gets the extreme: acquittal or a higher penalty. You cannot penalize a defendant who wants a jury trial but can measure his attitude, especially if the defendant lies." Some add that the defendant's failure to plead guilty indicates that he did something wrong. Thus, the judges in Prairie City go along with the harsher penalty for jury trial, partly because they believe in it and partly because their view of a proper penalty is higher than the defense's and, in some instances, the prosecution's.

The Amateur Element of Juries

Earlier we discussed the effect trials have on the standards of proof used in plea bargaining. In this sense, trials serve to reinforce these professional standards of proof. Trials affect plea bargaining in another important way, by establishing boundaries on what actions are punishable. Juries are amateurs in the criminal justice process and their standards may diverge from the yardsticks embodied in legislative prohibitions. A defense attorney made this point by distinguishing between a strong case and a winning case. The state may have a strong case and sufficient evidence to prove the defendant committed the act, but still not have a winning case because a jury would not convict. He cited a hypothetical example of an eighteen-year-old charged with a sex crime, but love was involved. The evidence might be open and shut, but it is doubtful that a jury would convict.

Prosecutors are well aware of the distinction between a strong case and a winning one. Some types of cases are viewed as hard to sell to juries. Besides sex cases, they mentioned barroom brawls and drunk driving. The latter is of particular interest because of the large number of accidents involving drunken drivers. Jurors, however, generally view drunk-driving arrests as cases of "there but for the grace of God go I." Unless there has been a serious accident or injuries, jurors are very hesitant to convict. As a result, the state prefers to reduce the drunk-driving cases to reckless driving rather than to try them. Juries thus temper the formal law with a "commonsense" view of law enforcement. In University Towns, juries are said to be very reluctant to convict student marijuana users. Juries are also viewed as sympathizing with the young.

There are other types of cases where jurors would be inclined in the opposite direction. Consider, for example, a case in which the treasurer of a crippled children's charity embezzled thousands of dollars. One can imagine the indignation in the jury room when the jurors discussed those poor kids whose money was stolen. The case did not go to trial.

The jurors' probable reaction to a case is a critical consideration during plea bargaining. Thus the effects of jury trial must be measured not only by the impact on a specific case (did they convict or not?) but also by the effect it has on similar cases at a later point. Prosecutors have long memories of cases that produced extensive jury deliberations. As one prosecutor said while discussing a case with a colleague, "A year ago we had a case like this and the jury was out for over seven hours." Prosecutors like fifteen-minute jury deliberations (time enough to choose a foreman and take one vote for conviction). It is in this way that a few jury verdicts set the parameters for the disposition of future cases.

Why Cases Go to Trial

The American system of criminal justice is premised on a trial; but a variety of factors have made trials relatively rare events. The system has developed patterns that produce pretrial agreement in the vast majority of cases. From this perspective, trials represent an inability to reach agreement. Several factors relate to the inability to reach agreement: a fact dispute; the defendant's past activity, unrelated to the particular case; the seriousness of the offense; and the defendant's "irrational demands" for a trial. In discussing which cases go to trial, we will consider each of these tangible factors, as well as a less tangible factor of credibility maintenance.

Some cases present a real fact dispute. Two sets of witnesses may produce different versions of the event, or the evidence may be so circumstantial that what happened may be unclear. When there is such a fact dispute, cases are more likely to go to trial. For example, one prosecutor commenting on one such case said, "This type of case should go to trial." For the professionals, the function of the jury is to resolve such disputes, which obviates the need for them to settle it. We have already mentioned that defense will recommend a trial when evidence is weak. These two factors may be interrelated. Table 15 showed that a disproportionate number of sex and battery cases go to trial, and we reasoned that proof problems account for this. Thus, cases involving weak evidence and/or a real fact dispute are much more likely to go to trial in Prairie City.

The defendant's background plays a marginal part in the state's decision to go to trial. In cases where evidence is weak the state may not want to accept a reduction to a misdeameanor because of the defendant's past actions. In their view, some defendants need to be taught a lesson so they know that they cannot get by with such activity. Defense attorneys say that prosecutors sometimes mention that they are "leaning on this fellow." For example, one trial for second offense petty theft involved two females with a reputation for repeated shoplifting who had only been convicted once. Although the state's case was weak (and became weaker during the trial), the prosecution did not want to settle for a small fine or a dismissal; a loss at trial was preferable to simply letting the two off. This way the state conveyed the message—we are after you.

By far the most important factor relating to which cases go to trial is the seriousness of the offense; the more serious the charge the more likely a jury trial. Returning to table 15, recall that in property crimes such as burglary, theft, or forgery a defendant rarely demanded a trial. By contrast, in serious crimes like murder or armed robbery, narcotics defendants were more likely to have a trial. This difference relates to the penalty involved. In minor cases the penalty will be light (usually probation for first offenders). Thus one is risking a lot to have a trial, for if found guilty the penalty will be higher. In more serious crimes, however, the defendant has less to lose by going to trial. He knows that if convicted he will receive a long prison term no matter what, so he is more likely to try for the acquittal.

Viewed from this perspective, the decision to go to trial involves a rough calculation on the part of the defendant and his attorney: What are the chances of winning? What penalty if we lose? What settlement if we plead? The seriousness of the offense tends to slant the decision toward a trial because the relative differences in penalties are lessened. An additional factor, closely related to the seriousness of the charge is a supect's past felony conviction. In the next chapter we will examine in greater depth the Prairie City norm that a defendant with a past conviction will not receive probation. If a prison term is a certainty upon conviction, defendants are less hesitant to try to secure the optimum— an acquittal.

The factors we have discussed up to this point—a fact dispute; the defendant's past conduct; the seriousness of the charge; past conviction—are viewed by the participants as legitimate considerations affecting the decision to go to trial. Indeed, with the exception of the prosecution's evaluation of the defendant's conduct outside of this particular case, they are all sanctioned, or at least based on legal considerations. But one additional factor— a suspect's insistence on trial no matter what the possible outcome—is not viewed in the same way. It is viewed as illegitimate. Participants label defendants as irrational who refuse to recognize the realities of the criminal justice system and insist on a trial even when the state has a very strong case. For example, one defendant with several previous felony convictions was charged with armed robbery of a Colonel Sanders' restaurant. He was arrested shortly after the incident, with the money, and a gun stuffed in a bag with the Colonel's picture on it. In addition eyewitnesses identified the defendant during a line-up. In short, the state had as strong a case as it was likely to have, yet when the defense attorney conveyed the state's recommendation on a plea, the defendant termed the offer "ridiculous" and demanded a trial. The system—prosecutors, judges, and defense attorneys— consider such defendants as malcontents who demand a trial no matter what the evidence.

In analyzing why cases go to trial, one additional factor— unrelated to the individual case, or the individual defendant— needs to be considered. Each side needs to maintain their credibility with the opposition. Over the long run, each side may be aided strategically by calling the other side's bluff and going to trial. As we have already indicated, a lawyer with a reputation as a good trial attorney is in a slightly better bargaining position with the opposition. Such long-term strategic considerations, however, are limited by the law's focus on the individual case. In particular, the defense attorney's long-term strategic considerations are limited by his ties to the client. The final decision, whether to plead guilty or go to trial, rests with the defendant. In turn, defense attorneys are well aware that they face no personal penalty if they attempt to alter the situation but their client does. The client faces a term in the state penitentiary. In addition, the state is in a more favorable position to act on its stategic considerations because the state can offer major concessions if the case is weak (and therefore the defense may desire a trial). By offering a good deal the state does not have to try cases it does not want to. It is difficult to point to any particular case where the prosecution was seeking to maximize its long-range position, but several comments pointed in this direction. During an interview a state's attorney commented that, "You can't let a defense attorney plead out every case. Once in awhile you have to a make them try one." Shoptalk among the prosecutors also showed that one law firm had been winning too many cases.

Conclusion

Richardson and Vines assert that "the frequency of jury trials is a measure of the strength of the democratic values in district [Federal] court decision making." [6] Although our analysis is of lower state courts, the factors involved are the same as in lower Federal courts. Our analysis of Prairie City suggests that equating jury trials with democratic values leaves out too much. Trials function within a criminal justice system. The role structure of the participants, the perceptions of jury trials, and the variety of factors relating to why cases go to trial all mediate between "democratic values" and jury trials in Prairie City.

It is crucial to stress that juries function mainly to introduce nonprofessional standards into the criminal justice process. Jurors look beyond the technical aspects of law and express commonsense viewpoints. Professionals can argue technical points among themselves but at some point they must relate these standards to the general public and the community. The ready availability of jury trials means that each side can appeal to the people whenever they think the jury will give them a better deal. For this reason prosecutors and defense attorneys must evaluate their cases in terms of juries' reactions. Juries thus set the boundaries of permissable prosecution and conviction.

Jurors' hesitancy to convict in certain types of cases is one way in which they set the boundaries of a system. Sex and battery crimes, plus drunk-driving cases are viewed as hard cases to sell juries. Juries also sympathize with certain classes of defendants, particularly the young. Certain victims of crimes, such as barroom brawls, also make cases difficult to sell juries. Jurors' reactions, however, do not always work to the defendant's advantage. We noted, for example, that the embezzler of funds for crippled children was not likely to evoke sympathy. Implausible stories from the defendant also are hard to sell juries. The participants carefully evaluate present cases in terms of past ones where juries have hesitated to convict or have not convicted at all. These anticipations are taken into account in decisions on current cases.

It is significant that in Prairie City the law-and-order movement has not greatly affected juries. Defense attorneys felt juries were reasonably fair. But defense attorneys in their opening and closing remarks were increasingly mentioning law and order in an attempt to nullify its impact. In their remarks they also stressed the hope that jurors would disregard national attention to crime and judge their client on the evidence in the specific case.

---

[6] Richard Richardson & Kenneth Vines, *The Politics of Federal Courts* (Little, Brown, 1970), p. 88.

Juries in Illinois are restrained somewhat by law from expressing law-and-order sentiments because they have no control over sentencing (except in recommending the death penalty). This differs from Texas, for example, where juries have been handing out 1,000-year sentences.[7]

A major consequence of introducing laity into decision making in criminal justice is an increase in unpredictability. Professionals, by working together, develop common frameworks, and in Prairie City at least, the parameters are widely known. Juries, however, represent a constantly changing element. We already mentioned that certain jurors were unpredictable. In a way, the professionals resent this intrusion into their domain. In this sense, the guilty plea functions to buffer the system against a great amount of uncertainty from dealing with the laity. It is doubtful that if all sixty burglary cases of 1968 had gone to trial (rather than just four) that all would have been found guilty. But predicting the few that would have been acquitted remains all but impossible. One attorney summed it up by saying, "I've told defendants that no jury will believe their outlandish story and yet occasionally they win an acquittal (but only occasionally). On the other hand I've lost cases that I thought surely I would win." The guilty plea functions then to buffer the system against the extremes of acquittal and a high penalty.

---

[7] "Big Stick in Big D," *Newsweek*, July 20, 1970, p. 59.

Sentencing: The Choice Between Prison or Probation

CHAPTER 11

The defendant's primary interest is the sentence. Although reformers usually focus their attention on the process—the setting of bail; appointment of counsel; plea bargaining; etc—the defendant is primarily concerned with the outcome, the likely sentence. In theory, society can impose various sanctions on wrongdoers that range from informal pressures (social displeasure or social ostracism) to corrective attempts (counseling, job training, or mental health treatment) to formal punishment (prison). In reality the options are much more limited; the court has only two choices: prison or probation. Although a variety of additional alternatives are being proposed—such as community-based correctional facilities—at present the choice is between returning the guilty to society and maintaining limited supervision (probation), or removing him from society and having maximum control (prison).

Sentencing is a graphic illustration of the fact that criminal justice is a sorting process. Some defendants are classified as prisoners and others are categorized as probationers. The aggregate effects of this sorting are shown in the docket study. The 248 defendants charged with a felony during 1968 were winnowed down to 151 who were found guilty of a felony. Those convicted were divided almost equally along the two paths: 75 were sentenced to prison, 76 were granted probation. This chapter examines how these decisions are made; who participates; and what criteria are used.

The Sentencing Hearing

Prison or probation is imposed officially at the sentencing hearing, which is held several weeks after the suspect has been found guilty. At the sentencing hearing the probation officer submits his report, which is called the pre-sentence investigation, and makes a recommendation as to whether probation should be granted or denied. In addition defense and prosecution have the opportunity to call witnesses, as well as to make recommendations of their own. After listening to the three parties, the judge imposes the sentence. As we have noted throughout this study, however, formal court proceedings, held in public, are only imperfect guides to the decision-making process, which usually is informal and often secret. The real decision between prison or probation occurs prior to the sentencing hearing. Thus the sentencing hearing functions largely to formalize the arrangements previously agreed upon.

The contrast between the formal rules and the informal norms is highlighted by the role of the judge in the sentencing hearing. Although only the judge possesses the legal power to impose sentence, in practice the effective decision is made by others. For example, the probation officer makes a recommendation to the court about whether a defendant, who has been found guilty, should be granted probation or not. The judge does not have to follow that recommendation, but he does. Thus the effective decision on probation is the probation officer's recommendation, not the judge's. The length of the prison term similarly is set by the prosecutor, not the judge. After probation has been denied the prosecutor makes a recommendation to the judge as to the length of the sentence, a recommendation that is invariably followed by the judge.[1]

But the critical consideration in sentencing is not the process by which sentences are imposed but the substance of the decisions —the criteria that are employed in sending some persons to prison but placing others on probation. Through practice a set of informal norms—what we may call rules of sentencing—have developed in Prairie City. These rules of sentencing are not derived from the statute books or appellate court decisions (although they are based on them to a limited extent) but stem from practice in the community. These rules of sentencing are known to all the participants, which enables them to make judgments about the likely outcome of the case. These informal norms make sentencing not only highly predictable but also consistent. Let us examine the probation and prison decisions, paying particular attention to the criteria used in making these decisions.

---

[1] Chapter 5 discusses the norms of the court community that produce the limited role of the judge.

Probation and the Probation Officer's Recommendation

After the defendant is found guilty, the probation officer prepares a presentence investigation. The presentence investigation, which is not explicitly authorized by statute, provides the judge with information on the defendant's background, possible mitigating circumstances involved in the crime, and the suspect's chances for successfully completing probation. Unlike some states, where the presentence report is available only to the judge, in Illinois the report is also given to the opposing attorneys who thus have an opportunity to comment on possible inaccuracies, as well as to assess the basis for the final recommendation.

Although this is a critical report, it is nonetheless brief, mainly because the probation office has limited facilities. The report is based on a short interview with the defendant, a meeting with the family in their home, and a scrutiny of official court records. To prepare these reports (about 300 per year involving both felony and misdemeanor cases) and to supervise roughly 250 probationers a year, the Prairie City probation office has only two full-time employees. The large work load and the small staff preclude a more thorough investigation. These limitations mean that the defendant's personal problems or possible mental deficiencies or psychiatric maladjustments are not examined in depth. They will be mentioned in the report only if those interviewed have raised the issue. The probation office does not have the staff or the background to investigate these matters independently.

The most important part of the presentence investigation is the probation officer's recommendation as to whether probation should be granted or denied. The statute book is the starting point for assessing why some defendants are denied probation and others are not. Illinois law provides that all defendants, except those convicted of murder, rape, or the sale of narcotics, are eligible for probation. (In 1971 the Illinois legislature added armed robbery to the exemption list.) The law also sets forth guidelines for granting probation. According to Chapter 38, Section 117 of the Illinois Revised Statutes, a defendant

> May be admitted to probation when it appears that:
>
> [1] The defendant is not likely to commit another offense;
> [2] The public interest does not require that the defendant receive the penalty provided for the offense, and;
> [3] the rehabilitation of the defendant does not require that he receive the penalty provided for the offense.

The law further provides that probation may range from a minimum of six months to a maximum of five years, and the probation period may be extended for an additional two years, on a showing of "good cause."

The criteria for admitting a person to probation are, at best, vague. Although the statutes provide general guidelines for deciding who does not have to be imprisoned, the categories are so broad that officials may interpret them in numerous ways. For example, probation is allowed when "the public interest" would be served. This does not qualify as a criterion. Politicians and others have debated for centuries what the public interest requires and have not arrived at a consensus.

Given the broadness of the legislative guidelines, informal rules of sentencing have developed in Prairie City to structure the sentencing decision. We can isolate three rules of sentencing that fill in the details of the legislature's broad statement that probation should be in the public interest. Three categories of defendants will be denied probation: those convicted at trial; those with a prior felony conviction; and those convicted of aggravated battery involving a deadly weapon. Let us look at each of these rules and see how they may differ in other jurisdictions.

Rule one holds that defendants convicted at trial will be denied probation. As discussed in the previous chapter, the court system in Prairie City penalizes those who demand a jury trial; a stiffer penalty is handed out to those found guilty at trial than to those who plead guilty. One type of penalty is the denial of probation. Of the seventeen defendants found guilty at trial during 1968 only one received probation. Significantly, the lone exception involved a bench trial, not a jury trial. Otherwise the system operates under an iron-clad rule: defendants convicted by a jury trial will not receive probation. We need, however, to place this rule in perspective because not all cases or defendants are equally likely to go to trial. As we have seen, defendants accused of a serious crime, or with a previous record or charged with battery are more likely to demand a jury trial. Since these are also independent factors in denying probation, the trial prohibition is not as overwhelming as might first appear.

A second sentencing rule deals with a defendant's past conduct: defendants with a prior felony conviction will be denied probation. The assumption is that the defendant had one opportunity and failed. Because probation was not successful in the past—as shown by the subsequent conviction—probation is not likely to work this time, so a prison sentence is in order. The data on the disposition of the 1968 felony defendants illustrates the impact of this sentencing rule. Of the thirty-three defendants with a previous record who were found guilty of a felony, only one received probation.

Denying probation to defendants who were previously convicted is similar to, but not necessarily identical with, practices in other jurisdictions. In Kansas, Milwaukee, and Michigan, for example, "The defendant's criminal record is one of the most important factors influencing the probation decision." [2] These practices mirror Prairie City. A study of Los Angeles, however, found a slightly different pattern in which the critical element was the "length of the rap sheet." That is, the longer the list of previous arrests and convictions, the less likely the defendant was to receive probation.[3] The difference is that in Prairie City a single previous conviction is sufficient to deny probation, whereas in Los Angeles a single previous conviction might not necessarily produce the same results.

The third sentencing rule in Prairie City relates to the seriousness of the offense. Although, in theory, probation looks only at the defendant's potential for rehabilitation, in practice a number of communities also consider the seriousness of the offense. Those convicted of a serious offense are not likely to receive probation no matter how good their prospects for successfully completing probation.[4] In Prairie City aggravated battery with a deadly weapon (such as a gun or knife) is viewed as very serious. As a result, a defendant convicted of aggravated battery involving the use of a deadly weapon is not recommended for probation.

Although most communities appear to operate under a similar rule—a defendant convicted of a very serious offense will not be granted probation—there are differences in the exact details. In the three states studied by the American Bar Foundation, the rule was that defendants who seriously injured another person would almost never receive probation.[5] In Prairie City, however, the seriousness of the injury to the victim is not considered.

Having examined the three major factors that deny proba-

---

[2] Robert Dawson, *Sentencing: The Decision as to Type, Length, and Conditions of Sentence* (Little, Brown, 1969), p. 81.

[3] Lynn Mather, "To Plead Guilty or Go to Trial?" Paper delivered at the Annual Meeting of the American Political Science Association, Washington, D.C., September 5-9, 1972, pp. 7-8.

[4] Dawson, *Sentencing*, p. 88.

[5] Ibid., p. 89.

tion to defendants in Prairie City, it is helpful to state the rules positively: young defendants (who are, therefore, unlikely to have a previous felony conviction) and/or those accused of common property crimes, normally qualify for probation. Defendants with these qualifications are normally placed on probation for one year (the usual probation period in Prairie City).

An important feature of the sentencing rules in Prairie City is that they are known to all the participants. Through years of working in the criminal justice system, the prosecutors, defense attorneys, and judges know who is likely to qualify for probation. Defense attorneys estimated that they can predict the probation officer's recommendations ninety-five percent of the time. Similarly, one state's attorney commented, "Our assessment of the defendant is usually right down the line with the probation officer's report." Since the norms of who will qualify for probation are well known, each of the participants can make accurate predictions about the particular defendant's chances of qualifying.

The results of these recommendations also are predictable. As table 18 shows, the court follows the probation officer's recommendation ninety-five percent of the time. The judge never denies probation if it has been recommended. He will, on rare occasions, grant probation even though the probation officer has recommended that the defendant is unlikely to complete probation successfully.

The close congruity between the recommendations and the court's determination is no accident. In the first place, the court appoints the probation officer. Second, the chief judge discusses the recommendations with the probation officer before the court appearance. Chapter 5 illustrated that the chief judge does

TABLE 18

THE COURT FOLLOWS THE RECOMMENDATIONS
OF THE PROBATION OFFICER—1968

Probation Officer's Report	Court Action		
Probation recommended	Probation granted	84	(64%)
Probation recommended	Probation denied	0	
Probation not recommended	Probation denied	41	(31%)
Probation not recommended	Probation granted	6	(5%)
		131	

not hesitate to indicate when he thinks a defendant is not a fit candidate for probation, although the probation officer had recommended against a prison sentence. Thus the chief judge informally can affect the nature of the probation officer's determination. While the probation officer is tied formally and informally to the chief judge, he is independent if for no other reason than his over twenty years on the job. His position of independence is further supported by what one defense attorney termed his level-headed approach to the job.

Having examined the criteria used in Prairie City for placing defendants on probation, we should also mention the limitations placed on probationers. As a condition of probation, the court places a number of restrictions on the person, including periodic meetings with the probation officer, holding a job, staying out of places where alcoholic beverages are sold and, most importantly, not breaking the law again. If the conditions of probation are not met, the court may revoke probation and send the person to prison. If a violation of probation is alleged, the court holds a hearing. Although the defendant has certain rights at a hearing to revoke probation, the state's burden of proof in showing a violation is less than it would be if the suspect were tried for the same offense. Thus, if a suspect on probation is arrested for another felony, the usual practice is to revoke probation rather than attempt the more difficult task of trying the new case.

Prison Terms and the Prosecutor's Sentence Recommendations

The key consideration for defendants who are denied probation is the length of the prison term. As with qualifying for probation, the court system in Prairie City operates under a number of well-known, but informal, rules governing the length of the prison term. But before considering these informal working rules, it is best to discuss their basis in the law.

Illinois utilizes indeterminate sentences. The judge imposes a range of years, but the exact time served is determined by the Department of Corrections. Thus, if a defendant is sentenced to prison for one to ten years, the Department of Corrections might release him after one year (the minimum) or after ten years (the maximum) or sometime in between. While the statute books set the range of potential prison terms, they do not provide even minimal criteria for guiding the application of that pattern. By contrast, the legislature has enacted guidelines—albeit vague ones—for determining who should be placed on probation, but in sentencing no criteria are set forth. Thus local officials must fill in the blanks, unaided by even minimal criteria provided by the legislature or even appellate courts.

The amount of time a suspect serves in prison is determined not only by the range of years specified by the judge, but also by the rules of the Department of Corrections. Convicts who behave themselves in prison and adhere to the rules are rewarded with a reduction in sentence. This is officially known as "good time." If a prisoner qualifies for good time he will be released after eleven months on a one-year sentence. On a two-year sentence, he receives a three-month reduction, and so on. In addition to the good time schedule the Illinois Pardon and Parole board normally releases prisoners near the minimum of the sentence imposed. Thus a prison sentence of one to ten years effectively means eleven months, if the defendant conforms to prison rules.

In setting the prison sentence within the range allowed by the statutes, the key figure is the prosecutor. At the sentencing hearing the prosecutor will make a recommendation to the judge, a recommendation that is invariably followed. In turn, the prosecutor's recommendation is based on well-established policies of normal or modal penalties for a given offense.[6] In a forgery case the usual recommendation is one to five years; in burglary one to ten; and in armed robbery two to ten. There may be an upward valuation if the defendant has a long previous record, or if the crime is viewed as particularly heinous.

Negotiations over sentence proceed from these modal penalties. Defense attorneys know, almost without asking, what the prosecutor will recommend for a prison term, if the defendant pleads guilty and does not receive probation. The prosecutor's initial offer on sentence derives from a monthly meeting of the felony assistants and the state's attorney. Each case is reviewed, assigned to a particular attorney, and an initial offer arrived at. In most instances the initial offer is the model penalty for that crime. Although the meeting allows for an exchange of views on the proper sentence, there is seldom any discussion, a reflection that the policy on proper sentences is well known.

The defense attorney's response to the initial offer depends on

---

[6] The concept of the normal crime is derived from David Sudnow, "Normal Crimes: Sociological Features of the Penal Code in a Public Defender Office," *Social Problems* (1965), 12: 255. Lynn Mather reported similar findings: "To Plead Guilty, or Go to Trial?" Annual Meeting of the American Political Science Association, Washington, D.C., September 5–9, 1972.

the type of client involved. In most instances the defense attorney's primary goal is negotiating a low minimum sentence since the minimum is the effective amount of time most defendants serve. In some instances, though, the defense attorney's primary goal is negotiating a lower maximum penalty. In particular, if the suspect has a lengthy prior record, or is the type likely to have trouble in prison, the maximum penalty more accurately reflects the amount of time he will have to serve. In these cases the defense attorney will try to negotiate a lower maximum.

The concept of the modal penalty reduces bargaining over the sentence. In most cases, the prosecutor's initial offer is the one that is agreed to eventually, because the state's initial offer usually involves a one-year minimum, the primary goal of the defense attorney. The only types of cases where the participants engage in extensive negotiations are serious crimes such as murder or rape for which the minimum and maximum sentences are high. If the defense attorney believes the prosecutor is asking for too much, he can threaten to go to trial. In one case, for example, the state initially recommended a twenty-year-to-life penalty on a murder charge. The defense attorney argued that his client had participated, but unknowingly, in the murder and had not been involved in pulling the trigger. After extensive negotiations, the state agreed to accept a plea to voluntary manslaughter and recommended seven to twenty years. It is only in the most serious offenses, however, that the attorneys engage in extensive sentence negotiations.

The well-internalized norms of proper sentencing have as a prime advantage that they insure consistency. As one lawyer observed, "Sentences in this city are uniform. Consistency is taken into account and identical facts and identical past records draw the same sentence." He pointed to other counties, however, where there was no such consistency. The stress on uniformity is so well-internalized by all participants that defense counsel can use a deviation from the norm as a bargaining point. If a sentence recommendation is higher than normal, then defense counsel can use this deviation as a bargaining point to get his client what other defendants obtained. For example, one attorney stated that a particular assistant had been making slightly higher sentence recommendations than past assistants. This resulted in more negotiations over the proper sentence. To quote him, "the results are the same but there is more mickey mouse in getting the recommendation that other assistants would have begun with." Thus

the norms of uniform sentencing in Prairie City prevented a sin-
,gle assistant prosecutor from increasing prison sentence recommendations.

It is important to specify the sentencing agreement produced
by plea bargaining. The key phrase is "plea and apply," which
means that the defendant will plead guilty to the offense agreed
to. In return, the prosecutor agrees to support the probation officer's recommendation. Although neither side can definitely say
what this recommendation will be, past practices make them virtually certain what the recommendation will be. The prosecutor's
agreement in advance to support the probation officer's recommendation of probation virtually assures that it will be granted.
For if the probation officer recommends probation and the prosecutor concurs, naturally the defense attorney assents as well, and
the judge is unlikely to disagree. In a limited number of cases,
however, the prosecutor indicates he will not concur in the probation officer's report recommendation for probation. The substantive impact of this refusal to concur is minimal, however, for
in these cases the defendant has a long previous record and/or
has committed a serious offense and, therefore, is unlikely to
qualify for probation.

The phrase "plea and apply" involves a fine line between prob-
abilistic assessments and firm promises. This fine line is necessi-
tated by the division of power in the sentencing process. In accepting a plea the prosecutor cannot be opposed by the judge, but
in making a sentence recommendation he can be. It is considered
within the prosecutor's domain to accept a plea to a misdemeanor
or a less serious felony. In this area the prosecutor can promise
and deliver; but this is not so in sentencing. In sentencing only
the judge has the power to impose the sentence. Thus an agreement over sentence, negotiated between defense and prosecutor,
must be more circumspect than an agreement on the crime to
which the suspect will plead. Although the prosecutor cannot
assure that his side of the bargain will be adhered to, past practices of the court make it highly likely. Nonetheless, the agreement on sentencing is more limited than a similar agreement on
the charge.

When the Defense Counsel Attempts to Alter
the Rules of Sentencing

In Prairie City the informal norms on sentencing are stable
but not static. In particular the defense attorneys disagree with
the almost automatic denials of probation for defendants con-

victed of using a deadly weapon in an aggravated battery case. They believe this blanket prohibition is unfair and have used the probation hearing to challenge the rule. During the period of study four cases illustrated this attempt to have the rules changed. All four cases involved violence and the use of a deadly weapon. In each case the probation officer's testimony was virtually the same: he had recommended against probation because a deadly weapon was involved. It is somewhat anomalous that on occasion defendants convicted of armed robbery in Prairie City do get probation, but in aggravated battery cases with a weapon they do not. Let us examine the four cases where the norm was challenged.

Of the four cases, two were manslaughter and two were aggravated battery. But an examination of the events indicate that all four of the cases could have been manslaughter, or all four could have been aggravated battery. The only difference was that in two cases the victim survived the attack. For example in the Jones case, the defendant admitted aiming the gun "right between the eyes." The shot, however, just grazed the victim. In this and the other three cases similar types of abrasive relationships between the defendant and the victim were involved. Ill feelings between the defendant and the victim had been smouldering for a long time and, in each instance, some spark led to the confrontation. In each case a weapon was readily available. One other point of similarity should also be stated—none of the defendants had a prior felony record and all were generally model citizens except for the particular event.

During the probation hearings, the defense counsels called witnesses to document their central thesis—their defendant was a good citizen. In Mrs. Anderson's case, the point was made that she had worked at the same job for nineteen years, had never been in trouble, and had raised a family despite the alcoholic, abusive, and violence-prone husband from whom she was divorced. She had killed her ex-husband as he was attempting to steal tires from her car. The shot had been fired at long range and Mrs. Anderson had never believed the gun would hit the target. The other three defendants had similarly enviable records. Two had good, steady jobs and were raising families. The final defendant had a slightly blemished record but still came close to the ideal. In all four cases, the defense attorneys stressed that the defendants, except for this one act, had lived exemplary lives. One judge even conceded this point. Smith had been found guilty of knifing his brother-in-law. The judge commented that all the evidence indicated that he was a model citizen and did not need probation because probation was designed to rehabilitate the defendant. This defendant was already rehabilitated. He did not need rehabilitation, only punishment.

Besides stressing that their clients were model citizens, defense attorneys also argued that probation should be granted because there was little likelihood a future violation of the law would result. One standard for granting probation is the likelihood that the person will successfully complete the conditions of probation and not commit any future wrong. Attorneys felt this condition was met because the crime in question had been caused by an unusual, incendiary event that was not likely to reoccur.

Another argument advanced during the probation hearing was that it was not in society's best interest to impose a penitentiary term because it would only remove a steady worker from society and create great hardships upon the family involved. In some instances, a prison term would mean that the family would have to go on welfare.

Judges and prosecutors viewed these offenses from a decidedly different perspective. Whereas the defense counsel understandably looked at the case from the micro level of their client, judges and prosecutors proceeded from the macro level of society in general. As one judge put it, "A stab in the back is one of the most reprehensible acts in society," and the job of a judge was to demonstrate to the defendant that society would not tolerate such conduct. The chief judge commented in one case that "All society would be outraged if probation was granted in this type of case." The state's attorney's arguments perhaps best summarized the thinking of these participants. He stated that rehabilitation was a consideration in deciding whether to grant probation, but it was only one consideration. Punishment was also needed to deter others from committing similar acts.

These four cases point up the contrasting views on the proper place of probation in the criminal justice system. Defense attorneys argued that the rules be altered. The only striking outcome of these cases was the one in which the defendant was granted probation. The fact that Jones was put on probation was viewed as adding a new dimension to sentencing in Prairie City. However, even during the next week, it did not serve as a precedent for sentencing in the Smith case, which was virtually identical to the Jones case, but was decided by a different judge. The judge mentioned the Jones case but refused to be governed by it and imposed a prison sentence.

The defense attorneys strongly disagreed with the decisions in these four cases. Their disagreement should indicate that defense attorneys are not co-opted into the system and are not unwilling to challenge the major outlines of policy as some critics of defense attorneys have contended. The conditions under which they moved to alter the norms are also instructive. Defense attorneys were not arguing for a blanket change in the norm of denying probation to defendants convicted of using a deadly weapon in an aggravated battery case. Such a tactic would have met with little success. Rather, they felt these cases represented legitimate exceptions. As one lawyer put it, "If there ever was a case involving a death and the defendant should have received probation, that case was Mrs. Anderson's, nineteen years at the same job, and two teen-age daughters and yet she was sent to prison."

Conclusion

During plea bargaining the focus shifts from what the defendant did (guilt adjudication) to what to do with the defendant (sentencing considerations). Although the sentencing hearing is the final step in the case (excepting an appeal to the appellate courts) anticipation of this decision permeates the entire process.

We can best illustrate the importance of such expectations— as well as show the multiple dimensions involved—by viewing the process through the eyes of the defense attorney. He defines his task as obtaining the best possible outcome for his client given the constraints of the system. As was pointed out in Chapter Four, the lawyer approaches his job by asking, "Given the situation, what is the best that can be done for my client?" Here the lawyer is performing a counseling role for the client who is, of course, most concerned with the outcome. For example, in deciding whether to plead guilty or go to trial, the defendant is interested in the penalty if he pleads guilty and whether he will receive probation or not. In answering this question the lawyer must consider the following: in the past, have defendants with similar backgrounds been placed on probation? If probation is denied, what is the likely prison term? If the defendant is found guilty at trial, what will be the penalty? The system usually provides predictable answers to these and similar questions.

Probation is one of the most critical dimensions in the allocation of justice. In Prairie City, at least, the decision is made on the basis of well-known, but informal, standards. Participants can predict with a high degree of accuracy who will qualify for probation and who will not. Defendants convicted at a jury trial, those found guilty of aggravated battery where a deadly weapon was used, and suspects with a previous felony conviction normally are denied probation. On the other hand, first offenders charged with property crimes are admitted to probation almost automatically. Decisions on prison terms also are predictable. All participants agree that every effort is made to assure that defendants with similar backgrounds and who have committed similar crimes will receive identical prison sentences. The exact range of the prison term is determined primarily by the offense. For each offense there is a commonly accepted penalty.

The widely known informal rules on sentencing account for the largely routine nature of the sentencing hearing. Although only the judge can impose the sentence, through custom, supported by social sanctions, the judge defers to the recommendations of the probation officer and the prosecutor. The judge's sentencing power is limited to rare instances where recommendations are rejected or to sentences imposed after a jury trial. Since a finding of guilt at trial does not involve the prosecutor's prior commitment on sentence, the judge has more leeway in this area. Similarly, the defense attorney must play a largely reactive role in sentencing. His main bargaining points are consistency and the threat to go to trial. When these elements are removed, the defense attorney has little opportunity to negotiate a lower sentence, except in a case where the prosecutor may have difficulty winning at trial. Although defense attorneys have relatively little leverage on this key point, they are still able to achieve their major objectives. Defense attorneys want particularly to secure a low minimum for their clients if they are sent to prison and this usually is obtained.

CHAPTER 12 **An**

Assessment

This study was based on the simple notion that ours is a government of law *and* of men. The difference between the law of
the statute book and court precedents, and the living law—law in
action—are the officials who apply the law. The law is much like
the stage of a theater since it provides boundaries for the actors.
And, it is somewhat like the script of the play because it provides
the parts. But it is unlike the script because the dialogue is not
predetermined. The law creates a decision-making apparatus and
provides cues for the actors to make these decisions, but still
leaves ample opportunity for these officials to decide on the basis
of their discretion, judgment, reasoned opinion, or even prejudice.
We have argued that this is the politics of the administration of
justice. It is not necessarily, but in some cases resembles, electoral
politics. Instead, it is political because it allocates justice.

But, in stressing the importance of the legal actors who make
the decisions, we must not make the mistake that some others
have and assume that the actions of the officials are unbounded
or that discretion explains most. On the contrary, the process is
not random. It is rather that the actors develop informal policies
and norms that guide action: their working relations forge
bounds of trust and respect, or of tension and suspicion.

As a shorthand, we have termed these factors the social network, the social network that underlies the formal law. In summarizing our major findings about this social network and the
type of justice it produces in Prairie City it may be helpful to
return to the five questions developed in Chapter One: 1] Who
makes the decisions? 2] What standards are employed in making
these decisions? 3] How do the decision makers interact? 4] How
are the rights of the defendant protected? and 5] Who benefits
from this process?

By concentrating on these five questions we felt we could weld
the steps of the criminal justice process into an overall perspec-

tive. Although the participants work in steps (charging decision, plea bargaining, jury trial, etc.), they do not compartmentalize their thinking in these categories. Rather, the decisions made at one point are made with an eye to their impact at a later time.

Who Makes the Decisions?

As we have argued throughout this study, the formal definitions of power are not always useful guides to the exercise of that power. In some instances power delegated to one official has been usurped by the actions of another. In other instances the grant of power is notably ambiguous, which means that one actor may exercise more power than the law stipulates. By far the most important actor in Prairie City is the prosecutor. It is the state's attorney who decides which suspects will be charged with a crime; dominates the preliminary hearing and grand jury; conducts plea bargaining; and has a large say in the penalty enacted upon the guilty party. Notice, however, that while the prosecutor is the dominant official in most areas of law enforcement, in certain areas, particularly the setting of bail and the interpretation of Supreme Court decisions, the prosecutor plays only a minor role.

Second in importance to the prosecutor is the defense attorney. The defense attorney mediates between his client and the law. This mediation, while simple in theory, involves the defense attorney in several ambiguous relationships. He must work with the prosecutor in the sense that the bulk of his actual work is conducted with him. At the same time, however, his primary tie is to his client. The client's perceptions do not always agree with those of his attorney and in such a situation serious tensions may develop. The defense attorney on the whole views his task as mediator, trying to secure for his client the most desirable alternative given the working reality of the court, which is that acquittals are unlikely. Thus success is not defined in terms of winning or losing, but rather in terms of negotiating a settlement at the lowest end of the scale.

The judge is the most indirect decision maker in the Prairie City courts. Although in legal theory he possesses a great deal of power, in actuality the social network of the other legal actors, combined with the judge's own definition of his job, has resulted in a pattern of deferring to the decisions of other actors. The one exception is in bail setting, where the judge plays a critical role. It is only in the interpretation of Supreme Court decisions that the chief judge plays a dominant and largely unchecked role.

Otherwise the judge's power has been limited to one of potential intervention.

The prosecutor, defense attorney, and the judge then are the principal decision makers in the court system. In addition, several other actors are involved on occasion. In particular the police, the probation officer, and the jury make decisions of which the other actors must take cognizance. Their participation is of a different order than the other actors, however, for they are only sporadic decision makers. Whereas the defense attorney, prosecutor, and judge are in a position to shape the major outlines of the court system, the police, probation officer, and juries are confined to filling in the details.

An examination of who makes the important decisions in criminal justice must consider not only the relative powers of the actors but must also consider what the crucial decisions are. The formal law creates a number of steps in the history of a case: arrest; filing of charges; preliminary hearing; grand jury; trial and sentencing. Some of these steps are largely routine. By contrast the important decisions tend to be concentrated in a few stages. In Prairie City there are two significant decision-making areas: the filing of charges and plea bargaining. In the charging decision, the prosecutor reviews each police arrest and performs the functions usually associated with the preliminary hearing and grand jury—the elimination of obviously weak cases. We have noted that in other communities the charging decision takes on less importance. It is critical, therefore, in examining a community to isolate those stages where the important decisions are made.

The second critical stage in a case is plea bargaining. Plea bargaining, in turn, involves two components: guilt adjudication and sentencing. Often discussions between the participants merge these two questions, but for analytical reasons it is important to maintain this distinction, for separate sets of standards are involved for each question.

How Do the Decision Makers Interact?

Asking who makes the decisions is much like requesting an organizational chart. Such a chart, while a useful first step, often omits a critical dimension—the relationship between these actors. None of the actors are isolated. They are all cognizant of the likely actions and reactions of the others. Further, the principal actors deal with one another on a daily basis and such continual interaction creates important considerations of its own.

In examining the interaction between decision makers it is helpful to work on two levels: a macro level and a micro level.

At the macro level, the administration of criminal justice embraces a mosaic of institutions, each charged with upholding the applicable federal, state, and/or local laws. In examining these institutions, it is helpful to inquire about the nature of the system. Can we speak of a "system" in the administration of justice? *Newsweek* portrays a nonsystem composed of "a fragmented series of processes through which those offenders who are caught bump along from arrest to jail to court to improvised punishments that fit neither the criminal nor the crime." [1] In terms of overall coordination this is the case. Reiss and Bordua similarly categorize the administration of criminal justice as a loosely jointed system "held together at many points by microsystems of antagonistic cooperation and discretionary decision." [2]

The general assessments of *Newsweek* and Bordua and Reiss concerning the lack of coordination in the administration of justice apply to Prairie City. One is struck by the disjunctures. First and foremost is the disjuncture between the police and prosecutor. Although both work toward the same general goal, the types of organizations are radically different. The different focuses of the organizations, and the contrasting backgrounds of the principles combine to strain the working relationships between the police and prosecutor. The other end of the process, the sentencing of defendants, is also marked by major disjunctures. Judges and prosecutors send defendants off to the penitentiary which they have never seen. In turn the efficacy of these actions is measured by only a limited feedback system, how many defendants return to that court. The gulf between the local court and the penitentiary is measured in more than miles.

At the macro level, then, the Prairie City courts typify the American pattern of major disjunctures. The task of social control has been delegated to separate institutions—police, courts, corrections, and parole boards—and each isolates itself from the other. At the micro level within the court system, however, there

---

[1] "Justice on Trial," *Newsweek*, March 8, 1971, p. 17.

[2] Albert Reiss & David Bordua, "Environment and Organization: A Perspective on the Police," in David Bordua, ed., *The Police: Six Sociological Essays* (John Wiley, 1967), p. 26.

are more structured interactions. As George Cole has commented the local courts take on many of the attributes of a small town.[3] Not only is the number of legal actors very small, but these legal actors must by necessity work with one another almost on a day-to-day basis.

The small town character of the criminal courts places a stress on "cooperation." Such cooperation has been mentioned in past studies and with rare exception has been pictured as disruptive of the adversary model. Such negative connotations confuse advocacy with antagonism.[4] At least in Prairie City the "cooperation" between defense and prosecution was on the same order as the professional relations between two opposing attorneys engaged in civil practice. In a profession whose reason for being is conflict, the development of norms to mute and channel this conflict is to be expected.

In turn, the cooperation expected from opposing attorneys introduces important elements of social control in the system. The primary ingredient in such social control is the reputation of the actor. Given the small community of the court system, an individual actor can put one over on the opposition once but, in all likelihood, not twice. A lawyer who develops a reputation for not playing fairly will find his effectiveness decreased. In particular, this element of credibility works on the defense attorney. The prosecutor also feels the pressure of such expectations. Since most state's attorneys plan to enter civil practice, the attorney knows he is being judged on the basis of unspoken questions such as, "What type of lawyer would he make in my firm?"

The juncture of these restraints on prosecutor and defense similarly imposes important restraints upon the judge. Of all the actors, the judge is most removed from any potential sanctions. Nevertheless, judges are socialized to respect the agreements negotiated between opposing counsel. Judges need not accept these agreements, but do, for they realize that to reject the prosecutor's sentencing recommendation would shift much of the sentencing burden to their shoulders. Thus the judge also is restrained by the social system of the courts.

---

[3] George Cole, ed., *Criminal Justice: Law and Politics* (Duxbury Press, 1972), p. 212.

[4] Abraham Blumberg, "The Practice of Law as Confidence Game: Organizational Cooptation of a Profession," *Law and Society Review*, 1: 15–39. David Sudnow, "Normal Crimes: Sociological Features of the Penal Code in a Public Defender Office," *Social Problems*, 1965, 12: 254–276.

What Standards Are Employed?

Within these restraints imposed by the social network, the settlement of cases proceeds on the basis of standards known to all participants. We can best analyze the nature of these standards by employing a civil law model.

When interviews in Prairie City focused on plea bargaining practices, numerous respondents spontaneously compared plea bargaining in criminal cases to the settlement of civil cases. Such a comparison is more than a metaphor because participants do not see any major differences between the civil and criminal process. Attorneys normally expect to discuss and negotiate with the opposition, for the law, like any other human enterprise, requires communication. That the lawyers compare criminal and civil law should not be surprising since all the legal actors also are involved with civil cases. State's attorneys, while specializing in criminal law, have in the past practiced civil law and probably, more important, most intend to develop a civil practice at some future date. Thus participants stress that the plea bargaining is similar to attorneys discussing their personal injury cases.

Communication among attorneys and the settlement of cases is based on commonly perceived standards. Such common standards, at least partially account for the stability of the system. In Prairie City there is a great deal of stability in the criminal justice system because of the continuity of personnel. For convenience in summarizing our most important findings we can oversimplify slightly and say that in Prairie City there are three prime categories of standards: 1] professional-legal standards relating to proof, 2] standards imposed by juries, and 3] working norms relating to sentencing.

We have emphasized that prosecutors and defense attorneys are first of all lawyers who have experienced professional education that centers on what the law considers important and what it ignores. It should not be surprising then to find that lawyers talk in terms of the legal elements of the crime, and what can or cannot be proven. Past studies, however, have neglected this aspect of plea bargaining because they have concentrated largely on negotiations over sentence. Prosecutor and defense conduct a minitrial in the state's attorney's office. The state usually has the upper hand in these negotiations. If the case involves property the prosecutor is likely to have the stolen goods that were in the defendant's possession; if violence took place the prosecution has the victim's and witnesses' testimonies. In addition, in forty percent of the cases the defendants have confessed. Legal requirements for proving the case involve more than these factors, but the above should indicate that the prosecution usually begins with a fairly strong legal base.

Juries are also important in introducing standards for decision making. Both defense and prosecution must make decisions on the basis of what they think the jury will do. More abstractly, the primary function of the jury is to set the limits on which activities should be punished and which should not be. Notice here that the standards of the jury may differ from those of the professionals or the legislator. The juries introduce an essentially amateur element into the decision-making process. For example, there is a difference between a strong case and a winning case because the evidence of guilt may be more than sufficient, yet it may not be a winning case because the jury may be hesitant to convict. Although the jury decides only a relative handful of the felony cases, its impact should not be downgraded. The decision in one jury-trial case sets the standards by which future negotiations between defense and prosecution are conducted.

The standards of legal proof and the standards introduced by juries are concentrated to a large extent on guilt adjudication. The formal standards for sentencing are much less specific. Normally the legislature provides a range of penalties, as well as an option for probation in certain types of crimes. Otherwise only the broadest and most vague guidelines are laid down to guide the sentencing decision. Further, the reasons for imposing a given sentence do not have to be justified to a higher court. As a consequence there is little, if any, hard law on standards for sentencing. All this suggests that the most important determinants of the sentence are the actors' views. We have argued that in Prairie City a number of working norms have developed. These working norms are not written down but have widespread currency nonetheless. Virtually every participant that was interviewed discussed these working norms. Some of the more important working norms on sentencing are: longer prison terms for those convicted by a jury (the jury trial penalty); denial of probation to defendants with a prior conviction; denial of probation to defendants convicted of aggravated battery where a deadly weapon was used; generally probation granted to first offenders in a property offense. In addition, the social criteria for deciding which defendants would be placed on probation were also largely understood. Indeed, one of the major attributes of an attorney was his ability to predict whether his client would qualify for probation.

In examining standards for decision making, we also need briefly to review our findings about discretion. All respondents readily acknowledged that discretion does occur and that the system could not function without it. However, it appears that the term "discretion" has been so broadly used in past studies that its utility now has been compromised. Some of what has been termed "discretion" is better referred to as the working norms of sentencing. In addition, one must make a distinction between discretion and judgment. In judgment, the legal official decides on the basis of standard criteria, particularly the strength of the evidence. By contrast, in discretion the official has the opportunity to substitute his own standards. We concluded that the Prairie City prosecutors office exercises less discretion than past studies would lead us to believe. Indeed, the defense attorneys criticized the prosecutor for not using their discretionary powers more.

How Are Defendants' Rights Protected?

Dealing empirically with the problem of how to protect the defendant's rights is obviously a difficult task for due process automatically evokes normative concern. We have suggested, however, that the protection of a defendant's rights must look beyond the formal law and the formal mechanism designed to accomplish the laws intended purpose. The protection a defendant receives under the law occurs within the framework of the social network of the courts. The institutions of preliminary hearing and grand jury; the possibility of pretrial release; and the recent expansion of rights granted by the Supreme Court allow the officials a great deal of latitude in transforming the black letter of the law into practice. By far the most important ingredient is the official's sense of justice.

The magistrate has instituted a variety of policies that move to mute the effects of economics on the administration of justice. Use of pretrial release, as well as ready appointment of counsel for indigents, have resulted in expansion of the law's protection. By contrast the chief judge is in open disagreement with the goals of the Supreme Court as stated in *Mapp* and *Miranda*. As a result, the direct impact of these decisions have been less than their advocates had hoped. Even here, however, the informal court process is an important consideration. Attorneys have been able to produce changes in the interrogations tactics of one detective, not by formal court hearings, but by informally raising the issue.

Who Benefits?

In asking "Who benefits?" our primary concern is with the outcomes of cases. This is an important transition for much of the current literature focuses more on procedures and less on actual outcomes. Some dimensions of this question will be dealt with shortly under the author's normative assessment of the Prairie City courts. For now we should summarize briefly some of those who benefit. Our assessments must be considered as tentative because we lack the studies that would provide the necessary guidelines for drawing firm conclusions.

The poor are among the beneficiaries of the Prairie City system. As we have just noted, the arraigning magistrate has instituted policies that mute the effects of poverty. In the same manner we found that the young tend to be advantaged by the policies followed in Prairie City. The poor do receive a different type of justice than the not-so-poor, but the duality is not as sharp as in some other communities. This suggests that the penalty attached to poverty is a relative one; some communities attach a higher price to impoverished defendants than others.

Another major beneficiary of the Prairie City courts is the defendant arrested for a minor crime. The prosecutorial dominance of the charging decision results in the failure to file charges, as well as the reduction in the seriousness of some cases when charges are filed. In addition, the state's attorney does not place a great stress on prosecuting misdemeanors, preferring a more laissez faire attitude. In felony cases, on the other hand, fuller enforcement is the goal of the office.

But Is This Justice?

In this section I want to assess the quality of justice in Prairie City. What biases are found in the system? What inherent problems do the courts encounter? How does this city compare to other communities? At various times throughout the research similar questions were raised by the participants. They were genuinely concerned with the quality of justice in the community and wanted the author's own assessments. In this section I want to try and spell out some of these assessments. It should be indicated that I am not proceeding from a comprehensive theory of justice. Instead, the purpose is to raise and evaluate some problems for which clearcut answers are not readily apparent. Rather, it seems to me that many of the positive qualities of justice in Prairie City are purchased at a price. For example, a prime attribute of justice in Prairie City is that it seeks to avoid disparities in treatment, but the price that is paid is a decrease in the individualization of justice. Similarly, many of the reforms being advanced attempt to rationalize the system but the increase in efficiency that accompany such reforms raises some new problems.

These questions and probings about the quality of justice seem to me to be appropriately treated in a conclusion as long as it is understood that these are the author's own thoughts and opinions. Throughout this work the emphasis has been on understanding and explaining how the courts administer justice to the streams of defendants that pass through its portals. Normative evaluations have been avoided. As we argued in the introduction, a separation of findings from the author's value position is imperative. All too often studies have presented a variegated mixture of findings and evaluations that makes it difficult to separate the findings from the author's condemnation of the practices. In value-free research, however, it does still seem appropriate for the author to voice his own impressions and judgments apart from the findings.

Some Conditions of Justice

As this research progressed from initial interviews through observation to the original draft and then the final distillation, one thought kept returning—if criminal justice is going to work it will most likely work in a community such as Prairie City. This is not to suggest that this community is "perfect." That is too much to ask. But it is to suggest that the assumptions of American criminal justice require certain social foundations and working capital. It seems to me that Prairie City to a large extent possesses most of these conditions.

Consider for example the size of the community. Our urban courts are overwhelmed by the press of cases. With such staggering caseloads, the main thought is clearing the docket and little time is left for thoughts about justice. On the other hand, justice in rural America often leaves much to be desired. The problem is the opposite of urban courts. Where the urban courts have too many cases, the rural courts have too few. Why too few? For one thing the few cases that do arise are not sufficient to allow the officials to develop the necessary expertise. But even more importantly the relatively few cases mean that each case is overly important.[5] In a small community it is very difficult for the courts

---

5 Emile Durkheim, *The Division of Labor in Society* (The Free Press, 1933), p. 72.

to maintain the proper distance between the individual defendant and the aroused citizenry.

Prairie City fits a middle category. Unlike the urban courts it is not overwhelmed by clogged dockets. But unlike rural areas it has the critical mass necessary for the development of expertise by the court officials. Prairie City has also been spared the agonizing public dialogue over crime in the streets and largely has been able to retain that necessary distance between the individual defendant and the community.

A less subjective look at Prairie City shows that it has been spared many of the ills identified with the criminal courts. Indeed many of the reforms advocated for the nation have to a certain extent taken root in Prairie City. Take, for example, the problem of delay. In some communities the time from arrest to adjudication averages six months to (in some cases) a year. In Prairie City cases come to trial six to ten weeks from the date of arrest —certainly a model of the speedy justice that Chief Justice Burger has been stressing. Closely associated with delay and clogged dockets are overcrowded jails. Some urban jails are filled to double or triple their intended capacity. In Prairie City the jail is half-empty. Some jails are so ancient that they have deteriorated beyond the point of repair or even upkeep. The Prairie City jail, while not modern, is very definitely not medieval.

But the conditions of the jail, average length of time from arrest to trial, and the docket count are only physical attributes. Far more important, it seems to me, are the people who run the system. In the words of Ramsey Clark, the former United States Attorney General, many of the problems of criminal justice stem from a failure of court officials to internalize a sense of justice. To a certain extent the officials of Prairie City are cognizant of this larger problem of justice. In turn, they also possess the necessary skills required for manning their positions. The prosecutors are by and large able young attorneys. The defense attorneys are on the whole much better than average in the skills of advocacy. Unlike the urban defense attorney who has been painted as a virtual outcast of the legal profession, the defense attorneys in Prairie City have standing among their colleagues. To be sure none of these lawyers qualify as the top echelon of the bar, but such a requirement makes little sense. Unfortunately many legal reforms speak fondly of recruiting the best lawyers to be judges without realizing that such talents would be lost in the criminal courts. The day-to-day activities of the lower courts present few of the complicated legal issues that the upper echelon of the bar is equipped to handle.

From outward appearances, and the usually adopted measuring sticks, then, the court system of Prairie City is fairly progressive. It has avoided the problems that plague many systems, has adopted many of the reforms being advocated, and has taken seriously the justice component in the phrase "the administration of criminal justice." The cracks in the system, therefore, cannot be explained on the basis of too much of this or too little of that. Nor can the faults be corrected by the infusion of men of good will. With the exception of the chief judge, the court officials are largely men of good will.

Prairie City and Reformed Justice

A useful way to compare Prairie City to other communities is to use the typology developed by Klonoski and Mendelsohn as part of their discussion of the relationship between the legal system and the larger political community. They posit two ideal types of communities—an exchange model and an elite-bar model.[6] As used here, an ideal type is not a normative standard but rather a distillation of many factors. It is ideal in the sense that we do not expect communities to fit neatly into one category or another. We expect communities to fall somewhere between the two ends of the continuum. The advantage of ideal types is that they highlight important features necessary for analysis.

One end of the continuum is the exchange model, which is very similar to unreformed, machine-dominated city politics. In this type of community the courts and police will have important links to the political leaders. For example, judges and prosecutors secure their positions by work for the political party. Further, the police force will be ill-trained with promotions based not on merit but rather on ties to the party, or personal ties to the command personnel. As a result, the standards for deciding cases will be largely particularistic—hence the term, "exchange system." If a defendant has ties to the local political machinery, he will be treated more leniently than the defendant who lacks such ties. Numerous inequities will be apparent in the administration of justice according to Klonoski and Mendelsohn.

By contrast the elite-bar model closely follows the reformed

---

[6] James Klonoski & Robert Mendelsohn, eds., *The Politics of Local Justice* (Little, Brown, 1970), pp. 14–17. The authors also develop a third type—the communal system—but a discussion of this type of community has been omitted here.

model of politics. Selection and promotion will be on the basis of merit. The police and court officials will have no ties to the party machinery. The stress is on professionalism. In short, the elite-bar model will have all of the outward manifestations of a reformed, well-ordered law enforcement apparatus.

The elite-bar model has been held up by the reformers as the picture of what justice should be like. Klonoski and Mendelsohn, however, suggest that even here the system will be biased. "The inequities in the allocation of justice are much less visible and much more difficult to pin down in this type of system." Nonetheless inequities will be present. "In all probability, the outputs of the system will be biased against those of low status . . ." [7]

Working with this distinction continuum of exchange model to elite-bar model of justice, Prairie City lies much closer to the elite-bar model than the other. It does not represent a perfect fit but the essential outlines are met. Party involvement in Prairie City justice is minimal. Respect for the law is held as a major ideal. Differential treatment of defendants on the basis of race, economic status, or party affiliation does not occur on any overt basis. The question then remains, are the Prairie City courts biased as Klonoski and Mendelsohn suggest? Are those of low status treated similarly or differently from others? Further, what additional implications are there about a well-ordered, fairly well-run criminal court system? I think the Prairie City court system represents three issues that merit comment. In my view the quality of justice needs to be assessed along three dimensions: 1] bias against low-status defendants; 2] strains on the individualization of justice; and 3] problems raised by the "efficiency" of the system.

Status Bias

Klonoski and Mendelsohn suggest that an elite-bar community will be biased against those of lower status. In one sense this pattern does not develop in Prairie City. As previously mentioned the efforts of the arraigning magistrate to reform bail procedures and to appoint counsel for indigents greatly lessen the penalty attached to poverty. In another sense, however, the system does appear to me to be biased against the lower status groups. This bias is not necessarily an overt one but rather a bias stemming from the application of the informal working norms of the system. The background of the legal actors in Prairie City is pri-

---

[7] Klonoski & Mendelsohn, eds., *Politics of Local Justice*, p. 16.

marily middle class. Such experiences fail to provide any links to the type of people most likely to appear in court. Martin Levin suggested this same type of bias in his discussion of judges.[8] He concluded that judges in Minneapolis had little empathy for lower-class defendants. I think the same conclusion applies in Prairie City. In chapter 5 we argued that the chief justice in Prairie City falls in the same category as the Minneapolis judges —an upper-middle-class official who often views defendants as parasites upon society.

The attitudes of the chief judge seem to me the clearest indication that the system represents a bias against low-status individuals. But even beyond the chief judge's attitudes, two other points illustrate a parallel bias. Take, for example, the prosecutors' handling of misdemeanor cases.

The dominant attitude was that many of these cases should not be before the court. On more than one occasion state's attorneys expressed the view that defendants should settle these cases on their own. These defendants were not deemed to fall within the law's protection. This attitude, while a reasonable one from the perspective of administrative convenience and regularity, ignores the overwhelming fact that the courts are in many instances the only agency that can provide social services, albeit limited ones, to such people. This attitude was typified in the state's attorneys handling of husband-wife fights. One gained the impression that the state's attorneys had little understanding of the problems involved and chose to remove themselves from such issues rather than deal with them.

In a more focused and direct manner, I think the bias against low status was most apparent in the policies involved in aggravated battery cases. The working norm was that a defendant convicted of using a deadly weapon would not receive probation. The basis for this working principle was the obvious seriousness of the offense. In some cases the victim lived only because of the luck of the draw. Not discounting the seriousness of the offense, however, the policy in essence derived from middle-class abhorrence of lower-middle-class use of force in settling arguments. The middle-class actors were unable to make, or apply, relevant distinctions involving the nature of the offense. No matter what the victim's provocation, this was not considered.

The answer to this problem is not immediately obvious for the

---

[8] Martin Levin, "Urban Politics and Policy Outcomes: The Criminal Courts," *Journal of Legal Studies*, 1972, 1: 202–208.

opposite side of the coin is undue relativism in enforcement of the law. Studies of the police have found, for example, that a knifing among blacks is treated very differently than knifings among whites. In the former it is a cutting, in the latter, a major fight. In the former event, no arrest is likely to be made; in the latter a felony arrest is more likely to be forthcoming.[9] Defining one group as outside of the law's protection for racial or other reasons seems to me equally as wrong as rigidly applying the same criteria to both. The fundamental failure in both instances is the inability to make socially relevant distinctions about the types of behavior.

Individualization of Justice vs. Mass Processing

Closely linked to the question of handling aggravated battery cases is the larger question of individualization of justice. Individualization is a prime benefit claimed for the common law. Each incident is to be considered and resolved on the specifics of the event. Just as no two automobile accidents are ever the same, no two burglaries are the same. The individualization of justice seems premised on a small work load, yet criminal law is a mass operation. It is much like a factory that is supposed to produce Brooks Brothers suits, but is actually confronted with the need to supply Robert Hall. The breakdown of individualization, however, is not confined to criminal law. A recent study of tort law and automobile accidents suggests that while the tort law is individualistic in theory it is actually categorical in practice.[10]

Consider some of the tension points mentioned earlier in this study. Sentencing for example is supposed to be individualistic— the penalty should be tailored to the person and the crime. In reality this tailoring is mediated, at least in Prairie City, through broader categories. First-offense burglars receive probation, second offense burglars draw one to ten. Such rules of thumb, or informal policies if you prefer, have one central advantage—they insure uniformity. The disparity in sentences is a problem receiving increasing attention. Where one has a rule of thumb, as well as the norm of Prairie City that like cases should be treated alike, the problem of disparities is greatly diminished. The problem still remains, however. Have the categories been applied properly, or are they used as a way to avoid examining whether defendant X should be treated like all the others or, is his case so unusual it deserves individualized attention?

---

[9] Jerome Skolnick, *Justice Without Trial* (John Wiley, 1966), p. 172.

[10] H. Laurence Ross, *Settled Out of Court* (Aldine, 1970).

The problem of categorization is not a new one. Sudnow, for example, in his study of a public defender's office raised this very point. He entitled his study "Normal Crimes" and depicted defense attorneys, as well as prosecutors, making a cursory examination of a case and then assigning it to a predetermined category.[11] His criticism seems to me to go too far because it ignores a very basic requirement of any organization, to say nothing of human thinking—the need to use categories. Just as a child learns that a four-legged creature called a cat and a different looking four-legged creature termed a dog both fit under the same rubric of animal, so human thinking requires reducing the world to manageable proportions. Without categorization thinking is impossible. The problem then is not one of the existence of categories but rather the proper use of these categories.

The elite-bar, reformed nature of justice in Prairie City seemed to me unable to grapple with this question of the proper application of categories. The state's attorney's office was primarily a law firm busily applying society's rules and the working norms that had developed. The defense attorney believed that the prosecutor failed to exercise discretion when he should, a criticism with which I tend to agree. The categories became too predetermined and were on occasion applied without considering mitigating factors.

I am suggesting, therefore, that the working norms on sentencing have a primary advantage—they tend to assure equal application of the law. At the same time, however, the categories become ends unto themselves and the elimination of disparities can result in too little individualization of the law.

But even more troublesome are the deviations from individualization caused by the internal dynamics of the social system. A defendant's case is decided not only on the basis of what he did, what can be proven about his conduct, and the norms that have developed for dealing with such behavior, but also on the status and power considerations surrounding the legal actors. The defendants operate under a short time span—their case. By contrast the legal actors must also be cognizant of the larger time span of maintaining their bargaining position. Neither defense nor prosecution wants to deal from weakness. Therefore at some point the dictates of an individual defendant are supplemented by a con-

---

[11] David Sudnow, "Normal Crimes: Sociological Features of the Penal Code in a Public Defender Office," *Social Problems*, 1965, 12: 255–265.

cern for improving one's position overall. One prosecutor reflected upon this question and said:

> If I had ten DWI's for that month and at the end of the month I would have looked back and realized that all had been reduced to reckless driving, I wouldn't have felt right. Unconsciously, in the back of your mind, you have the notion of evening up.

Similarly, an informant pointed to various combinations of defense attorneys and prosecutors. One defense attorney had not won a jury trial against a particular prosecutor in almost two years. On the other hand, a prosecutor had not won a trial against another defense attorney for a long time.

To take another example, on occasion one would hear a prosecutor comment to the effect that attorney X had not been to trial for a long time. He would further add that you have to let these attorneys know they can not bargain out all their cases—sometimes they have to go to trial.

I have suggested then that the individual case is also judged against the wider concern of the attorneys' need to maintain their bargaining position. Let us be careful, however, to place this in proper perspective. Such pressures were not operating most of the time. Yet the pressures were there. This problem has usually been treated under the heading of "mass bargaining of cases." Some studies have found that a defense attorney will somewhat willingly accept a high penalty for one defendant in return for leniency for the rest of his clients. Such mass bargaining definitely does not occur in Prairie City. But the same type of problem exists. In placing this problem in perspective, we should also note that such considerations of long-term strengthening of position are by no means confined to criminal practice, for civil practice appears to involve many of these same considerations.

Efficiency

In considering the type and quality of justice in Prairie City we also need to examine the outputs of the system. The end results have been examined rarely. Instead, studies of the American legal system have concentrated on procedure, particularly due process of law. But, apart from the procedures that a community follows, we need also to know something about the end results. Does this community send more defendants to prison than other communities? If so, why? Does this community prosecute more suspects than another? Again, if so, why? To examine these out-

TABLE 19

SENTENCING IN PRAIRIE CITY COMPARED
TO THE REST OF DOWNSTATE ILLINOIS

	1970 Prison population per thousand
Prairie City	1.768
Average-downstate	.482
Minimum	.042
Standard deviation	.335

Source: State of Illinois, Department of Corrections, *Population Analysis of the Illinois Adult Prison System*, 30, June 1970.

Comparison is based on all forty-nine downstate Illinois counties with a population of over 25,000.

puts of the Prairie City court system, table 19 compares the study city to other communities in Illinois with a population over 25,000.[12] Two conclusions emerge from this comparison.

First, Prairie City prosecution of misdemeanors falls in the middle range. There is a twofold explanation of this finding. The prosecutor's office in Prairie City is well organized and therefore experiences no difficulty in efficiently processing minor misconduct. On the other hand, the office views these offenses as not very serious. In addition, the charging decision operates to eliminate a fair number of arrests for minor misconduct prior to the filing of charges.

The data on felony prosecutions and sentencing, however, show a remarkably different pattern. In both instances, Prairie City is on the top rung of high enforcement. Only a few communities prosecute more felony cases than Prairie City but the data suggest they are less successful. Probably the truest indicator of the output of the courts is the number of defendants sent to prison. Here Prairie City is the highest county in the state. Why? Is justice more vindictive than elsewhere? I doubt that. As we have argued throughout, the prosecutor is definitely not a law-and-order crusader. Alternatively the high prison sentences might reflect long prison terms. Again one doubts this explanation. Recall that in the sentencing chapter, we found that the vast majority of prison sentences were the minimum allowed by statute.

---

[12] For a fuller discussion and analysis of this data see David Neubauer, "Policy Outputs of Illinois Trial Courts: An Exploratory Examination," Paper presented at the Annual Meeting of the American Political Science Association, Washington, D.C., September 5–9, 1972.

This, coupled with the release practices of the parole board, which adheres to the minimum, argues then that the length of the term is not the crucial variable.

The crucial variable is volume coupled with efficiency. The elite-bar model stresses efficiency and regularity in procedure. This feature is dominant in Prairie City. On the whole the Prairie City prosecutors are better equipped than most offices to process cases and gain convictions. They are on the whole good trial attorneys. As a result, more people are sentenced to prison. A similar conclusion has been found in studies of police departments. In general, the more professionalized the department, the more likely they are to arrest. The broader question then is: are the ends of justice best served with such an efficient system that sends more people to prison? Without additional data we should not extend our discussion of Prairie City too far, but it is probative that high prison sentence rates will result from many of the procedures in practice in a community like Prairie City. This proposition requires careful scrutiny for its implications are many, not the least of which is that the court applications of sanctions are only indirectly related to the problem of crime in that community. It further suggests that increased reform will produce more crowded prisons. In short, the end result of reforming the courts requires much greater attention because in correcting one set of problems in the courts we might be creating another set.

STATE'S
ATTORNEY'S
QUESTIONNAIRE

The complete state's attorney's questionnaire is reprinted here in order to illustrate the nature of the prefieldwork stage of the research. Other questionnaires were prepared for interviewing judges, defense attorneys, and the police but are not reprinted here because of their length. Since these questionnaires are parallel to the state's attorney's, little would be added by reprinting them.

The questionnaire was developed on the basis of the relevant literature, which is cited throughout the body of this work. The questionnaire forces one to set forth the major concerns of the study. After a preliminary draft was prepared it was pretested in University Towns and a number of modifications were made prior to interviewing in Prairie City. Thus the questionnaire was tied to one particular court structure (that of University Towns) and, therefore, had to be modified in midcourse in Prairie City to take account of the different court structures.

A second important aspect of its application was noted in Chapter Two. The questionnaire was never used in its entirety for any one prosecutor (or other legal actor). Rather, it was a guide for interviewing. As a general-purpose questionnaire it was too detailed for certain legal actors and not detailed enough for others.

Interview Schedule—State's Attorney and Staff

How is your office organized?

Does one man handle arraignment court or do you rotate?

How are cases assigned to your assistants?

Since you've been in office, has there been an expansion in staff?

When the police have arrested without a warrant whom do they see in your office?

What type of evidence do you require before requesting a warrant?

In your experience have the police brought in cases lacking evidence necessary for a charge?

Do the police tend to overcharge when they first bring a case in?

At what stage in the proceedings do you feel you know enough about a case to make an assessment of chances of successful prosecution?

What do you do with husband-wife fights; girl friend-boy friend fights? Do you discourage prosecutions when you believe complaint may later hesitate to cooperate?

In preparing a case for prosecution what problems do you face with a witness hesitant or unwilling to testify? Could you give me any examples?

Preliminary Hearing

When is it held?

Is it a significant stage in the criminal process?

Who testifies at preliminary hearing—arresting officer or just some officer swearing to the report?

Can you recall any instances where a judge did not think probable cause was established at preliminary hearing?

Do judges set a high level of proof at preliminary hearing?

How quickly are weak cases eliminated?

Do you dismiss any cases before presentation to the grand jury?

We hear a lot about the grand jury being obsolete. Do you think that it is true? Any instances where grand jury failed to return indictments requested by the state's attorney?

I imagine the closer one gets to actually trying a case in court, some cases don't look as strong as they once did. Do you then dismiss these cases?

Do you ever have borderline cases where you are not sure if you have enough evidence to prosecute? What do you do then? Can you give me any examples?

Do you talk much with others in the office when you have hard cases? Is there pretty much agreement on what cases to prosecute and which not to? Why are certain cases dismissed?

Bargaining

People disagree on whether or not so many defendants should plead guilty. What do you think?

What strategies are appropriate for state's attorneys to follow on guilty pleas?

> What types of cases do you think should be tried?

> What incentives are there for a defendant to plead guilty?

> If you lose too many cases at trial will this affect guilty pleas?

What part does a judge play when a defendant pleads guilty?

> Some judges want to know ahead of time what has happened. Other judges wait until the defendant pleads guilty in court. What about this community?

What do the police think about plea bargaining? Would they rather lose a case than have a defendant plead guilty to a lesser charge?

> When a plea has been arrived at, do you talk to the police about it?

On a guilty plea, do judges generally accept the prosecutor's recommendations on sentence?

What degree of supervision is there on plea bargaining?

To what extent is state's attorney and defendant's discussion of a case similar to pretrial in a civil case?

Search and Seizure

How often are search warrants used in this county? How important are search warrants?

When the police come in with a request for a search warrant what procedures are followed?

What type of information do judges require before they will issue a search warrant? Do they ever decline to issue a search warrant?

If a search warrant is used does this present problems or complications? Has evidence ever been suppressed because a search warrant was defective?

As a general rule on police searches, do the police usually rely on consent of the suspect when requesting a search?

Do the police have a consent to search form which they use?

In reviewing cases for prosecution, can you recall any instance where a search warrant should have been obtained but wasn't? What happened? Can you tell me about it?

Do you have many problems with search and seizure—legality of evidence?

The law on search and seizure is not always clear. Is there anything in particular which gives police the most difficulty?

From a prosecutor's perspective, are there any police search practices which present problems? Any that might be improved?

What do you think of suppression of evidence? Does it result in improved police procedures? Does suppressing evidence do anything besides upsetting the police?

What do the police think of search-and-seizure law? What's their reaction when evidence is suppressed?

How do judges view suppression of evidence? Have judges ever indicated how they feel about suppression of evidence?

Communications with Police

What communications do you have with police?
> Do you talk with officers after a case about what could have been done better?
>
> During the last few years there have been major changes in law relating to the police procedures. Have you ever had general meetings with the police on what these changes in the law meant?

If the police have a question about the law, whom should they ask for advice?

Do the police bring questions about the law to the prosecutor?

Do the police ask the city attorney for legal advice on a regular basis?

Do city attorneys and the prosecutor perform different functions for the police?

Do you think there is enough communication between the police and the prosecutor's office?

How could communication be improved?

Some police departments are very concerned about what happens in court—especially convictions. Other departments don't seem to place the same emphasis on successful convictions. What about local departments?

Do the police know what happens in a particular case? How do they know?

Do you ever get any reactions from the police when a case is dismissed?

What would you like to see in the way of police training?

Have there been any police practices which your office didn't think were right?

What do the judges think about police practices? Have they ever indicated practices they don't like? Improvements they would like to see?

How do the police feel about local judges? Do they ever comment on things they like or dislike?

General

How would you describe the job of being a district attorney—what are the most important things you should do in criminal cases?

The district attorney has to work with the police every day. What should the relationship be between the state's attorney and the police? PROBE: Should the district attorney be primarily concerned with prosecuting cases and reflecting police concerns, or should the district attorney be concerned with enforcing rules designed to control police practices?

Some say that a state's attorney should not prosecute defendants where the police may have violated the law, others say that the judge is the only one who should decide. What do you think? Should the district attorney refuse to prosecute or should the decision be left up to the judge?

People disagree on the responsibilities of judges. Some say a judge should be an administrator or overseer of criminal justice. Others say that isn't proper, that the judge should treat the police and state's attorney as independent agencies. What do you think?

Stop and Frisk Law

What's been your experience with stop and frisk law? Have you had many cases involving stop and frisk? Could you describe them? Are many cases prosecuted under the law?

Have the police brought cases under the stop and frisk law that your office thought the law was being used incorrectly?

With something as new as stop and frisk, I imagine no one was quite sure exactly how the law should be handled. Were there any discussions, formal or informal, held on the meaning of the new law? With whom?

Have any of the judges commented on the stop and frisk law? Have they provided any guidance on the proper scope of the new law?

What communications have the police had over the meaning of the law?

CODING KEY
FOR
DOCKET STUDY

The complete coding key for the felony docket study is reprinted here. The coding key is a modification of the one used by Lee Silverstein in *Defense of the Poor*, pp. 207–212. A preliminary form was constructed, used for a few cases in the court files, and found wanting. Therefore, a new form was prepared, incorporating the available data in the court files. At a later stage information from the prosecutor's files was used to supplement the data available in the official court records.

The docket study referred to throughout the study is based on the universe of 1968 felony charges filed. Because of the manner in which the official records are kept, the sample does not agree with the official court records of number of cases filed and number of felonies. If a charge is filed in Prairie City, it is given a docket number. If the defendant is later indicted by the grand jury the first case is dismissed and the grand jury indictment is given a new number. This practice artificially increases the actual number of charges and dismissals. Therefore, the docket study views a case in its entirety and records it as one case and not two.

The second point to keep in mind concerning the felony sample centers on the defendant. The felony sample includes 318 defendants. However, a proportion of these 318 cases involve multiple but separate charges. Therefore, the bulk of the analysis employ a subsample termed "defendant deck" that encompasses 248 defendants. If a defendant was charged with multiple charges, the defendant deck incorporates the charge to which he pled or was found guilty and discards the other charges but records these additional charges under column 55. The defendant deck also discards cases where defendant was charged but never adjudicated (due to suspect fleeing the jurisdiction, or other reasons). The defendant deck views the process from the eyes of the participants who focus not on entries in the docket book but on defendants. It also represents the effective number of suspects processed by the court for the given year.

One other point concerning the docket study also must be kept in mind. The docket study focuses on defendants, not cases. Thus if three suspects are charged with one count of burglary, three entries are made although the official records carry this as a single case. Again, this represents operational reality better than a strict accounting of docket entries.

DOCKET STUDY

S.A. Number _____

Docket Number _____

1,2: Study number

3: Deck number

4: County

5–8: Number

9: Year—use last digit of year

10–11: Crime originally charged/most serious offense charged
    01: Arson
    02: Assault
    03: Battery
    04: Burglary
    05: Auto theft
    06: DWI
    07: Embezzlement, fraud
    08: Forgery, bad check
    09: Larceny
    10: Murder
    11: Manslaughter
    12: Narcotics, possession
    13: Narcotics, sale
    14: Rape
    15: Robbery, armed
    16: Robbery, unarmed
    17: Indecent liberties

18: Other sex offenses

19: Other

Specific Charge Chapter 38

12:1 = misdemeanor   2 = felony

13: Total number of charges filed_____

14–15: Age_____

16–18: Date charge originally filed_____

19–21: Date of preliminary hearing_____

22–24: Date of indictment_____

25–27: Date of final disposition_____

28–30: Date atty. first appeared_____

31–33: Date def. released on bail_____

34: Preliminary hearing

> 1: waived
> 2: no probable cause
> 3: probable cause

35–37: Amount of original bail in hundreds_____

38–40: Final amount of bail

41: Motion to reduce bond

> 1: No
> 2: yes–denied
> 3: yes–denied, s.a. objects
> 4: yes–accepted s.a. objects
> 5: yes–accepted s.a. concurs or silent

42: Release on bail
   1: no remanded to sheriff–mitimus.
   2: yes–posted 10%
   3: yes–surety bond
   4: ROR
   5: notice to appear
   9: no data

43: Defense attorney   name
   1: private atty.

2: assigned counsel
3: public defender
4: no attys.

44: Status of defendant
1: not indigent
2: court rules indigent
3: court denies indigency

45: Grand jury
1: def. waives indictment by grand jury
2: indictment–true bill
3: no true bill

46: Summary of case disposition in nontrial cases
1: at or soon after preliminary hearing
2: prior to grand jury
3: between grand jury and trial

47–48: number of prosecution witnesses at grand jury or trial

49: Motion to suppress Chap. 38–114–12
1: not made
2: mo./no argument/mo. denied
3: mo. denied
4: mo. granted

50: Motion to produce confession Chap. 38–114–10
1: not made
2: mo. statement produced
3: mo. no statement produced

51: Motion to suppress confession Chap. 38–114–11
1: not made
2: mo. made–suppressed
3: mo. made–not suppressed
4: made–no arguments–denied

52: Waiver of rights by defendant
1: refusal to waive rights
2: oral statements of oral waiver but no written waiver
3: written waiver
4: no data

53: Statement or confession
1: none
2: oral admissions only

    3: confesses to crime
    4: confesses to additional crime

54: Not convicted
    1: motion to dismiss
    2: nolle prosequi
    3: return as parole violator
    4: lack of prosecution witnesses
       or evidence
    5: probation violation
    6: juvenile/mental proceedings
    7: convicted companion case
    8: convicted another jurisdiction
    9: lack of prosecution

55: Defendant pleads guilty
    1: one or several charges dropped
    2: charge reduced
    3: pleads to original charge
    4: reduced to a misdemeanor
    5: other charges dropped

56: Trial outcomes
    1: jury trial–guilty
    2: jury trial–not guilty
    3: bench trial–guilty
    4: bench trial–not guilty

57: State's attorney original recommendation
    1: concur in probation
    2: not concur in probation

58–59: s.a. minimum sentence recommendation

60–61· s.a. max.   "   "

62: Sentence
    1: fine only
    2: fine plus ct. costs
    3: bond forfeiture
    4: jail
    5: probation
    6: not sentenced

63–65: Amount of fine in hundreds_____

66–68: length of jail term min._____

69–71: length of jail term max._____

72: Probation officer's report
    1: no report–none requested
    2: recommends probation–probation granted
    3: recommends probation–probation denied
    4: recommends no prob.–probation denied
    5: recommends no prob.–probation granted

73: Prior record
    1: record shows prior felony conviction
    2: record shows no prior felony conviction
    3: record silent

74: Probation record
    1: probation successfully completed
    2: probation still in progress
    3: report of violation
    4: probation extended
    5: probation violation–contempt of court
    6: probation violation–probation revoked

75–76: term of probation / 2d digit portion of year

77: Physical evidence
    1: search warrant used
    2: search without a warrant

78: Search report
    1: yes
    2: no

BIBLIOGRAPHY

Books

Lucius Barker, and Twiley Barker, *Civil Liberties and the Constitution.* Prentice-Hall, 1970.

Lucius Barker and Twiley Barker, *Freedoms, Courts, Politics: Studies in Civil Liberties, With Revisions.* Prentice-Hall, 1972.

Theodore Becker, *Comparative Judicial Politics.* Rand McNally, 1970.

Theodore Becker, *Political Behavioralism and Modern Jurisprudence.* Rand McNally, 1964.

Peter Blau, and W. Richard Scott. *Formal Organizations.* Chandler, 1962.

Abraham Blumberg, *Criminal Justice.* Quandrangle, 1967.

Jonathan Casper, *Criminal Justice—The Consumer's Perspective.* Government Printing Office, 1972.

George Cole, ed., *Criminal Justice: Law and Politics.* Duxbury Press, 1972.

Congressional Quarterly. *Crime and the Law.* Congressional Quarterly, 1971.

Robert Dahl, *Who Governs?* Yale University Press, 1961.

Kenneth Culp Davis, *Discretionary Justice: A Preliminary Inquiry.* Louisiana State University Press, 1969.

Robert Dawson, *Sentencing: The Decision as to Type, Length, and Conditions of Sentence.* Little, Brown, 1969.

Kenneth Dolbeare, "The Federal District Courts and Urban Public Policy: An Exploratory Study." In Joel Grossman and Joseph Tanenhaus, eds., *Frontiers of Judicial Research.* John Wiley, 1969, pp. 373–404.

Kenneth Dolbeare, *Trial Courts in Urban Politics.* New York: John Wiley, Inc., 1967.

Edwin Driver, "Confessions and the Social Psychology of Coercion." In Marvin Summers and Thomas Barth, eds., *Law and Order in a Democratic Society*. Merrill, 1970, pp. 71–90.

Emile Durkheim, *The Division of Labor in Society*. Translated by George Simpson. The Free Press, 1933.

David Easton, *A Systems Analysis of Political Life*. John Wiley, 1965.

Daniel Elazar, *Cities of the Prairie*. Basic Books, 1970.

Robert Emerson, *Judging Delinquents*. Aldine, 1971.

Arnold Enker, "Perspectives on Plea Bargaining." In *Task Force Report: The Courts*. Government Printing Office, 1967, pp. 109–119.

William Flanagan, and Edwin Fogelman, "Functional Analysis." In James Charlesworth, ed., *Contemporary Political Analysis*. The Free Press, 1967, pp. 72–85.

Jerome Frank, *Courts on Trial*. Atheneum, 1969.

Lawrence Friedman, and Stewart Macaulay. *Law and the Behavioral Sciences*. Bobbs-Merrill, 1969.

John Gardner, *Traffic and the Police*. Harvard University Press, 1969.

Erving Goffman, *Encounters*. Bobbs Merrill, 1961.

Sheldon Goldman, and Thomas Jahnige, eds., *The Federal Courts as a Political System*. Harper & Row, 1971.

Edward Green, *Judicial Attitudes in Sentencing*. St. Martin's, 1961.

Neal Gross, Ward Mason, and Alexander McEachern. *Explorations in Role Analysis: Studies of the School Superintendency Role*. John Wiley, 1958.

Joel Grossman, and Richard Wells, *Constitutional Law and Judicial Policy Making*. John Wiley, 1972.

Joel Handler, *The Lawyer and His Community*. University of Wisconsin Press, 1967.

Michael Hindelan, "Equality Under the Law." In Charles Reasons and Jack Kuyendall, eds., *Race, Crime and Justice*. Goodyear, 1972, pp. 305–317.

Fred Inbua, and John Reid. *Criminal Interrogation and Confessions*. Williams and Wilkins, 1962.

Herbert Jacob, *Justice in America*. Little Brown, 1965.

Herbert Jacob, *Justice in America*, 2nd ed. Little Brown, 1972.

Herbert Jacob, and Kenneth Vines, eds., *Politics in the American States*. Little, Brown, 1965.

Herbert Jacob, and Kenneth Vines, eds., *Politics in the American States*, 2nd ed. Little, Brown, 1971.

Thomas Jahnige, and Sheldon Goldman, eds., *The Federal Judicial System*. Holt, Rinehart and Winston, 1968.

Howard James, *Crisis in the Courts*. David McKay, 1968.

Harry Jones, ed., *The Courts, The Public and The Law Explosion*. Prentice-Hall, 1965.

James Klonoski, and Robert Mendelsohn, eds, *The Politics of Local Justice*. Little, Brown, 1970.

Wayne LaFave, *Arrest: The Decision to Take A Suspect Into Custody*. Little, Brown, 1965.

Harold Lasswell, *Politics: Who Gets What, When and How*. Meridian Books, 1958.

Karl Llewellyn, and E. Adamson Hoebel. *The Cheyenne Way*. University of Oklahoma Press, 1941.

Donald McIntyre, ed., *Law Enforcement in the Metropolis*. American Bar Foundation, 1967.

Donald Matthews, *U.S. Senators and Their World*. Random House, 1960.

Martin Mayer. *The Lawyers*. Dell, 1966.

Robert Merton, *Social Theory and Social Structure*. Free Press, 1957.

Frank Miller, *Prosecution: The Decision to Charge a Suspect with a Crime*. Little, Brown, 1969.

Neil Milner, *The Court and Local Law Enforcement*. Sage, 1971.

Raymond Moley, *Politics and Criminal Prosecution*. Minton, Balach, 1929.

Donald Newman, *Conviction*. Little, Brown, 1966.

Arthur Niederhoffer, *Behind the Shield*. Anchor, 1969.

Dallin Oaks and Warren Lehman, *A Criminal Justice System and The Indigent*. University of Chicago Press, 1967.

Herbert Packer, *The Limits of the Criminal Sanction*. Stanford University Press, 1968.

Talcott Parsons, "The Law and Social Control." In William Evan, ed., *Law and Sociology*. Free Press, 1962, pp. 56–72.

Talcott Parsons, *The Social System*. The Free Press, 1951.

Jack Peltason, *Federal Courts in the Political Process.* Random House, 1955.

Richard Quinney, *The Social Reality of Crime.* Little, Brown 1970.

Albert Reiss and David Bordua, "Environment and Organization: A Perspective on the Police." In David Bordua, ed., *The Police: Six Sociological Essays.* John Wiley, 1967, pp. 25–55.

David Reissman, *The Lonely Crowd.* Yale paperbound, 1961, abridged ed.

Richard Richardson, and Kenneth Vines. *The Politics of Federal Courts.* Little, Brown, 1970.

H. Laurence Ross, *Settled Out of Court.* Aldine, 1971.

Robert Salisbury and John Heinz, "A Theory of Policy Analysis and Some Preliminary Applications." In Ira Sharkansky, ed., *Policy Analysis in Political Science* (Markham, 1970), pp. 39–60.

Joseph Schlessinger, *Ambition and Politics: Political Careers in the United States.* Rand McNally, 1966.

Glendon Schubert, ed., *Judicial Behavior.* Rand McNally, 1964.

Edwin Schur, *Law and Society.* Random House, 1968.

Edwin Schur, *Our Criminal Society.* Prentice-Hall, 1969.

Ira Sharkansky, ed., *Policy Analysis in Political Science.* Markham, 1970.

Lee Silverstein, *Defense of the Poor.* American Bar Foundation, 1965.

Jerome Skolnick, *Justice Without Trial.* John Wiley, 1966.

Frederick Suffet, "Bail Setting: A Study of Courtroom Interaction." In Richard Quinney, ed., *Crime and Justice in Society.* Little, Brown, 1966, pp. 292–307.

Kenneth Vines, "Courts as Political and Governmental Agencies." In Herbert Jacob and Kenneth Vines, eds., *Politics in the American States.* Little, Brown, 1965, pp. 239–287.

Kenneth Vines, "The Judicial Role in the American States: An Exploration." In Joel Grossman and Joseph Tanenhaus, eds., *Frontiers of Judicial Research.* John Wiley, 1969, pp. 461–495.

John Wahlke, Heinz Eulau, William Buchanan, and Leroy Ferguson, *The Legislative System.* John Wiley, 1962.

Patricia Wald, "Poverty and Criminal Justice." In President's Commission on Law Enforcement and Administration of Justice, *Task Force Reports: The Courts,* Government Printing Office, 1967, pp. 139–151.

Stephen Wasby, *The Impact of the United States Supreme Court: Some Perspectives.* Dorsey Press, 1970.

Richard Watson and Ronald Downing, *The Politics of the Bench and Bar.* John Wiley, 1969.

James Q. Wilson, *Varieties of Police Behavior.* Harvard University Press, 1968.

Periodicals

Albert Alschuler, "The Prosecutor's Role in Plea Bargaining." *University of Chicago Law Review,* 1968, 36:50–112.

Charles Ares, Anne Rankin and Herbert Sturz, "The Manhattan Bail Project; An Interim Report on the Use of Pre-Trial Parole." *New York University Law Review,* 1963, 38: 67–95.

Theodore Becker, "Surveys and Judiciaries, or Who's Afraid of the Purple Curtain." *Law and Society Review,* 1966, 1:133–143.

"Big Stick in Big D." *Newsweek,* 20 July 1970, p. 65.

Abraham Blumberg, "The Practice of Law as a Confidence Game: Organizational Cooptation of a Profession." *Law and Society Review,* 1967, 1:15–39.

Irvin Bromall, "Lawyers in Politics: An Exploratory Study of the Wisconsin Bar." *Wisconsin Law Review,* 1968, 3:751–764.

Henry Bullock, "Significance of the Racial Factor in the Length of Prison Sentences." *Journal of Criminal Law, Criminology and Police Science,* 1962, 52:411–417.

Arthur Burnett, "Search Warrants: Impact and Application of *Chimel* and *Spinelli* and Related Problems." *Federal Bar Journal,* 1969, 29:170–199.

Jerome Carlin, Jan Howard, and Sheldon Messinger, "Civil Justice and the Poor: Issues for Sociological Research." *Law and Society Review,* 1966, 1:9–89.

Robert Cipes, "Crime, Confessions and the Court." *Atlantic Monthly,* September 1966, pp. 51–58.

George Cole, "The Decision to Prosecute." *Law and Society Review,* 1970, 4:331–343.

"Court Approves 'Negotiations' for Sentences." *St. Petersburg Times,* 11 February 1971, Section B, p. 1.

Julian D'Esposito, Jr. "Sentencing Disparity: Causes and Cures." *Journal of Criminal Law, Criminology and Police Science,* 1969, 60:182–194.

Donald Dowling, and John Yantis, "Defense of the Poor in Criminal Cases in Illinois." *Chicago Bar Record,* 1966, 47:216–299.

Richard Engstrom, "Political Ambitions and the Prosecutorial Office." *The Journal of Politics,* 1971, 33:190–194.

Howard Erlanger, "Jury Research in America: Its Past and Future." *Law and Society Review,* 1970, 4:345–370.

Edward Fisher, "Plea Bargaining in Traffic Cases." *The Prosecutor,* 1969, 5:91–105.

Joseph Goldstein, "Police Discretion Not to Invoke the Criminal Process: Low-Visibility Decisions in the Administration of Justice." *Yale Law Journal,* 1969, 69:543–594.

John Griffiths, and Richard Ayres, "A Postscript to the *Miranda* Project: Interrogation of Draft Protestors." *Yale Law Journal,* 1967, 76:300–319.

Herbert Jacob, "Judicial Insulation—Elections, Direct Participation, and Public Attention to the Courts in Wisconsin." *Wisconsin Law Review,* 1966, 801–834.

"Justice on Trial." *Newsweek,* 8 March 1971 pp. 17–46.

Alfred Kamin, "Bail Administration in Illinois." *Illinois Bar Journal,* 1965, 53:674–686.

John Kaplan, "The Prosecutorial Discretion—A Comment." *Northwestern Law Review,* 1965, 60:174–193.

Jack Ladinsky, "The Impact of Social Backgrounds of Lawyers on Law Practice and the Law." *Journal of Legal Education,* 1965, 16:127–144.

Wayne LeFave. "Search and Seizure: The Course of True Law . . . Has Not . . . Run Smooth." *University of Illinois Law Forum,* 1966:255–389.

Lawrence Leiken, "Police Interrogations in Colorado." *Denver Law Journal,* 1970, 47:1–53.

Martin Levin, "Urban Politics and Judicial Behavior." *The Journal of Legal Studies,* 1972, 1:193–225.

Donald McIntyre, "A Study of Judicial Dominance of the Charging Decision." *Journal of Criminal Law, Criminology and Police Science,* 1968, 59:463–490.

Maureen Mileski, "Courtroom Encounters: An Observation Study of a Lower Criminal Court." *Law and Society Review,* 1971, 5:473–538.

Frank Miller, and Lawrence Tiffany, "Prosecutor Dominance of the Warrant Decision: A Study of Current Practices." *Washington University Law Quarterly,* 1964:1–23.

Stuart Nagel, "Disparities in Criminal Procedure." *UCLA Law Review,* 1967, 14:1272–1305.

Donald Newman, "Pleading Guilty for Considerations: A Study of Bargain Justice." *Journal of Criminal Law, Criminology and Police Science,* 1956, 46:780–790.

Dallin Oaks, "Studying the Exclusionary Rule in Search and Seizure." *University of Chicago Law Review,* 1970, 37:665–757.

John O'Shea, "The Preliminary Hearing in Illinois: Nature and Practice." *Illinois Bar Journal,* 57:556–560.

"Prosecutorial Discretion in the Initiation of Criminal Complaints." *Southern California Law Review,* 1969, 42:519–545.

Arthur Rosett, "The Negotiated Guilty Plea." *The Annals of the American Academy of Political and Social Science,* 1967, 374:70–81.

Lee Silverstein, "Bail in the State Courts—A Field Study and Report." *Minnesota Law Review,* 1966, 50:621–652.

Jerome Skolnick, "Social Control in the Adversary System." *The Journal of Conflict Resolution,* 1967, 11:52–70.

Alexander Smith and Abraham Blumberg, "The Problem of Objectivity." *Social Forces* 1967, 46:96–105.

Albert Somit, Joseph Tanenhaus, and Walter Wilke, "Aspects of Judicial Sentencing Behavior." *University of Pittsburg Law Review,* 1960, 21:613–619.

David Sudnow, "Normal Crimes: Sociological Features of the Penal Code in a Public Defender Office." *Social Problems,* 1965, 12:254–276.

Evelle Younger, "The Challenge of the Prosecutor's Office." *Prosecutor,* 1968, 4:209–215.

Michael Wald, Richard Ayres, David Hess, Mark Schantz, and Charles Whitebread II, "Interrogations in New Haven: The Impact of *Miranda.*" *Yale Law Journal,* 1967, 76:1519–1648.

Bertram Wilcox, and Edward Bloustein, "Account of a Field

Study in a Rural Area of the Representation of Indigents Accused of Crime." *Columbia Law Review*, 1959, 59:551–574.

Cases

Bivens v. Six Unknown Named Agents 403 U.S. 388 (1971).

Brown v Beto 5th Circuit, 377 F.2d 950 (1969).

Brown v. Mississippi 297 U.S. 278 (1936).

Chimel v. California 89 S. Ct. Reports 2034 (1969).

Gallegos v. Colorado 3rd U.S. 54 (1962).

Gideon v. Wainwright 372 U.S. 335 (1963).

Mapp v Ohio 367 U.S. 643 (1962).

Miranda v. Arizona 384 U.S. 436 (1966).

North Carolina v. Alford 400 U.S. 25 (1971).

Santobello v. New York 404 U.S. 257 (1971).

Public Documents

Administrative Office of the Illinois Courts, *1965 Annual Report to the Supreme Court of Illinois*. Springfield, Illinois.

Administrative Office of the Illinois Courts, *1967 Annual Report to the Supreme Court of Illinois*. Springfield, Illinois.

Administrative Office of the Illinois Courts, *1968 Annual Report to the Supreme Court of Illinois*. Springfield, Illinois.

Illinois Revised Statutes 1967. West Publishing Co.

Gene McNarry. *1971 Annual Report, St. Louis County Prosecutor's Office*. Clayton, Missouri.

The President's Commission on Law Enforcement and Administration of Justice, *The Challenge of Crime*. Government Printing Office, 1967.

The President's Commission on Law Enforcement and Administration of Justice, *Task Force Report: The Courts*. Government Printing Office, 1967.

The President's Commission on Law Enforcement and Administration of Justice, *Task Force Report: The Police*. Government Printing Office, 1967.

Report of the National Advisory Commission on Civil Disorders. Government Printing Office, 1968.

U.S. Dept. of Justice, Federal Bureau of Investigation, Crime in the United States, *Uniform Crime Reports–1970*. Government Printing Office, 1971.

U.S. Department of Justice, Federal Bureau of Prisons. *Statistical Report 1966*. Government Printing Office.

U.S. Department of Justice, Law Enforcement Assistance Administration, "Commission Proposes Hundreds of Methods to Reduce Crime, Improve Criminal Justice." *LEAA Newsletter*, 1973, 3:12.

U.S. Law Enforcement Assistance Administration and U.S. Bureau of the Census. *1970 National Jail Census*. Government Printing Office, 1970.

Unpublished Materials

Irvin Bromall, "Wisconsin Lawyers in Politics: An Exploratory Study." Paper presented at the Midwest Conference of Political Scientists, Purdue University, Lafayette, Indiana, April 27–29, 1967.

Kay Calavan, "A Statistical Survey of Champaign County Criminal Court Dockets," circa 1969, Department of Anthropology, University of Illinois.

Lief Carter, "The Limits of Order: The Influence of Professional Autonomy, Uncertainty, and Interpersonal Trust on Prosecutorial Behavior." Paper presented at the Annual Meeting of the American Political Science Association, Washington, D.C., September 5–9, 1972.

Kenneth Dolbeare, and Phillip Hammond, "Local Elites, The Impact of Judicial Decisions and the Process of Change." Paper presented at the Annual Meeting of the American Political Science Association, New York City, September 2–6, 1969.

James Eisenstein, "The Federal Prosecutor and His Environment." Paper presented at the Annual Meeting of the American Political Science Association, Washington, D.C., September 2–7, 1968.

Samuel Funderburk, "A Study of Sentencing Tendencies of a Florida Misdemeanor Court: 1962 and 1966." Master's Thesis, Department of Political Science, University of Florida, 1967.

Gene Mason, "Judges and Their Public; Role Perceptions and Role Expectations." Ph.D. dissertation, Department of Political Science, University of Kansas, 1967.

Lynn Mather, "To Plead Guilty or Go to Trial?" Paper presented at the Annual Meeting of the American Political Science Association, Washington, D.C., September 5–9, 1972.

David Neubauer, "Counsel for Indigents: An Empirical Examination of the Criminal Justice Process." Paper presented at the Annual Meeting of the American Political Science Association, Washington, D.C., September 2–7, 1968.

David Neubauer, "Policy Outputs of Illinois Trial Courts: An Exploratory Study." Paper presented at the Annual Meeting of the American Political Science Association Convention, Washington, D.C., September 5–9, 1972.

Index